TRAITORS

The Worst Acts of Treason in American History
from Benedict Arnold to Robert Hanssen

TRAITORS

The Worst Acts of Treason in American History
from Benedict Arnold to Robert Hanssen

Richard Sale

BERKLEY BOOKS, NEW YORK

This book is an original publication of The Berkley Publishing Group.

A Berkley Book
Published by The Berkley Publishing Group
A division of Penguin Group (USA) Inc.
375 Hudson Street
New York, New York 10014

Copyright © 2003 by Richard Sale
Text design by Julie Rogers
Cover design by Jill Boltin
Cover photo by Nonstock/Fredik Boden

PRINTING HISTORY
Berkley edition / November 2003

Library of Congress Cataloging-in-Publication Data

Sale, Richard T., 1939–
Traitors : the worst acts of treason in American history from
Benedict Arnold to Robert Hanssen / Richard Sale.
p.   cm.
Includes bibliographical references (p.) and index.
ISBN 0-425-19185-0
1. Traitors—United States—Bibliography.   2. Spies—United States—Biography.
3. Treason—United States—History.   4. Espionage—United States—History.
5. United States—Politics and government—Case studies.   I. Title.

E176.S23 2003
327.12'092'273—dc21   2003052450

Printed in the United States of America

10   9   8   7   6   5   4   3   2   1

Dedication

This book is dedicated to my many fathers: Phil, Baba, Courtney, Vince, Pat, Larry, Fritz, Milt, Dave, Bozzorg, the two Jacks, Bill, and many who don't even want to be indicated here. It is you who have taught me about the tradecraft of intelligence and the inner workings of foreign policy and that, no matter how high its ideals, even the United States has ulterior motives in whatever it does in the world.

And this book also goes to my wife, Carol, the great gift of life God gave me.

Contents

Preface

I want to say at the outset that I am writing biography, not history. I was trained as an historian with my major emphasis on historiography. But it must be understood that the following narratives are basically miniature biographies, very constricted in space, in which I have tried, with some few telling essentials, to convey the lives of these famous traitors. I have tried to do it in the fewest words and with as much power and color as possible.

I have also, within my limits, tried to be a dramatic artist. Biography, like history, was once real life: a living, fluid, full experience, being suffered, undergone, rejoiced in, despaired of, by people just as frail as ourselves. I have tried to produce not only an account of what happened, but a connected account, illuminating the motives and idea of the actors, the influence of circumstances, the play of chance and the unforeseen.

We have so often been told that some villain is a "Benedict Arnold," that the name acts as a stop sign on the road. We recognize what it indicates, but the act of recognition discourages any further reflection as to what it means. It seemed to me essential to try and write biographical essays of traitors that would place them solidly in their economic, historical and political times.

My aim has also been to give the kind of account that would prompt a reader to want to reach out to fuller and more comprehensive versions than mine, but hopefully will not feel that they have been short-changed or led astray by having read what I have done here.

The Makings of a Traitor

A British intelligence official once said, "A good espionage operation is like a good marriage. Nothing out of the ordinary ever happens in it. It is uneventful. It does not make a good story."

"The spies who interest us are the ones who did not get caught and who therefore are not to be read about," a Central Intelligence Agency manual observes to its recruits.

It is a chilling truth that the really successful traitors in history remain unknown to us. They are still out there somewhere. Who knows who Perseus was, the Soviet spy who passed secrets from the U.S. atomic bomb program in the 1940s? Or the spy recruited by the KGB's Second Directorate who was very active in Jimmy Carter's presidential campaign? Or the scientist code-named "ZENIT" whom the Soviets had placed deep inside TRW, the U.S. defense contractor, in the 1970s?

The spies whose names we know are spies who failed.

Successful traitors have managed to elude both scrutiny and pursuers. They led long and peaceful lives, making quiet withdrawals from offshore bank accounts, their treachery a matter of note to no one but themselves, their former handlers, and perhaps the baffled damage assessors of various intelligence agencies who cannot quite lay a finger on why certain of their operations failed or were blown.

Before their unmasking skyrocketed their names into the headlines of newspapers, the lives of the more famous traitors in the espionage firmament such as the Britisher Kim Philby, the Rosenbergs, navy spy John Walker Jr., or the CIA renegade Aldrich Ames were essentially uneventful, most of them lacking in exotic glamour of any kind. In many cases, there was nothing personally or outwardly remarkable about the traitors themselves. Some were married and had children. Outside the home, many led the ordinary life of an ordinary person. He or she usually worked in a government office where they performed regular duties and kept regular hours. At work they appeared to obey all the rules and to bring to their job some degree of purpose or propelling ambition.

It is one of the more sinister ironies of traitors that their excellent job performance often acted to cloak the seamy underside of their life and aided them in obtaining promotions that would place them in positions where they had access to even more highly secret information than before.

U.S. Navy radioman John Walker Jr., who stole codes that allowed the Soviets to read over one million top secret messages on the movement and operations of U.S. ships and submarines, ruthlessly recruited his brother, his son, and a best friend Jerry Whitworth to keep up a steady flow of stolen data to Moscow. Yet to all outward appearances, Walker was a model navy employee.

"Chief Warranty Officer-2 Walker is intensely loyal, taking great pride in himself and the naval service. He possesses a fine sense of personal honor and integrity, coupled with a great sense of humor. He is friendly and intelligent and possesses the ability to work in close harmony with others," gushed a 1972 performance review.

At the time of this report, Walker had been spying for the Soviets for four years and just given the KGB U.S. Navy and other codes that were passed to North Vietnam to help it ambush and shoot down U.S. fighters and bomber jets.

Army Sergeant Clyde Conrad, who had served in Germany from the 1970s until his retirement in 1985, was one of the most damaging spies in all of U.S. history. Recently I talked to Paul Redmond, retired chief of counterintelligence for the CIA, who said that the case of Aldrich Ames "didn't rate in the same charts" as the Conrad case in terms of damage to U.S. interests. This is because a top target of any hostile spy service is to gain access to the operational war plans of the enemy. Conrad, over a period of years, gave the Soviets detailed lists of how NATO forces in Germany would respond to a sudden thrust into West Germany by Soviet armored forces, including release of nuclear weapons.

Yet to his superiors in the army, Conrad was a wonder. "Clyde was always in the office day and night, typing, copying, and doing all paperwork that makes a (war) plans shop tick," one supervisor said.

Another wrote, "An absolutely outstanding NCO . . . an administrative genius . . ."

But then the world has always been taken by the outside of things.

Didn't our mothers advise before we left the house for school, "Comb your hair. Wash your face. Make sure your nails are clean. Shine your shoes." We are all taught at an early age that to *appear* is the same as to *be*. We present to those who can confer advantages a very highly edited version of ourselves in order to extract advantages.

ARE THERE DIFFERENT kinds of traitors? Does one type predominate over another?

Miles Copeland, one of the CIA's early legends and a personal friend, now deceased, said that there are four types of traitor. Type one is the spy who is spotted by an alert KGB recruiter, whose potential is assessed (do they have access to classified or other valuable information), who is then slowly conditioned to spy, and who is then "managed" according to KGB principles.

Another type is the walk-in. This is a person with access to classified information who usually has some intelligence experience that enables him or her to walk into a foreign embassy and offer services without being spotted by counterintelligence watchdogs. Accused FBI spy Robert Hanssen, arrested last February, was such a spy, although Hanssen did his walk-in by mail. John Walker Jr. was another. Walker actually appeared in the lobby of the four-story old gray stone mansion of the Russian embassy on Sixteenth Street in Washington with a highly classified document in his hand. After a hurried interview with a startled Soviet who had to ensure that Walker wasn't a plant or a provocation sent by the FBI, the Soviets accepted Walker's offer and plunked a hat on his head, then smuggled him out a side entrance and bundled him into a waiting car. A few hours later the Russians let their new recruit out on a Washington side street.

The third spy type is the long-term agent or defector-in-place, usually recruited in their youth, who at the time of their recruitment were far removed from the sensitive information desired by their handlers and who took years to work their way into a useful position. Kim Philby, the British traitor, was just such an agent. Recruited at Cambridge, he married a communist, then later became part of the foreign policy establishment. The longer he stayed, the more valuable he became. He ended up running the Soviet spy hunting operations for British intelligence until mounting suspicions forced him to resign. Even then he was able to work for British magazines until he finally fled to the Soviet Union after a long and brilliant career for the Soviets.

There is a fourth type that Copeland calls the "Willy" after an actual CIA case. A "Willy" is someone who spies for one intelligence service, like the Soviets, but is convinced by his handler that he is working for another, more friendly power. This is often called a false-flag recruitment. Never mind that espionage does not consist of spying for countries hostile to the United States; spying for allies of the United States still legally makes you a traitor. Jonathan Pollard, a top U.S. spy for Israel, learned this after Defense Secretary Casper Weinberger intervened with the court to ensure Pollard got a life sentence for his spying for Israel.

Jerry Whitworth, who FBI agent Courtney West described to me as being "one of the most deadly spies in U.S. history," was a navy radioman, who was convicted of working for John Walker Jr. to help steal navy codes and operational plans in the event of a U.S.-Soviet war. He was sentenced to 365 years in prison. When Walker recruited his friend, he told Whitworth that the top secret information they were selling was being given to Israel, a beleaguered ally of the United States, and for years Whitworth seemed satisfied to believe this.

How does the enemy spymaster snag his mole? Through recruitment.

Recruitment is the jewel of the crown of any intelligence service. "The best case officer is the busiest case officer," the CIA tells its prospective espionage managers. "Turning" a hostile security officer or taking a Soviet diplomat or confidential secretary and getting them to work for the United States as a double agent—this is considered the acme of counterespionage, defined as the penetration of the enemy's secret service.

The Soviet handlers of John Walker Jr. and Jerry Whitworth were awarded the highest Soviet honors. The Soviet official in the San Francisco consulate that entrapped FBI counterintelligence agent Richard Miller rose very rapidly in the KGB as a result of the case. "The case officer is always a kind of elite in any intelligence service," said the CIA's former Soviet expert Fritz Ermarth.

The statue of Nathan Hale may stand outside the old agency head-quarters, but Major John Andre, the British Army officer and secret agent who recruited General Benedict Arnold to get from him plans to betray West Point (which would have cut the colonies in two at a key time in our Revolutionary War), is seen as more admirable for a simple reason: Andre was the mover, Arnold simply the moved. "Hale is just a poor messenger boy who got caught," a CIA official told me. "Little glory in that."

The urgency and care that goes into recruitment depends in large degree on the kind of secret information to which the potential traitor has access. Men like Philby or Ames, who have access to Soviet spies being hunted by the services of the United States and Britain, are extremely valuable, but of far more value are obtaining a country's war plans or compromising its military communications systems.

Recruitment consists of several steps: identifying the kind of information that must be obtained and identifying the people who have this information, determining who among these people can safely be approached, and then picking one as a target. The case officer then checks on the operational data he has accumulated on his target, including range of social contacts, club, hobbies (especially those that include group activity), and the various personal services he employs from a maid to a dentist.

The focus is on the prospective target's weaknesses. A defector from the MFS, the East German state security service, Werner Stiller, explained to U.S. counterintelligence officials how it was done, at least by the KGB. Stiller said that KGB recruiters taught the acronym MICE in classes on recruitment approaches to Americans. MICE stood for money, ideology, corruption/coercion, and ego.

Of all the motives, ideology was discarded as outdated certainly by the 1960s. But during the 1930s, when the Soviet government launched an enormous effort to penetrate the U.S. government to gather industrial secrets, many Americans were sympathetic to communism. James Agee, a writer at *Time* magazine, proudly wrote his priest in the 1930s, "Of course, I am a communist."

In the 1930s, America was full of communist romantics who saw democracy as an economic failure because of the depression, and who turned to the Soviet Union both as a leader of the "progressive" forces and the chief barrier in the struggle against rising fascism in the world.

To these men and women, the "I" in MICE was very real. Laurence

Duggan, a liberal working in Franklin Roosevelt's New Deal government, was described by his Soviet handler as "soft . . . cultural and reserved . . . under his wife's influence."

With his position in the U.S. State Department's Latin America division, Duggan was seen as a way to get to Noel Field, an American working in the U.S. State Department's European division, a target of top priority for the Soviets at the time.

As a reward for supplying sound information from U.S. "neutral" outposts on the intentions and capabilities of Germany and Japan, Moscow wanted to give a money payment to Duggan. His Soviet handler Boris Bazarov reacted in alarm, warning his superiors that Duggan "will reject the money and probably consider the money proposal as an insult."

Months before, another Soviet handler had purchased a beautiful crocodile toiletries case engraved with Duggan's monograms. Duggan had "categorically refused" to accept even that gift, saying that, "he was working for our common ideas . . . and not helping us because of any material interest."

Those quaint days are long gone. As Stiller said of the KGB, "We were told that if an American expressed belief in our ideology, we were to reject him as a provocateur [double agent]. We did not expect the capitalist Americans to accept our ideology. Our trainers emphasized that money was the proven path to obtain the loyalty of most Americans."

When a Soviet diplomat asked walk-in John Walker Jr. in 1967, "Is your coming here politically or financially motivated?," Walker didn't hesitate to answer. "Purely financial. I need the money," he said.

When the Russian started to ask Walker if he had ever read Karl Marx, Walker said rudely that what he wanted was a lifetime contract. He would supply the Russians classified information in return for a weekly salary of $500 to $1,000, "just like an employee."

Money and a sense of having personal preferment by any means appeared to lie at the base of Benedict Arnold's treachery. Always obsessed by making money, Arnold was true to character in his treachery. His asking price? 20,000 British pounds sterling, a princely sum for those days.

Money was the precipitating factor in Ames becoming a walk-in. Panicked over expenses connected with a divorce, he saw selling secrets as the only way out.

But was that his only motive? "He wanted to make an impact on history. . . . How many people have a chance to nudge history in one direction or the other? But he did. He really did," said David T. Samson of the CIA.

So ego is involved too, as it would be with Walker and Conrad.

"I would say ego is second only in importance to money as the motive that spurs a traitor," said Stuart Herrington, the army colonel who hunted Conrad down.

Certainly coercion becomes a factor once the traitor turns over his first stolen documents. "All spies think they can control the situation," Herrington said. "They say to themselves, 'I'll just give them this.' But it doesn't work that way. You've taken their money, and they are in control." A door slams shut behind them, and there can be no turning back.

Treason is a drastic act. One traitor's wife said to him after his conviction, "I wish you had done anything but this."

To betray one's country is to annihilate a very intimate part of the self. Our lives are not only personal, but social. They involve not the present, but a past lived in common with others. What can cause a man to, as one Soviet defector put it, "drop a curtain" over his past school experiences, his love for his mother or father, his schools and activities, the close friends he had while growing up, his old loyalties and past ties?

Just how does the traitor turn his or her back on all of this?

Paul Redmond once said to me, "You can't generalize about traitors." I beg to differ. What traitors share in common, no matter what their case may be, is the fact that they are criminals and criminals share certain characteristics. Too often by merely recognizing that treason is a crime, we stop our minds short of exploring more deeply what the word "criminal" really means. For example, one of the most common myths about criminals is that they are someone just like us who simply made an unlucky slip, which was followed by another slip until it was too late for them to turn back and live like a normal law-abiding human being.

This is not at all correct, at least according to prominent and highly regarded criminal psychologists such as Dr. Samuel Yochelson and Dr. Stanton Samenow, who have written a three-volume work on the criminal personality.

According to them, criminals are people who do not think at all like the rest of us do. To these psychologists, being a criminal isn't a difference of degree in behavior or of thought, but of kind.

If we look at the life of a traitor, we soon find that long before the final, fatal defection occurs, there lies behind the traitor a lifetime of little defections, of small dishonesties, of a general feeling of being superior to existing rules, of disdain for common decency and for what is good and trusting in people in favor of an exaltation of self at the expense of others.

John Walker Jr.'s early life was full of storms and squalls. The father was a failure, the mother a nag. Loud arguments, slammed doors, brawls, and drunken lectures were the norm. At an early age, Walker began to give in to little displays of meanness: he stole eggs and threw them at street cars, rolled used tires down a hill at passing cars, threw rocks through the windows of a Catholic school.

He and a friend soon began to steal money from the pockets of unattended winter coats at school functions. They stole coins from the church canisters where donations had been left for the poor or to help the church to pay for prayer candles.

Later Walker and his friend were setting fires. One night, out shooting at empty bottles and cans, Walker went and began firing at headlights out in the distance on a highway.

Aldrich Ames's home was unhappy. His father, Carleton, was an irresponsible man. He came from River Falls, Wisconsin, where, during World War II, he was teaching at a community college. But in his mid-forties, with three children and a wife to support, he suddenly dropped his teaching job and went to work for the CIA, becoming a spy in Burma. It wasn't a job he did well. One of his performance reviews said of him, "He has no redeeming values. I don't see any hope for him ever to improve." Faced with catastrophic defeat, Carleton Ames took to drink to console himself. Of the three children he had, all would turn out to be alcoholics.

"Rick" Ames, as Aldrich was called, would be remembered by his friends for loving "fantasy games," for being a practical joker, and for liking to act in plays. Yet he too had a dark, rebellious, self-indulgent side. He once shoplifted a candy bar from a café. With a new BB gun, he shot out the side windows of the school principal's car. With a friend, he stole a delivery boy's bicycle. When he became especially hungry, he would go and steal money from his father's wallet to treat himself to meals.

He liked to perform magic tricks because of the element of deception that made the trick work. Knowing a trick of course meant he was in possession of information denied the audience.

He once worked with a fellow magician to perform an elaborate trick involving a séance on a group of friends at a party, but he never told anyone afterward the role he played. *"Never,"* said the magician friend. "Do you know how rare that is? Most people want to take credit, but Rick got his kicks from fooling people."

When he was twenty, Rick went to the University of Chicago, consumed by a passion for acting. He barely passed his first year, and flunked out by his second. Unable to confront failure, he began to drink, like his father.

What does this indicate, if anything?

Many people flunk out of school, come from broken homes, or have deep-seated psychological problems, but they don't betray their countries. So what elements are added to a traitor's character that makes him the kind of unfeeling human being he is?

The traitor is, first of all, a person who believes that he or she is entitled to the satisfaction of his whims and impulses and appetites, no matter what the consequences. To the mature adult, moral life consists of being able to select intelligently among strikingly opposed courses of conduct by using common sense to make real to one's mind what effects following the first will mean as opposed to following the second. If we pursue one set of actions, we will reap affection and admiration; if we follow the other, we will be scorned or despised or ignored. One offers the rewards of accomplishment, praise, and favorable notice, and the other the pains of disgrace. There is also the consideration of whether the choice we select will aid in the development of the good of the self or whether the course we choose yields to whatever in us is impulsive, dishonest, or weak.

But the traitor, like the criminal, doesn't bother to deliberate. "I have a character flaw that never got corrected," Ames told an interviewer. "If someone else says, 'Hey, you got to do this,' and I don't want to, I don't argue about it, I simply don't do it. What's odd is that I react in this way without ever considering the consequences. I never look ahead. I just do what I want."

Traitors, like other criminals, tend to see themselves "as the hub of every situation, never as one of the spokes," Samenow says. A convict once told him, "I made myself a little god at every turn. . . . I always wanted to feel like a king."

"Spies almost always think they're something special," wrote Colonel Stuart Herrington, the U.S. Army spy hunter who headed the investigation of Conrad. "When someone such as Clyde . . . looks in the mirror, he sees the world's cleverest, boldest and most enterprising fellow. Entering a crowded room, the Clyde Conrads of the world gaze on the assembled masses with pity: These are the ordinary slobs who don't have a clue about

how one makes it big in life. Only he, the spy who leads an adventure-
laden dual life, has overcome the odds and broken the code that leads to
riches and fulfillment."

Because of his exaggerated notion of his own capabilities, the traitor
sees himself a master of some great shadowy unseen empire. He never sees
himself as obligated to anyone or having to account for his actions to anyone. Jack Devine, Ames's boss at one time and the CIA station chief in
Rome, discovered this one day in a sinister incident.

It occurred many years before Ames became a traitor. Ames was at the
time only a mediocre case officer, very poor at recruiting new spies or assets, which was an important part of his job. Yet in spite of this, Devine
told me that "there was always some grandiosity" about Ames, some "exaggerated narcissism" to be seen in his personal makeup.

Devine spoke of one time when Ames had failed a polygraph test and
then hadn't bothered to come in for the makeup. Devine was furious, and
when he encountered Ames in the hallway, really let Ames have it. "Ames
didn't say anything. He didn't say, 'Hey, my cat got hit by a car and I
couldn't come in or my wife was sick.' He didn't make any excuses. He
didn't counterpunch. He absorbed the blow," said Devine.

But then something chilling occurred.

"Ames's eyes glistened and grew hard, and I could see, at that moment,
for the first time, that Ames was thinking, 'Why am I, a great man, being
pestered by this midget and paid flunkey?'" Devine said, adding, "It was
really startling, watching his eyes start to glisten."

Because of an inner insufficiency, the traitor always has to have the
upper hand, but he gains it not through fair competition, but underhand-
edly by dishonest stealth. He loads things in his favor without others
knowing, because his secrecy affords him a sense of superior mastery.
Traitors enjoy deceiving people, and enjoy the fact others are unaware of
the sinister intentions behind the benign façade.

Ames, as we've seen, enjoyed deceiving people and approached everything as a kind of role to be played, both in his professional and personal
life. As a high school friend observed, "He once said to me, never express
your real feelings."

A traitor, like most criminals, is a superb dissembler who can teach a
chameleon to change color.

To friends of John Walker Jr. the navy spy gave two entirely different
impressions. To Joey Long, Walker was a rambunctious adventurer who

was polite, respectful, honest. To Jack Bennett: ". . . believe me, what you see on the surface with John is not what you get. Trust me. I knew him like a brother, better than anyone else. Jack is cunning, clever, intelligent, personable, and intrinsically evil." With Bennett, Walker performed all sorts of mean, petty crimes and both ended up being arrested for burglary.

All traitors appear to have an ambition to achieve and stand out to bolster their exalted self-image. But in the traitor, the drive to distinction is twisted and unscrupulous. There is desperation about it, as if not to be everything means you will end up being nothing. The end goal of accomplishment, to add significance to life, gets lost.

In the case of Benedict Arnold, we see that his superior boldness, battlefield ability, drive, and tactical genius that made him a key actor in the victories at Fort Ticonderoga and Saratoga were not coupled to any principle of loyalty. In the end, he simply was a superior capacity for sale, and the British thought him worth more of a price than his fellow countrymen.

The road to accomplishment for the ordinary person is simple: it means applying present efforts and resources to present problems. But the traitor, like the criminal, lacks the grit for gradual growth and instead must start out at the top. When they find that's denied them, they lapse into grandiose fantasy. Says Samenow, the criminal fantasizes that he "is the medal of honor combat hero, the super secret agent, or the sleuth who cracks a murder case that has stymied an entire police department."

There is a pathos in Walker and accomplice and fellow-spy Jerry Whitworth sitting and drinking in Virginia, talking of their spying, and Whitworth saying, "Isn't it a shame that no one will ever know how good we really were?" Or Clyde Conrad in a café turning to his Hungarian handler and saying to him, indicating to a soldier accomplice, "Tell my buddy here, what they think of me in Hungary." To Hungary, he was a legend, the greatest Soviet spy since World War II.

What is equally amazing is that no matter what crime the traitor commits, he may acknowledge that his actions are criminal, but he never sees himself as being one, says Samenow. Thomas Cavenaugh, employee of Northrop who tried to sell classified Stealth secrets to the Soviets to pay off his debts, rationalized his act by thinking of how corrupt the U.S. government was. By withdrawing from Vietnam after 55,000 American servicemen had died there, the U.S. government had sold out. If the U.S. government had sold out, why shouldn't he?

Caught by the FBI in a sting operation, convicted and sentenced to two life terms in the federal penitentiary at Lompoc, California, he later told a reporter, "I didn't try to sell us out. . . . I'm not a would-be traitor. I was giving (the Soviets) information because I thought that's what they wanted to hear in order (for me) to get the money . . . ?"

To him, his crime was really only poor judgment. "I know what I did was wrong and stupid. But I sincerely do not belong around killers, homosexuals and mentally unstable people," he said.

When John Walker was confronted with the fact that the information he sold resulted in the deaths of U.S. pilots in Vietnam, he refused to believe it. He was too important a spy and Russia would not have passed such valuable information to a mere ally. Besides, he said, the Soviets posed no real military threat to the United States, and a war between the two wasn't a real possibility. ("Walker apparently forgot what the Soviets did in Afghanistan, Nicaragua, and Angola," said a U.S. intelligence official in reply.)

A traitor is without remorse. A convict told Samenow, "I turn people on or off as I want. My idea in life is to satisfy myself to the extreme. I don't need to defend my behavior. My thing is my thing. I don't feel I am obligated to the world or to nobody." John Walker expressed similar sentiments.

Another convict said of the patrons at a neighborhood bar where he mixed drinks, "All the people there were checkers or pawns waiting for me to deal with them as I wished and sacrifice as I wished."

Ames apparently felt the same way. As a spy for the Soviets, his first concern was to protect himself, and as an employee for the CIA, he knew who was secretly working for America. In the end, for $1.6 million, he compromised over a hundred spies, and turned over for execution twenty-five more, of which ten were executed. One was a retired officer and grandfather in his fifties who was taken to a cell, made to kneel, and shot with a pistol in the back of the head. The shot in the head was a piece of Stalinist tradition. The exiting bullet acts to make the face unrecognizable.

Ames's reaction? It was their fault. The Soviet spies had changed sides. They were playing a dangerous game. "They were not innocent men," he said to a reporter.

It may be that because Philby or Walker or Ames or Hanssen all got satisfaction in acting as they did that we can assume all traitors are activated by love of the same objective or ruled by the same dominant forces of character. But in the group of men and women we'll examine in this book, we'll discover that each act of treachery is as individual as a snowflake or a leaf.

The Traitor as Hero:
BENEDICT ARNOLD

The crown o' th' earth doth melt. My lord!
O wither'd is the garland of the war.

—WILLIAM SHAKESPEARE, *Antony and Cleopatra*

The way up is exactly the same as the way down.

—T. S. ELIOT, *THE WASTELAND*

1

★ ★ ★

To THOSE OF us who know Benedict Arnold chiefly as the historical cliché that depicts him as the embodiment of mercenary treason, it may come as a surprise that two names, George Washington and Benedict Arnold, blazed like torches throughout the American Revolution. To minds of the time, they represented colonial heroism at its highest, finest, and most inspiring.

As late as 1780, before the British surrender at Yorktown ended the war, many Europeans and Americans regarded Arnold as the greatest battlefield commander produced by both sides. When a French historian sat down to write a history of the war, his first volume was devoted to Arnold, "the Hannibal of the North," whereas Washington got only a footnote.[1]

The difficulty with most current historical accounts of Arnold is not simply the venomous contempt with which they treat their subject, but that the authors tend to view Arnold's military career through the lens of his treason, as if the second were more important than the first. I differ with them because Arnold seems to me to be a figure of genuine tragedy. He was an insecure man with a tremendous compulsion to prove himself to other people, yet on the battlefield, his spirit was unquenchably determined, his heart the embodiment of effective wrath, full of the drive that wants to "hurt the enemy, in any way possible, with any weapon; to destroy not his will to exist, but his ability to make that will effective."[2] His talents were mighty and towering, and his contributions in founding American freedom so enormous, that to see him collapse in moral darkness is a startling and horrific sight.

If he is our greatest traitor, he is also our saddest.

ONE OF THE most striking things about Arnold's career is its rollercoaster character. Nothing about it went as expected. It was up in glory like a rocket one minute, sputtering back to Earth in failure and reversal in the next.

As a man, Arnold had a mind and character that seemed most at home in extremes. He went from a cowardly child to a daredevil, from a man of poor means to a rich one, from an aggressive, head-down fighter for the cause of liberty and independence to a despised and mercenary turncoat.

The marvel is that throughout his turbulent history, his innate characteristics are persistent. There is an incredible love of self, a love of accumulating money, a craving for social esteem mixed with an addiction to reckless self-assertion, plus a passionate, stubborn love of being his own law. Thus the same impulses propelled him first to success in business, next to glory in war, and finally to ignominy and ruin.

By the time our hero was born in Norwich, Connecticut, in 1741, the Arnold name, once great in the eyes of the world, had decayed to a feeble shade of its former luster. Arnold's great grandfather Benedict had been governor of the colony of Rhode Island following Roger Sherman. His son, Benedict II, however, managed to lose the greater portion of the family fortune so that by the time we come to Benedict IV, the traitor's father, we find the family in very poor straits. Benedict IV, apprenticed as a cooper, lived a modest, circumscribed life until he fell in love and married Hannah More, who belonged to a leading social family with a very large fortune. At a single stroke, Benedict IV found himself installed among the highest social circles of the town, part of the preferred and idolized set that worked all the levers of worldly power.

At first, Benedict IV very much enjoyed the cold pride of rank and precedence. Every Sunday, with all eyes following him, he would stroll down to the very foremost pew of the church, leaving to loiter behind him, at the very rear of the edifice, his unfortunate brother Roger who had not risen in life as he had, but who had remained but a simple cooper.

When Benedict IV had a son in 1738, it was named Benedict, but died in less than a year. When another son was born in January 1741, he too received the name Benedict. It was our hero's first hour. But the good days were fast fading for Benedict IV. He had become a successful merchant-shipper with a brisk trade in Long Island and the West Indies, but a severe financial depression caused by turmoil in Europe soon brought about the calamitous crash of his business. Crushed, he quickly retreated for strengthening and consolation to a tavern. Till then, like most New Englanders, Benedict IV drank heavily and regularly, but drinking went from being something to do to being instead the only thing he did.

As the first ebbed out in her husband, Mrs. Arnold tried to imbue her son, Benedict, with a spirit of submission to the mysteries of fate. Some have said her religious gloom undercut Benedict's self-confidence, but she was a warm, affectionate woman who had a drunken bankrupt for a husband and who had lost two children to illnesses. Since she had suffered much from it, she had good reason to talk of resigning oneself to the vagaries of God's will.

In one letter, she wrote to Arnold, "Keep a steady watch over your thoughts, words and actions, be dutiful to superiors, obliging to equals and affable to inferiors. Always choose that your companions be your betters." In a constant succession of other letters, she would urge her son to submit gracefully to God's will in all things, to show humility, to "seek the guidance of the Holy Spirit."

She might as well have been teaching a cow to curtsy because there was nothing submissive in Arnold's character. From an early age, he stole, he tied buckets to the tails of cows, and one night he set alight some stolen barrels of tar, making the biggest blaze ever seen in the budding town of Norwich. When the town constable arrived, Arnold confronted him, words flew, and Arnold suddenly whipped off his coat and offered to fight the official. He was only fourteen.[3] He was about five feet seven, but compact and powerfully built, with black hair, swarthy skin, hard gray-blue eyes, a hooked nose, and an almost feminine mouth. He seemed to be made a courage, yet his grit was the product of exerted will, not a quality occurring naturally to his character. He would later admit, "I was a physical coward until I was fifteen." So behind the invulnerable persona there lurked the drive of an imperious will to succeed.

His mother had two cousins, Daniel and Joshua Lathrop, both Yale graduates who became apothecaries and business partners in the general merchandise trade, rising to become two of the town's wealthiest citizens.

At the age of thirteen, Arnold became their apprentice. It was the Lathrops who taught Arnold the intricacies of trade. They sold drugs, French wines, and even exotic goods like woven silks from India. Arnold lived with the other apprentices at Daniel Lathrop's Georgian mansion where Arnold and the other boys were waited on by slaves and driven about town in the Lathrops' splendid chaise and horses. Arnold took away from this a love of rich living that he never fully lost.

When he was twenty, the Lathrops encouraged Arnold to move to New Haven, and with their money, helped set him up there as a junior partner as part of a plan to expand their business. Three years later, Arnold had formed a partnership with one Adam Babcock, and they soon owned three ships and traded in horses, rum, molasses, pork, grain crops, and timber. Arnold made long trading voyages to Canada and throughout the Caribbean. He was a tremendously hard worker, energetic, prompt, conspicuously efficient, full of purpose and drive, and possessed of a great power to compete. He was keenly intelligent, always paying meticulous attention to detail. In his travels, he saw a great many things and remembered what he saw.

As a trading merchant, he could be shady and unscrupulous. For example, in one transaction Arnold paid a Jeremiah Pennusston for a load of cordage in such a confusion of French currencies that it took Pennusston some time to discover he had been drastically shortchanged.[4] Nor did Arnold pay much attention to existing British law except to break it. Like John Hancock, the bulk of Arnold's profits came from smuggling, which was widely winked at by traders and merchants of the time.

It's no surprise to discover that when war broke out, Arnold was one of the wealthiest men in New Haven, yet a shadow lay across his success, due entirely to his volatile temper. Arnold was a very flammable man, apt to bridle at any interference, who suffered from the unfortunate habit of concluding disputes by turning to swords, pistols, or fists. When a crewmember of his had asked for a raise in pay and been refused, the man plotted to inform on Arnold's smuggling to the authorities. Arnold was the grim spirit behind a boisterous party who seized the man in a tavern, flogged him, and drove him terrified from the town. In another instance, Arnold took a dislike to a suitor of his beloved sister, Hannah, and drove off the annoying and offensive wooer by firing bullets at the man's heels. Arnold fought two duels in the West Indies, and among the more staid of

New Haven's town fathers, was generally known as a turbulent, uncontrollable, and unruly individual.

But Arnold was a hot-blooded man in every sense. Those Arnold loved, he loved with headlong affection and with all the force of his soul. His sister, Hannah, was a major character of his biography. He stayed close to her all his life, leaving her to care for his children after his first wife died, and returning to have her care for him following his first failures in the military.

In the late 1760s, Arnold was utterly smitten by the daughter of the local sheriff, Margaret Mansfield, who came from a family with a solid local reputation and respectable financial means. We know little about her beyond the fact she was sickly as a child, but since Arnold did everything wholeheartedly, he courted his Margaret like a being obsessed, seeming to see in union with her the "foundation of happiness or misery," in George Washington's words. She finally consented to be his wife, and they married in February 1767. She would bear him three children, and his love for her was intense. He surrounded her with luxuries and built for her one of the finest mansions in New Haven with a fine view of Long Island Sound, a defiant assertion that his abilities were not to be determined by having a failure for a father.

IT WAS APRIL 1775. The news of the clash at Lexington and Concord swept through the colonies like a storm through tossing trees. Something unendurable had ended. "Uncommon parts need uncommon times for their exertion," the great English writer and critic Samuel Johnson had said, and suddenly, for many, there shimmered in the air the hope of making a glorious name, of having a career that might be brilliant, great, and important.

Men flocked to Boston in droves.

The American Revolution, of course, was actually not a revolution but a war of succession and a civil war. It did not, at first, attempt to replace or alter the accepted character of political and legal authority. No one quite foresaw the ultimate dimensions of the struggle. When George Washington left for Boston, he'd told his wife in Virginia he expected to be back in a year. No one but a handful of professional radicals believed that the war would mean permanent separation from the Crown. Even fewer believed the colonies had any real chance of winning such a conflict. When Washington was named colonial army commander-in-chief, he rushed from the room. The task lay beyond the scope of his abilities, he said, and he seemed suddenly drowned in self-doubt. With tears in his eyes, he somberly told radical Virginia firebrand Patrick Henry, "From this time . . . I date the decline and ruin of my reputation."[5]

But one thing was already clear to colonial strategists: any major British threat to their liberty was likely to come from Canada. It was one of the colonists' principal strategic conceptions. The core of the rebellion centered in Massachusetts, and the British might try to stage an invasion that would drive south, cut off New England from other colonies, and move to crush out the rebellion at its source.

In 1774, Samuel Adams, leader of Boston's Sons of Liberty, and an incendiary who sought complete severance from Britain, had sent a secret agent by the name of John Brown to Quebec, to not only test the loyalty of the French-speaking inhabitants there, but to also find out about the condition of the forts at Ticonderoga and Crown, which controlled Lake Champlain, a 135-mile-long watery road to the headwaters of the Hudson. Brown, a lawyer from Pittsfield, Massachusetts, had worked for Arnold's cousin, Oliver, a man Arnold heartily disliked. In an eager and glowing report, Brown said that the forts should be quickly taken if hostilities began.

Within days of the Concord clash, Arnold, now a captain of the New Haven Company of the Governor's Foot Guards, marched his small group of men to Cambridge, where he soon appeared before the Massachusetts Committee of Public Safety. In terse, powerful words, he outlined a bold plan to take Fort Ticonderoga and a place called Crown Point. Arnold emerged from the meeting no longer a captain, but a full colonel with orders for "a secret mission." But unknown to Arnold, Brown had already set plans in motion to have Ethan Allen accomplish the task. Allen was a huge, hulking man in a faded green coat. He had been a ranger in the French and Indian War and a speculator, and was also a wayward, unruly, hard-drinking outlaw full of bravery but utterly lacking in character and brains. He was also a traitor.[6]

Arnold was to gather 400 men and proceed, but he had hardly begun to organize when there came the unwelcome news that Allen was already moving to seize his prize. Not waiting to assemble his men, Arnold raced off with an orderly at breakneck speed, finally encountering the hulking Green Mountain Man himself. The Vermonter towered over him, but there was that odd element of menace in Arnold, a readiness to use force that always made people pause. As Arnold stood looking Allen in the eyes, something in the bigger man apparently gave way. He agreed that he and Arnold should share something like a joint command. The morning of May 10, Arnold and Allen and eighty-three Green Mountain Boys squeezed into boats, crossed Lake Champlain, and at 4 A.M., attacked a fort so decayed, its main gate couldn't fully close. There is a priceless image of the two men, Arnold and Allen, racing each other to be first inside the fort. Arnold, on the left, was faster. The forts, manned by only forty-eight men, half of whom were invalids, fell in less than ten minutes.

Allen's men, fanning out, discovered some rum and proceeded to get raucously, jubilantly, and recklessly drunk. There were wild scenes of Arnold snatching belongings out of the hands of Allen's drunkards and trying to give them back to the terrified British captives, but his efforts did no good. Amid the chaos, Allen, his face reddened by rum, suddenly reeled up to Arnold and declared that he had, in fact, never agreed to a joint command. A belligerent minion of Allen's put the muzzle of his musket to Arnold's chest, saying he would shoot Arnold then and there if Arnold didn't concur. All steel nerve, Arnold locked eyes with the man. The man lowered his musket and wobbled away.

But Allen's group snubbed Arnold. Since Arnold commanded no men, how could he get credit for the capture? For fours days, an idle, furious Arnold fired off letters to Massachusetts asking to be relieved. Then a white sail appeared in the water of the lake: Arnold's men had arrived from Massachusetts.

Only Arnold instantly saw that taking the forts was one thing, but holding them was another. For the sake of their own safety, the colonies must control the waters of Lake Champlain. Arnold put together a small force of fifty men, and using a previously captured schooner equipped with cannon, sailed boldly up the lake. On May 18, he pounced on the Canadian town of St. Johns, capturing the sloop, a British sergeant, and twelve British soldiers. Arnold had, on his own initiative, launched the first successful American invasion of foreign soil in American history. His efforts also forestalled a British attempt as a counterattack since he had seized and made off with their transportation.

As far as he was concerned, Arnold had performed his mission with thoroughness, zeal, and dedication. His brain was suddenly afire with plans about how the colonies could conquer Canada. He was convinced that a quick-hitting strike of pulverizing impact would bring all of Quebec province into the patriot camp, and he sent off a detailed plan to the Continental Congress.

Now, like a leaf in a tornado, Arnold was sucked into a vortex of numbing confusion. He was always slow to see the character of the political currents swirling around him, and with miraculous denseness, he understood nothing of the balancing of interests, the backstairs intrigues, and the double-faced schemes that are an essential part of politics. He also seemed to lack any feel for the structure of the government he'd been so eager to serve. Arnold's enemies, including Brown and a cowardly tavern-keeper named James Easton, had gone to the Continental and Massachusetts Congresses to try and blacken Arnold's name and give Allen the credit for the capture of the forts. But the fact was that the capture of the forts, in widening the war, placed Massachusetts squarely in the hot spotlight, and few politicians at that stage wanted final separation from the Crown. The result was that when Easton complained that Arnold had interfered with a successful mission sponsored by Connecticut, Massachusetts quickly stepped aside to let Connecticut be the sponsor and bear the brunt of the angry blame sure to come from the Crown. Arnold was, in effect, demoted and ordered to place his men under Connecticut command. The man whom his men had praised as "a humane, tender officer" and who had carried out his part in good faith was now being cast aside in favor of a virtual incompetent, General Hinman, called "King Log" because he was so congenitally incapable of decisive action.

Afflicted horribly with the gout, Arnold resigned, letting Easton and Brown, his enemies, take command of his men. As he always did when his feelings were hurt, Arnold headed for "the safe, happy asylum" of his home. In the past, his marriage had always helped him "to bear down any misfortune," but when he arrived, he found his sister, Hannah, hurrying with a frightened, ashen face down the stairs. Margaret, barely thirty, was dead, dying only days after his father-in-law had abruptly passed away.

ARNOLD'S DETAILED PLAN of conquest for Canada seemed as dead as Julius Caesar, but a pair of eyes had watched Arnold's foray up to St. Johns with keen interest. They belonged to a wealthy member of the old New York aristocracy. The new commander of the Hudson-Champlain theater, Philip Schuyler, was forty-two years old, tall, erect, and every inch the patrician. In the summer days of 1775, seizing the north seemed to many an easy accomplishment to effect, especially since colonial intelligence knew that the British commander in Canada, Sir Guy Carleton, had transferred most of his troops to help besiege the colonials at Boston, leaving Montreal unmanned. Schuyler's plan was to take a force to Fort Ticonderoga and then proceed to take Montreal and Quebec, bringing Canada into the war on the side of the colonies. If the invasion was a success, it would probably mean the British would sue for peace.

Schuyler assigned a group to take the traditional water route, but there was another route known only to traders and trappers, and woodsmen like Washington. It meant a trek through the dense, unbroken, forbidding forests of Maine to emerge and surprise Quebec on its flank. The deciding weight as to who would command the second segment would come from Commander-in-Chief Washington. Washington was very tall, six feet four, and Arnold was only average in height. Washington was an aristocrat. Arnold merely a merchant. But when they met in August, both instantly liked what they saw. Above all things, Washington hated inactivity, and Arnold was vigorous and enterprising, full of that drive to close in on the enemy that is the mark of the born field commander. The two quickly became warm friends.

Arnold was given the rank of colonel. Thanks to his friendship with Washington and Schuyler, he once more had a military career, and he was full of relief to know that fate had once again placed his feet on his life's true path. But Arnold now faced vast difficulties. Like a line of ants, Arnold's men struggled up impassable rivers, marshes, and swamps, bearing their homemade boats upon their backs. They stopped amid walls of dense woods to fell trees and hack paths through impenetrable brush and bramble thickets. Arnold soon found his soldiers had begun to flag. It was late September, and the country was as harsh and terrible as the weather. Numb and without energy, Arnold's men wandered into spongy quagmires where they sank in muck up to the knees, they were buffeted by bitter winds and blinded by stinging flurries of snow. Their clothes froze stiff as iron in the cold. The blight of diarrhea fastened on them, and then came cold, relentless rain with gusts lashing the trees and making them all sway one way.

In one of the finer moments of the war, Arnold held a council of war, asking his men if they felt up to going on. Without hesitation, they voted yes. Arnold's leadership had made them believe in themselves and in the inevitability of their success.

On November 2, General Richard Montgomery, Schuyler's second in command, took St. Johns and began to head for Montreal, but for Arnold's force, floundering in the wild, it was now an all-or-nothing race against time. The hungry men began to eat their cartridge boxes, their lip salve, even their leather moccasins, hobbling ahead barefoot the next day. They ate a pet dog. They learned to make a thin soup consisting of boiling candles in water. They even ate shaving soap.

Men began to die.

Finally, ravaged by smallpox, shivering from cold, hobbling from frostbite, his men tumbled out of the woods like so many scarecrows, emaciated, enfeebled, their vital fires almost gone out. But they had survived.

In the meantime, General Montgomery, who was in command, had taken Montreal without a fight and moved east to join with Arnold as chief commander before Quebec. Montgomery, Irish, tough, and only forty,[7] was mercurial and introspective, and Arnold marveled at his rapid changes of mood, but each was a born fighter, with a well-read military mind, and each found much to respect in the other. They were friends from the first.

They faced the canniest commander in North America, Sir Guy Carleton. Carleton had fought in the French and Indian War and had many gifts, which included a grave, self-possessed calm and a temperament of relentless tenacity. His forces had entered the town, raising the number of its defenders to 1,800 men. Now he lay in wait inside Quebec's walls.

On New Year's Eve, a blizzard struck, and so did the colonials. An initial volley killed Montgomery, his arm still raised in the air, just after he'd cried to his faltering men, "Come on, my good soldiers, your General calls you to come on." As Arnold raced up a blind street, ahead of his men, calling for a cannon, he was fired on by British troops behind a barricade and took a bullet in his calf and went down. Some of his men kept on and almost broke through before they were beaten back.

A deep gloom settled on the small army, but not on Arnold. Lying in a hospital bed, Arnold wrote to his sister, "I have no thoughts of leaving this proud town until I enter it in triumph."

Now a brigadier general and a famous man, Arnold used his sick, scanty, and faltering force to keep up a paper-thin siege of Quebec for an incredible five months. With the approach in May of heavy British reinforcements, Arnold was forced to move to Montreal. Beginning to ride again, Arnold damaged his wounded leg when his horse fell on an icy road.

He was the last man to leave Canadian soil. He took a force south, leaving behind a trail of scorched earth and charred ruins of St. Johns. Reaching the shore of Lake Champlain, Arnold dismounted his horse, shot him, and then got in a canoe, held steady by an aide, and paddled away, grimly defiant to the last.

When he met with his old patron Schuyler, Arnold's only thoughts focused on beating Carleton in battle. Even though he still limped from his leg wound and was wracked by rheumatic pains, he pronounced himself ready "to strain every nerve" in their forthcoming duel. But Congress was busy looking for a scapegoat, someone on whom could be pinned the blame for the failure of Canada, and Arnold's old enemies, Brown, Easton, and others, who had been with Montgomery's command, were filling the ears of congressional delegates with charges. These included the allegation that Arnold had been a thief, had helped spread smallpox among his men, and had threatened to give captured boats back to the British at Ticonderoga. The charges were malicious and entirely false, based mainly on Brown's injured fury at Arnold's having denied him a promotion he said was promised him by Montgomery.

Schuyler had urged Arnold not to engage his critics, but Schuyler himself had problems in the person of Major General Horatio Gates. Schuyler and Gates hated each other. The real difficulty with the feud lay with the fact that each had at his back a major faction. In Congress, New Englanders like John Adams and John Hancock loathed Schuyler, calling him a coward and unfit to command. They also hated him in part because of sectional rivalry: Schuyler was from New York and was seen as belonging to the group that had tried to unlawfully grab the Hampshire Grants— what is today called Vermont. To the colonial aristocracy who sought to preserve its power over the rising American masses, Schuyler loomed a hero, while to the New Englanders, Gates, they said, epitomized the worthy man of the people.

Schuyler and Gates couldn't have been more different. Schuyler had an attractive versatility of personality. He was bluff, hearty, and straightforward with his men, and suave and diplomatic with equals and superiors. Gates was sycophantic with superiors, and a martinet with his men. The two men abraded at other points. Where Schuyler was elegant, tall, and stately, Gates was fat and stooped, out of breath, and had a red face peering through heavy spectacles. He was nicknamed "Granny Gates" by his men.

Gates was the son of a British serving woman, a commoner in background. He served in Portugal under Brigadier General John Burgoyne, and then had seen combat in the New World. He had retired from the British Army with the rank of major when it was clear his lack of background and income would prevent him from purchasing his way up the British military ladder as so many others, like Burgoyne, had done. He had prepared to spin out his days drinking and gambling.

When the war came with the Crown, Gates's past military experience quickly gave him a prominent place, and he just as quickly became a focal point for those who belittled Washington and felt contempt for Schuyler. Unfortunately, Gates was a born intriguer who soon saw that the key to outranking his rivals lay with Congress. His keen eye had soon fixed where the sources of power lay and who worked the invisible threads that meant advancement. In no time, he was testing expertly for weak points, searching out those spots susceptible to the infections of flattery. He was seen at Congress often, making friends, fanning the flames of faction, and smoothing his path.

The Congress quickly decided that short enlistments, lack of money, and smallpox, not Arnold, had been the cause of the collapse of the Canadian campaign. Brown had been forced to slink snarling into the background after Gates had stepped in and quelled the slurs being cast on Arnold by the court of inquiry by saying, "The United States must not be deprived of this excellent officer's services at this important moment."

And important it was.

The British fleet would be sailing down Lake Champlain, and Gates appointed Arnold to stop them. The only problem was that the Americans lacked anything resembling a fleet. As the British under Carleton cumbersomely disassembled huge deep-water ships and carried them across almost impassable rock shoals to get them to Lake Champlain, Arnold hastily built a fleet of flat-bottomed ships. What plagued him greatly was the quality of the crew. "You ask for a sailor and they send you a tavern waiter," he stormed.

Grave news came. On August 22, the British had inflicted a smashing defeat on Washington at Long Island. Other defeats followed at White Plains and Fort Washington, leaving British General William Howe the option of sailing up the Hudson toward Albany, with Carleton coming down from Canada to join him. Carleton was still smarting from a jeer made at him by Lord George Germain, who was in charge of conducting the war from London. When the attempt to invade Canada collapsed in 1776, Carleton had trumpeted his success to Germain only to have come sailing back, "I am sorry you did not get Arnold, for of all the Americans, he seems to me the most enterprising and dangerous."

Germain was right and how dangerous Arnold was to him was made clear on October 11, when Arnold made a stand at Valcour Island. The fight between the two fleets seesawed back and forth. Arnold was everywhere, doing everything, exhorting, expostulating, planning, sighting guns, limping quickly over decks grown slippery with blood, issuing orders, maneuvering boats. His face was blackened with gunpowder, his hair was singed, and yet he kept dashing from gun to gun, the fury of battle upon him. From half past twelve until dark, the guns blazed and the battle raged, and then finally quiet fell.

Arnold's fleet had been shot to shreds, but he spotted a gap in the British line and slipped through. Arnold's battered boats made it to Buttonmold Bay ten miles from Crown Point, and after his men unloaded their ammunition, Arnold himself torched the *Congress,* his flagship. Arnold then burned the buildings at the fort and destroyed his remaining fleet. Exhausted, his force finally reeled into Fort Ticonderoga.

He had suffered a tactical defeat but a great strategic victory. Arnold had saved the American Revolution.

2

★ ★ ★

GLORY, REPUTATION, WHAT is said in praise about a man near and far when he is dead was what Benedict Arnold aimed for. To have men look at him as at a god, to stand out in his own and in others' eyes, endowed your life with meaning, and glory was what his soul craved most, cost what it would.

Yet in the aftermath of Valcour, the glory Arnold sought—the recognition of his supreme excellence in battle—seemed as far from him as when he had started the war. Early 1777 dawned as a dark low point for the cause. Everywhere the colonial armies were in retreat. George Washington had briefly rallied the revolution with small victories at Trenton and Princeton, but with the public, enthusiastic fervor for the war had waned. To make things worse, Congress, which had responsibility for the day-to-day conduct of the conflict, made the sudden and inexplicable decision to make war on military merit. On February 19, the delegates, anxious to keep the military subordinate to themselves, promoted five brigadiers to major generals over Arnold, the first on the list, and over Nathaniel Greene, one of Washington's finest commanders in the field, who was second.

This recklessly selfish and densely ignorant reasoning quickly reversed itself when a real threat appeared in the form of a British advance on New

Jersey. Arnold, not the new political appointees, was called to defend Philadelphia, and William Howe, the British commander, soon retreated to Staten Island. In April, Congress would again rely on Arnold to repel a British invasion of Danbury, which he did in a hard, mean-fought fight. The British again withdrew, and a guilty Congress in May 1777 finally made Arnold a major general, but without restoring his military seniority. Arnold was too sensitive to the opinion of others not to be cut to the quick. He resigned in bitterness from the army, but Congress did not act on the resignation because it found itself enveloped by a new crisis of extraordinary intensity: British General Johnny Burgoyne had appeared before Fort Ticonderoga, easily captured it, and now stood poised to mount a terrible, massive invasion down the Hudson.

The dreaded fear of dismemberment from the north rose up like an old ghost.

Gentleman Johnny Burgoyne was born in 1723 to parents who had waited nine years to have a child. It was whispered by the malicious that he was a bastard, but this appears not to be true. He was sent to Westminster School in London, and at fourteen, joined the Third Troop of Horse Guards as a sub-brigadier. In 1737, burning for glory of distinction, he began his military career in earnest. He was a tall, handsome, witty man, a person of courteous charm, and an excellent card player. But when George Germain gave Burgoyne the command for the northern invasion, his lordship had made a major blunder. He took a task that required methodical engineering skills and a deep knowledge of forest warfare and gave it to a kind of British Custer. Burgoyne was a cavalryman as opposed to a general. A general is patient, diligent, methodical, holding a comprehensive, prudent view that is coupled with a readiness to annihilate any enemy before him. By contrast, a cavalryman is given to a thirst for glory, to thoughtless haste and reckless show and this Burgoyne was soon to display. It is hardly surprising that Burgoyne's plan miscarried from the first. It would have been smarter for Burgoyne to have floated his force of 7,200 down Lake George to the Hudson and move on to Albany to be joined by St. Leger and his force of Indians moving in from the west, but Burgoyne came overland, dragging a long wagon train heavily laden with carts and cannon. Schuyler was quick to react. He dispatched Arnold in haste to block him and soon Burgoyne's advance had slowed to a crawl. It took him three weeks to advance twenty-seven miles.

Next, Arnold rushed west to attack the force commanded by St. Leger and his Indians, already blunted by a battle in the Mohawk Valley, Arnold used man-killing forced marches and a resourceful campaign of disinformation that alarmed St. Leger's Indian allies and caused them to desert. Defeated, St. Leger turned back.

Once again, Arnold was a hero.

But he was now to step blindly into the deadly pit of the feud that existed between Philip Schuyler and Horatio Gates, and he would climb out of it an altogether different and deeply scarred man. The festering rift between the two commanders had gotten worse after the capture of Ticonderoga, when Congress, infested with Gates's backers and sponsors, abruptly replaced Schuyler and Gates, ordering the former to present himself and explain how Ticonderoga had come to be lost. Shortly thereafter, a crestfallen Schuyler left to speak to Congress.

What was soon to emerge to the eyes of all who could see was that Gates saw the war mainly as an instrument for his own advancement and a means of increasing his prominence and power. At the Battle of Trenton, he had simply not shown up to support Washington, snubbing him without explanation as part of his continuing effort to undercut and belittle his commander-in-chief, but now Gates was chief in command, and military men knew him to be a cautious, tidy, unimaginative man—an excellent administrator and trainer of troops, but a man more likely to protect an army than to make it fight to its fullest capacity. (In his whole military career, Gates would not get within two miles of any front line.) Washington was intelligent enough to know that Arnold had what Gates lacked—the genuine spirit of decision, which does not consist of acting at all costs, but of not hesitating to move when an irresistible inner conviction compels you to. Washington had assigned Arnold to Gates because he saw Arnold's abilities as able to put an end to all fuzziness, delays, and indecisiveness. The contrasts were immediate and unfavorable: Gates was fifty, feeble, stooped, and nearsighted, while Arnold was thirty-six, virile, muscular, intense, and a battlefield genius.

It was September 19, 1778. Dense fogs covered the ground between the camps, and when the day finally dawned, Arnold looked over a dense, filmy white sea in which nothing could be seen but the tops of some of the trees. What carried clearly on the cold air was the sound of the enemy's drums beating to quarters. Gates seemed sure that the British would march straight at him, but the fog cleared, and through the dense fall foliage, colonial scouts caught glimpses of scarlet and blue uniforms and the deadly glitter of sunlight on weapons over on the left.

Arnold once again displayed abnormal speed in interpreting the opportunities that opened before him. Instead of waiting for the British to impose their battle plan, Arnold would surprise them by a savage attack in the woods, fighting Indian style. A hard smash from the right at the British would throw them off balance. Surprise bred shock and shock bred disintegration and loss of morale. Errors accumulated, and disaster followed.

According to one witness, Ebenezer Matoon, Gates reacted to the British assault by being timid and paralytic. Gates wanted to conduct only a reconnaissance in force and the incredulous Arnold said to Gates, "That is nothing. You must send a strong force." Gates, stung, and always conscious of the dignity of his place, had replied, "General Arnold, there is nothing for you to do. You have no business here." But another officer, General Benjamin Lincoln, supported Arnold's advice about sending reinforcements. Arnold now began to pile in units thick and fast, seven regiments in all. He electrified his men, cantering in front of the line on his black horse, waving his sword, and urging them on with the cry, "Come on, boys! Hurry up, my brave boys!"

As the battle thickened and grew in ferocity, Arnold again and again galloped back to the paralyzed and indecisive Gates, begging, entreating, beseeching his commander for more men to hurl against the British center, which was beginning to show dangerous weakness. But no order came from Gates. Gates would take the British attack inside his fortifications, like a turtle inside its shell.

Arnold led charge after charge, "with the fury of a demon,"[8] again rushing back to Gates where he urged, begged, and pleaded for more men. Gates's reply was to ask Arnold to release a group of Arnold's men to guard his headquarters.

When Arnold saw an opening, he once again galloped back to Gates. He pleaded for more men to attack the British/Hessian reinforcements in the rear. Gates hung fire, but then reluctantly gave the order. But, moved by envy, he refused to let Arnold lead the charge. Balked, hearing that a priceless opportunity was being allowed to be lost, Arnold, in a frenzy of frustration, shouted, "By God, I'll put an end to it." He jumped astride his horse, but Gates hustled an aide after him with a direct order for Arnold to come back. Arnold had to submit.

Darkness fell, and the battle, which had raged for six hours, sputtered out. All that could be heard were the terrible cries of the wolves moving among the dead and wounded.

GATES NOW SHOWED plainly the stuff of which he was made. He didn't bother to notify his commander-in-chief, Washington, of his victory, but instead reported to his political base in Congress. And he began to tell shameless lies. The battle had drastically boosted Arnold's reputation and severely lowered his own, so in his report to Congress, he ferociously snubbed Arnold, leaving out his name, calling his men only "a detachment of the Army."[9]

Arnold was in a foul mood. Freedom meant scope of action, an absence of interference, the ability to change plans, and at every step he had been thwarted, countermanded, and made the victim of meddlesome and wrong-headed supervision. On September 20, Arnold called for a full-scale assault while the British were reeling, but Gates had refused. Now Arnold sulked in his tent, fidgeting, choking with fury and unexpected resentment.

The gratuitous slights, the misleading reports, the hogging of credit were bad enough, but the splinter that caused the collapse of the whole came in the form of orders Arnold received on September 22, relieving him of command of Morgan's men, who would now be under the direct supervision of Gates. Even in the best of times, Arnold was rarely in full control of his temper, and that evening he went storming into Gates's tent. Enraged shouts and curses flew back and forth, and Gates's archery hit Arnold in some very sore places, especially when he reminded his subordinate that he wasn't sure whether Arnold retained the rank of major general, referring to Arnold's threat to resign after he had been passed over for promotion. Gates had a keen eye for what would hurt.

October 7 was a warm, still, autumn day. Crimson and pumpkin colors streaked the dense green cover of forest trees. It was two o'clock in the afternoon, and Gates and his officers were at lunch, dining on ox heart, when the scattered firing of muskets was heard like the snap and popping of a cane field set afire. Burgoyne, at the head of 1,500 regulars, had sent his wagons toward the American left.

Full of pent-up frustration and impatience and drinking heavily, Arnold listened to the complete pandemonium, and he peppered arriving aides with endless, anxious questions as to what was happening. He saw

Gates outside his tent, receiving messages, always looking through the importunate Arnold as though his talented subordinate were made of air. News that nothing decisive was being done finally raised Arnold to a fit of murderous fury. Ignoring the fact that he had no command, he downed a dipper of rum and ordered his black charger, Warren, to be saddled, then vaulted aboard. Shouting "Victory or death!" Arnold dug in his spurs and galloped away. The flustered Gates called for Major John Armstrong to order Arnold back, but it was too late. Armstrong would not be able to catch up.

The battle raged with a fury beyond words, and suddenly Arnold, astride his horse,[10] raced out amid the clouds of the bullets and shot. He was so overwrought, his waving sword struck a rifleman on the head, leaving him startled but unharmed. "What regiment is this?" Arnold shouted at the officers.

"Colonel Latimer's, sir."

"Ah, my old Norwich and New London friends," said the excited Arnold. "God bless you! I'm glad to see you! Now, come on, boys! If the day is long enough, we'll have them all in hell before night!"

Suddenly the rear of Burgoyne's strong point, Breymann's Redoubt, was exposed! Shouting and urging haste, Arnold led a charge. He was everywhere, urging, goading, shouting, waving his sword with savage vigor, when his luck ran out. Bullets thudded dully into his black horse, which instantly went down, kicking and screaming, flinging Arnold clear. As he clambored to his feet, sword drawn, a Hessian bullet hit him in his bad leg, and he toppled over with a groan.

Arnold was still gallant to the core. When he saw an American about to revengefully bayonet the Hessian who had shot him, he cried out; "Don't hurt him! He's a fine fellow! He only did his duty."

Thanks to the determined and energetic Arnold, the key enemy points were carried. But as he lay on the ground, in great pain, someone asked him where he was hit. He whispered hoarsely, "In the same leg." Then, as though he dimly glimpsed his future, he said, "I wish it had been my heart."

A few days later Burgoyne surrendered to Gates, the greatest British defeat in the war up till that time.

3

With Philadelphia, Benedict Arnold's star had begun to fade.

His wound had left him without spirit or energy, and life suddenly seemed to have entirely lost its savor. After the battle, Horatio Gates ignored Arnold entirely, never even taking the trouble to make the usual inquiries about his health, much too busy romancing the Congress with plans to have himself put in George Washington's place.

After months of hobbling about in an Albany hospital, his wounded leg two inches shorter than the other, Arnold finally went to Valley Forge to see his old friend and commander-in-chief. Congress had still persisted in refusing to restore his seniority, but apparently the sight of his friend Arnold being unable to stand without leaning on an aide moved Washington to the heart. In July 1778, he promised to give Arnold command of Philadelphia, the capital city of the colonies, now that the British were leaving. (Sir William Howe had returned to England to explain why he had so utterly failed to suppress the rebellion and in his place had come Sir Henry Clinton who immediately decided to vacate Philadelphia and make New York the new center of his operations.)

If Washington displayed a singular lack of judgment by giving the command to Arnold, Arnold manifested even less common sense in accepting it. The British occupation had left the city in appalling condition, its neat squares and commons trampled to a smelly, hoof-trodden muck of horse manure and scattered pieces of debris. The sides and roofs of shops and houses were missing, and all the fences had been pulled up, burned as firewood for the troops. Whatever the Crown's soldiers coveted—valuables, silver, apparel, cows, sheep, dogs—they had simply taken away. Even tombstones had been uprooted and scattered by the soldiers. In every city block, broken-down vehicles lay abandoned at the curbs, rotting horse carcasses still harnessed to some of them.

Only one area had been left entirely untouched—the city's Tory strong-hold, a square-mile enclave of handsome brick and stone mansions sur-rounded by neat orchards and formal gardens. One of the nicest of these belonged to Judge Edward Shippen the IV, a loyalist from one of the old-est families in Pennsylvania. He had a daughter, Peggy, eighteen, who was beautiful, vivacious, and fascinating. She was also a traitor. In winning her love and admiration, Arnold would fulfill his fate. She would capture Arnold's heart, and he would lose himself in the splendors and frenzies of passion until he at last toppled into the abyss of dishonor and disgrace.

Arnold had never understood anything of politics, but in Philadelphia, everything *was* politics. Savage differences had split the population. A venomous feud was taking place in town between the Tories and the Whigs, a New World version of the ugly, unending war between the few and the many. Leading the Whigs was the figure of Congressman Joseph Reed, a former (and disloyal) aide to Washington, a man never particu-larly scrupulous about how he advanced his career. Reed was a compla-cent, self-satisfied person who saw things in blacks and whites, which means he saw them falsely, and he had the born demagogue's gift of over-simplification, able to dress up his social prejudices as moral laws. To Reed, his party, called the Whigs or "patriots," embodied all that was good, and the Tories or "conservatives," all that was dark and evil. Shortly after Arnold arrived, Reed, in a fit of vindictive savagery, had pro-posed that 500 Tories of all rank and conditions of life be hanged and their property confiscated for the cause. What thwarted this slaughter was Washington's order that Arnold was to take "every prudent step" in his power to make secure individuals "of every class and description," no matter what their political beliefs. Arnold had enforced the order, and Reed had exploded in fury. (Even so there *was* vengefulness—hundreds of Tories were prosecuted in the courts, and several Quaker collaborators were publicly hanged.)

No wonder that in Philadelphia an astute grasp and an adroit handling of delicate factors was an essential requirement of the situation. But Arnold, rash and haughty as ever, took pleasure in scandalizing Reed by taking up with a set of men that embodied everything Reed was pledged to loath. They were powerful New York conservatives such as Robert Livingston, John Jay, and Gouverneur Morris, whom Reed regarded as unprincipled parasites who had thickened off of profits made from the war but for whom Arnold had developed connections and affections. Reed lived next door to Arnold and had a good view of the opulent dinner parties to which he was not invited.

It wasn't entirely perversity on Arnold's part. Arnold had always enjoyed men of social polish and precedence, beginning with Philip Schuyler and Washington, partly because they enjoyed the social standing that he was trying to acquire, and partly because he was a man of poise and polish himself. An observer, watching Arnold in Quebec, had said of him, "An officer bred at Versailles could not have behaved with more delicacy, ease and good-breeding." It was also part of Arnold's tragedy that he was an unideological man whose loyalties were determined by his affections. At Fort Ticonderoga, he had spent more time talking with two captured British soldiers with whom he felt he had more in common than with Ethan Allen's rowdy semi-literates. Arnold's battlefield heroism, after all, consisted of defying unpleasant consequences. On the battlefield, this is sublime; in politics and social life, the same attitude is often suicidal.

Arnold's grandiose style of life soon began to rub Reed where he was very raw. Arnold sported a sumptuous coach, thoroughbred horses, and liveried servants, mainly because Arnold was not the kind of man to live modestly. Money to him was only happiness in potential, a framework, and Reed spluttered as he watched Arnold move into the venerable Penn mansion only recently occupied by British General Howe. Arnold quickly contacted a suspected Tory named Joseph Stansbury to act as his agent, lavishly buying china, silver, and incredibly expensive wines. Arnold also hired a coachman, a housekeeper, and a groom for his horses and was soon living more opulently than his predecessor had.

Yet, grandiose living aside, Arnold was almost broke. (For an intelligence officer, someone living beyond his or her means should have been of instant concern.) Congress had not yet reimbursed him for the money he had spent in raising men or for the losses related to his abandoned business in New Haven, nor had it paid him for the 2,500 pounds it owed him for his expenses in Canada. In fact, Arnold had received no back pay for three years and had to maintain his household and headquarters out of his own pocket. This was bad enough, but then an unlooked-for disaster occurred: he fell in love with a Tory belle, and his anxious need for money redoubled overnight.

The love of Arnold and Peggy Shippen most certainly had its source in irresistible sexual attraction, but it also showed that, even in love, Arnold desired to excel. Peggy was famous for her ability to fascinate men. "We were all in love with her," confessed A. S. Hammond, a British Army captain, and contemporary accounts abound of men who were taken with her, including John Andre. Born in 1760, she was the fourth daughter of Judge Shippen, and the family's spoiled darling. It is Andre's sketch of her that survives and what we see today is the peevish, oval face of a person used to getting her way. The eyes are sly, the expression is one of faint distaste, the nose is long, the face is short-chinned like a cat's, the mouth is primly shut, and the blond hair is piled high prettily on the crown of a pert head.

Unfortunately, when Arnold began courting his daughter, Judge Shippen was anything but pleased. To him, Arnold was a widower with children, soon to turn forty, a social nobody whom the war had whirled very high. The hero's physical handicaps made it worse. To Judge Shippen's eyes, Arnold was like a fine dog with a maimed paw. But Peggy's eyes saw none of this. What Peggy saw was an Arnold that was glorious and exalted. In him she finally found that restless, animal vitality, that vital, personal force, that fatal glamour that other men around her had always lacked. Arnold's wounded leg still caused him spasms of pain, yet using a special high-heeled boot and cane, the tough soldier came to be able to hop about the floor of Peggy's house, defiantly showing the father he wasn't a cripple after all.

Then Reed's storm broke over Arnold's head.

While the general had been busy being in love, Reed had been active in devising ways to disgrace and discredit his enemy. He began by launching libelous attacks on Arnold in the press. Arnold was always absurdly, ruinously touchy; any criticism filled him with such overpowering feelings of his own moral rectitude that they crowded out any trace of simple common sense. Instead of reining himself in, or trying to be less conspicuous, he chose conduct designed to infuriate Reed all the more. For example, when Congress belatedly paid Arnold $8,000 on his back accounts, Arnold requested the parole of a British prisoner and sent him to New York for various expensive personal items that included new glass for the windows of his carriage. Reed's group, working with the energy of loathing, soon produced an eight-point indictment of Arnold's conduct as commander that alleged illegal deals for personal gain as well as his "discouragement and neglect" of patriots and his courting of the Tories.

Was Arnold guilty? Without doubt. But of what? In all of human dealings, even marriage, there creeps in a sense of accounting—a summary of what has been given versus what has been received in return. It's clear that by this time, Arnold clearly felt shockingly shortchanged by his country. The most simple ethics of childhood teach that the right deed is commended, the wrong criticized and deplored. Arnold had abandoned his business and family and given of himself and his talents in the tireless service of the Cause. He won great glories in war and had saved the revolution, only to be discredited, snubbed, and mortified by men he felt were far inferior to himself. If others cared nothing for his welfare, he would care nothing for theirs. So there came now little, sordid attempts to line his pockets.

The British had brought in tons of European and East Indian goods and anyone selling them to the pent-up demand of the patriots could reap skyrocketing profits. As a businessman, Arnold had always looked to his own self-interest as the paramount law of action in the conduct of his affairs. He began to use his position to make wholesale purchases of goods at low prices, ostensibly for the army, but in fact partly for himself. He used partnerships in schooners, agreements with aides, Tory middlemen, and other questionable business schemes and associates to do this. But such practices were *questionable,* not *illegal.* Neither Congress nor Washington had specifically prohibited such activities. But whether the law forbids a thing or not is one issue and a sturdy sense of doing right is another. Arnold's schemes were ignobly selfish, and where a person of delicate conscience would have felt this, Arnold felt nothing of the kind.

Part of Arnold's tragedy lay in the fact that he held a stronger hand with Reed than he thought, but he didn't play it. Reed's indictment was very shaky, based almost entirely on rumor and hearsay, missing any solid proof. Reed of course scrambled about frantically to get it, but it stayed just out of his reach. But since Reed knew he had right on his side, he didn't hesitate to start to say things that were not true about a man he did not like. He got a colleague to dredge up John Brown's old booklet of charges, knowing full well that Congress had already exonerated Arnold of all of them and sharply rebuked Brown for making them in the first place.

Arnold, in a temper, asked for a court-martial to clear his name, and, under pressure, resigned from his command in February 1779. His court-martial was scheduled for May, but was then postponed, and throughout this time, Arnold's raw and edgy mood was whipped into something approaching hysteria, his gaze fastened with such feverish intensity on the hatefulness of Reed and his own rectitude that he lost all sense of measure. And at his side was Peggy who fed in him what was blind, making it darker still.

With the insistence of a spoiled, self-willed woman, Peggy for months had staged fits of resentful hysterics over Judge Shippen's refusal to have Arnold enter the family. Over time, Peggy's tirades had grown tedious, and the judge at last had weakened, as she had known he would. Peggy and Arnold were married on April 9, 1779, in her father's drawing room, Arnold leaning on the arm of an aide during the ceremony. Arnold still owned a fine house in New Haven, where his sister and children lived, and he had purchased the Mount Pleasant mansion for Peggy as a wedding present. Yet in less than a month, the marriage quickly flowered in the disfiguring growth of treason.

Certainly new historical evidence has revealed that Peggy was in on the treachery from the first.[11] Kindred spirits make groups, and marriages. For any human creature, being in love is hardly a clear-sighted time of life. A predominant concern is to please, to show ourselves pliable and receptive, and, above all, to be able to change. But Arnold in love appeared like someone floating adrift, with no foothold anywhere in hard reality. His passion seemed to have robbed his mind of decision and direction. He had been living for so long in an overwrought emotional atmosphere harboring a long-nursed sense of injury and isolation, that it had created a sensitivity so acute that only Peggy's special touch could quiet and calm it. What did she whisper to him, one wonders? What promises of gain or recompense or belated recognition did she envision if her husband would only switch sides?

Unfortunately, Peggy's had been a callow, young woman's privileged life—a round of fancy cotillions and dress balls, with much admiring attention paid her person. She loved the select, the choice, the exclusive, which to her were a matter of class. The evacuation of the British had plunged her into dismay, disappointment, and despair. At a stroke, her family and social set had become social outcasts, living in constant fear and hissed at by the mob as being "mistresses and whores" of the British officers. She had always hated the patriots for their ignorance, their uncleanness and poor dress, their primitive manners and coarse pleasures. She also abominated the patriots' idea of liberty whose practice meant robbing others of their rights if someone else's view wasn't identical to their own. In her eyes, inner virtue was reflected in superior place, and as far as loyalty to country was concerned, her attitude seemed to embody Cicero's remark, "Our country is wherever we are well off."[12]

Arnold at first seems to have fought the seductive pull of her arguments. He still felt loyalty to "his brave boys." In the middle of May, he wrote to Washington for an opportunity to "render my country every service at this critical time," stating that "no public injury or insult" could make him forsake his country. But this was just empty words. Arnold had loved and served the Cause, but an ideal has life only through the power we give it to direct our acts and Arnold's hopes for the revolution had withered dead. He had believed in it, but it had not believed in him. The strong, surging excitement, the tingle, and the zest he'd once found in serving the revolution had faded and gone flat. He had at last begun to think there was another world.

His wife began a correspondence with Sir Henry Clinton's chief of intelligence, Major John Andre, one of her former dancing partners. The letters were written in code to disguise their real purpose, which was to determine what the British would be willing to pay if Arnold switched sides. In the meantime, Arnold used Joseph Stansbury, the Philadelphia Tory who had helped him to furnish his house, to make his initial approaches, sending the British news of troop movements and other secret data in a carefully coded message. The British must have been utterly startled and surprised. Ever since Clinton had taken command, the British had redoubled efforts to corrupt colonial officers and a list of recruitable targets had been compiled. Arnold had proven to be such a hard, tireless, inflexible enemy that his name did not appear on it. But Clinton's reply must have brought Arnold to his senses with a jolt. It was Clinton's aide, Andre, who wrote with insulting offhandedness that he had no interest in seeing Arnold change sides. Arnold had no command, and was of no value to the Crown unless he could get one. Andre would be happy to receive secret intelligence, of course, but the British spymaster did not say what amount he was prepared to pay.

Arnold suffered an uncontrollable paroxysm of rage at the rebuff. Didn't the British yet know with whom they had to deal, the hero of Ticonderoga? The savior of Saratoga? But he sent some more information just the same, keeping the door to the British ajar.

When his trial finally came in December, Arnold would again let his theatric sense of righteousness get the upper hand. He would tediously spend his time parading his military accomplishments instead of poking holes in the tissue paper of Reed's charges. (For example, on the charge that he had used army wagons to offload a cargo from a schooner he partly owned, Arnold *had* offered to pay all expenses for the wagons out of his own pocket, but Reed had refused.) The court-martial would find Arnold guilty of only two minor charges, having dropped all the rest, and his old friend Washington would issue a reluctant reprimand. "Our profession is the chastest of all," he said. "Even the shadow of a fault tarnishes the luster of our finest achievements." He offered Arnold opportunities "to regain the esteem of your country."

It was intended as a kindness, but it went clear through Arnold like a shard of glass and seemed to sever any remaining feeling of friendship he felt for his friend and superior. "Reprimanded?" he shouted and stormed to Peggy. "For what am I reprimanded? Not for doing wrong, apparently, but because I might have done wrong; or rather, because evil might follow the good that I did."

Once more, his emotions had smothered his judgment, and once more his mind seemed to come to center on money. Not only was there Peggy to impress and support, but she had also given him a son, Edward Shippen. Arnold went around trying to secure fresh funds, at one point asking the new French minister for $12,000 to keep him in the field against the British. He was refused and began to convert his assets to cash, trying to sell the house at Mount Pleasant and in New Haven, and once again seeking contact with Clinton. This time Arnold used a man named Samuel Wallis, a militia colonel who was one of Andre's agents. Carefully concealing his identity, Arnold made it seem he was *already* in command of West Point, and asked for an annual stipend of 500 pounds sterling and 20,000 pounds sterling for the capture of the fort. "I demand a full and explicit answer," he said, signing himself as "Monk" after the Cromwellian general who had switched sides in the English civil war and who had gained a dukedom by doing so.

More messages passed and at last Andre agreed to the 500 pounds sterling per year and 20,000 pounds sterling for West Point, provided that 3,000 colonial soldiers and vast stores of ammunition came with it. He detailed other information Arnold might provide: the names of American agents, the number and position of troops and reinforcements, the location of supply depots, and the content of secret dispatches.

When Arnold asked Washington about West Point, the commander-in-chief was puzzled as to why such a vigorous, driving combative soldier as Arnold would seek such an undemanding command. True, Arnold's leg wasn't healed, and he could neither walk nor ride. Washington then offered Arnold command of the left wing of the army at Newport, Rhode Island, an active post of great honor for his friend. But when she heard of the offer, Peggy had hysterics again, and Arnold refused, persisting in his request for the command of West Point. With a weary sigh, Washington gave in.

On August 3, Arnold took command. The Hudson River still remained the most strategically important waterway in America. Arnold established himself in a gloomy mansion on the side of the river opposite the fort and began to work immediately to weaken the fort's defenses.

4

★ ★ ★

SARAH TOWNSEND, THE pretty, vivacious sister of one of George Washington's most effective spies, had the talent of mind that was able to extract what is essential to the meaning of any situation. Yet quite by accident, she had suddenly stumbled upon something baffling, tantalizing, and unusual, whose meaning she could not quite make clear to her mind—and it all had to do with the British and West Point.

She was used to seeing and being around the British. When British General Clinton had taken New York City, the Culper Ring of spies on Long Island had continued to operate there as a "stay-behind network," as it is called in the espionage trade. Her brother, Robert Townsend, had been a top agent of the ring, occupying a splendid vantage point—for the past four years, British soldiers had been quartered in the Townsend family home at Oyster Bay. Currently, British Army Colonel Simcoe had taken up residence there, and John Andre, Clinton's chief of intelligence, had often been known to visit.

Andre was a man with a singularly winning personality. When Henry Knox, Washington's 280-pound bookseller and chief of artillery, had been assigned to drag back to Boston the cannon and guns Benedict Arnold had captured at Fort Ticonderoga and Crown Point, Knox had stopped for a night at Fort George, where he shared a cold, small room with Andre, a

British prisoner of war, captured in the Canadian campaign. Knox, who had spent any unoccupied time in his bookstore voraciously devouring his stock, had a mind of vast interests and the intellectual depth of the scholar. To his surprise, Knox found his companion as well read as himself. The two stayed awake for hours, talking with tireless passion about history, the theater, classical literature, and military history, especially artillery. The next morning they had parted mutually stimulated, pleased, and impressed, Andre heading south for Pennsylvania and parole, Knox returning to the task of transporting his cannon.

In the Townsend household, there sprang up the usual attractions due to close, daily exposure of the opposite sexes that overcomes even national animosities, no matter how entrenched. Robert's cousin, Hannah, had already married Major Joseph Green of the British Army, and Sarah had received from Simcoe a Valentine and other tokens of esteem.

But Sarah had keen instincts that no courtesies or flattering tributes could blunt. Her interest had flared up vividly at the latest things she'd seen. First, the British were making inquiries about the shores of the Hudson River in the vicinity of West Point. Second, and even more puzzling, she had watched as a supposed Whig, whom she knew to be a British spy, entered her house and concealed a letter in a little-used cupboard downstairs. The instant the coast was clear, Sarah had retrieved the letter from its hiding place. It was addressed to a "James Anderson" and appeared only an ordinary business letter. But if ordinary, why place it secretly in a cupboard no one used? Sarah kept close watch on the cupboard, and a little later felt a rush of excitement as she saw Andre enter, pick up the letter, and hastily conceal it in his coat. He then casually picked up a dish of donuts still hot from the fire and walked casually out of the room.

Her suspicions alerted, Sarah was moved to act. Later that night, she crept into a room that adjoined Simcoe's who was engaged in a whispered conversation. Her cheek laid flat against the wall, she could hear the words "West Point" repeated several times. West Point again! She sat down and wrote a hasty note to her brother, Robert. She then sent for Captain Daniel Youngs of the British Army, a lifelong family friend, and told him fetchingly that she'd run out of a certain kind of tea she would need for her party the next evening. She said that a supply was to be had at her brother's store in New York, and she needed a messenger at once.

Before the night was over, Robert had her letter in his hands, and a little while later, it was in the hands of Major Benjamin Tallmadge, Washington's chief of intelligence.

Washington liked having around him young cavalrymen of dash, grit, and daring, and Tallmadge was such a man. He was young, tall, and, during his days with the dragoons, wore a deep blue sash across his chest.

When Tallmadge returned to his headquarters from running his operations, there was waiting for him not only the message from Robert, but one from Arnold as well. To Tallmadge, Sarah's information about British focus on West Point and a "Mr. James Anderson" was of interest; a spy in the Culper Ring had reported that British officers were talking about West Point and receiving letters addressed to a "Mr. Anderson."

But Tallmadge had other, pressing matters to look to, mainly a mysterious series of letters that were passing between sources in Rhode Island and a man named DeLancey in New York.

But then someone handed Tallmadge an already-opened letter from Arnold. Arnold talked genially of having received some supplies, and then said, "If a Mr. James Anderson, a person I expect from New York, should come to your quarters, I have to request that you give him an escort of two horses to bring him on his way to this place." Arnold also asked that Tallmadge come with him.

Tallmadge had the sharp mind of the case officer and an eye for odd coincidences that awakens suspicion. His blood had quickened at the mention of an "Anderson" in Arnold's letter. Talmadge, a student at Yale College along with Nathan Hale, had earlier known Arnold and thought him "knavish," but the dedication and fiery zeal with which Arnold had fought against the British had since redeemed him in Tallmadge's eyes. Except there now was this! Above all things, Tallmadge wanted Arnold to remain lulled and unalerted, so in his reply, the spymaster cheerfully agreed to accompany "Anderson" to West Point. Tallmadge added that he expected to join Colonel John Jameson and signed his letter, "with Every Sentiment of Esteem." The date was September 21, 1780.

Then Tallmadge got busy with other things.

Yet, as sharp as he was, Tallmadge was in fact lagging far in the rear of important events.

The increased British activity clearly indicated that Clinton was anxious to make a move. The French had arrived in Rhode Island in force, but they would probably stay there the winter. Fears of a French attack on

New York had faded with the arrival of fresh British fleet reinforcements. But the British knew that the year 1780 was a dark year for the colonial Cause. Morale was so poor that Washington feared his officers would resign in a body. Clinton also knew that West Point was key to the collapse of the rebellion. West Point was not one, but seven forts, had taken three years to build, and cost three million dollars. Clinton believed its capture would force the newly arrived French out of America, ending any fears of a move on New York or a sweep down from Rhode Island in the spring. Clinton needed to consult with Arnold about how the forts would be surrendered and what troops and assets would come with their capture. They would also need to discuss how to do this without risking any colonial countermove.

Detailed plans were prepared. Andre, accompanied by British Colonel Beverly Robinson, whose confiscated mansion had become Arnold's headquarters, was put aboard the British sloop *Vulture* and rowed ashore to meet Arnold. It was night, and it says much about Andre that he felt in good spirits and raised his face to the sky as if to drink in the still, endless, majestic beauty of the clear, starry night.

On September 20, 1780, when the two men finally met, Arnold was nettled to find himself still forced to bicker pettily over terms Andre only offered him 6,000 British pounds for the betrayal of the forts, but Arnold stubbornly insisted that he should get 10,000, and Andre said he would try to persuade Clinton to agree to the sum. They then discussed the possibility of trying to capture Washington along with the forts, but discarded the idea. Quiet hours passed as they talked. When it was time to have Andre rowed back to the *Vulture*, the two boatman complained they were too fatigued to try. Besides, Arnold had papers he wished Andre to see, and the two mounted horses and rode to the nearby house of a traitor, Joshua Hett Smith, described as "extremely stupid, sly, self-esteeming and childishly fond of intrigue."[13] A harsh, abrupt voice came out of the night in challenge—an alert American sentry. Arnold responded with the password. But Andre was now inside an American position, in contradiction to his orders.

Arnold eagerly showed Andre a detailed list of the garrison, the number of men required to defend each position, the artillery commander's plan of defense, and Washington's own military stratagems. But Andre then made another blunder. Impressed by the documents, he asked Arnold if he could take them to Clinton, probably to aid Andre in his argument for more money. Arnold reluctantly agreed, and the two men parted.

Immediately complications began. For one, overnight the *Vulture* had come under fire and retired a way down river. Smith told Andre that it was too dangerous to try and return to the *Vulture* and too dangerous to walk around dressed as a British major. Andre strongly objected at first, but then settled down. Disobeying Clinton's orders a second time, he took off his scarlet uniform coat and put on a fine claret-colored coat with gold-laced buttonholes lent to him by Smith. It was a mistake that would prove his doom.

Smith and Andre at last made their way through a silent countryside full of abandoned homes. Not a soul was in sight. The two spent an un-easy night, and then resumed at dawn. Andre saw the British lines ahead, and his soaring spirits loosened his tongue, and he talked of painting, po-etry, and the ache that rose in the heart at the wild beauty of the Hudson Valley. At that point, Smith and Andre split up. Andre had on him two passes from Arnold, one for water, the other for the land, whichever way he decided to take.

Andre, alone, was making his way through Westchester, wild country controlled by rival, roving gangs of royalist "Cow Boys" and rebel "Skin-ners"—criminals who used patriotism to cloak the fact they were thieves that preyed on people who blundered into their hands. Seeing freedom in sight, Andre's heart was electric with happy expectation, when suddenly three such men loomed up and stopped him, clearly intending to rob him. Andre, the intelligence professional, totally lost his poise. Instead of merely producing Arnold's pass, he tried to determine if the men were Whigs or Tories. In talking, he was tricked into identifying himself as a British officer. Why he did this remains a mystery. If they were Whigs, they would have honored Arnold's pass, and if Tories, they would have turned him in to the British. In either case, his safety would have been assured if he had simply waited and kept still. Instead, the three thieves took him into a field and into a dense thicket, where they made him strip. They stole his gold watch and some silver dollars, and then they made him remove his boots. This was fatal. In the stocking of the left one were three papers, all the plans given Andre by Arnold. The would-be highwaymen were sud-denly sobered and marched the prisoner at rifle point to North Castle, where he was turned over to military authorities, led by Colonel John Jameson.

Now, at last, coincidences began to converge.

Tallmadge had made his headquarters in New Canaan, Connecticut, across Long Island Sound, and two days later, he and his detachment of men had just returned from a lengthy, wearying reconnaissance of the enemy's lines at East Chester. After he dismissed his tired men, Tallmadge got ready to receive dispatches from one of his agents, Caleb Brewster, who regularly sent his agent reports across the sound by whaleboat. Once received, Tallmadge had ready a string of express couriers to whisk them on their way to Washington.

But Tallmadge had hardly settled in when he was informed that the army had taken a prisoner by the name of "John Anderson." Tallmadge felt a shock of recognition. Was *John* Anderson *James* Anderson?

He hurried to the headquarters of Jameson of the Light Dragoons. Jameson was a tough, stubborn man , but he wasn't a lazy one. (He wasn't a particularly bright one either.) While Tallmadge was receiving the news, Jameson had already sat down and written a report of the capture of "John Anderson", sending a copy to Arnold and forwarding the papers to Washington who was then on his way to West Point from a meeting with French Army Commander Comte de Rochambeau at Hartford. Jameson had also sent "John Anderson" under guard to the general commanding at West Point, Arnold.

The minute Tallmadge heard Jameson's account, he urged the man to turn the entire matter over to his handling and discretion. Weren't the documents captured from "John Anderson" plans of West Point written in Arnold's own hand? Jameson agreed the matter looked awkward for Arnold, but he was not to be awed by a subordinate like Tallmadge. He had to notify Arnold, his own superior, or risk being insubordinate himself, and he would continue to handle the affair as he thought fit, thank you.

Tallmadge blew up, pointing out that if Jameson had been thinking clearly, he would have sent both the prisoner *and* the documents to Washington. Jameson became greatly agitated. Tallmadge then told Jameson that he wanted to take a leave of absence from the army, because he wished to adopt a measure "offering to take the whole responsibility upon myself."

The mulish Jameson was horrified and refused. In his later life, Tallmadge never made explicit what the "measure" was, but most historians believe that he meant to seize Arnold and hold him until Washington arrived. If Tallmadge had been given authority, Arnold's career as a spy would have ended. Instead Jameson proved the rock immovable. The frantic Tallmadge finally got Jameson to agree to have "John Anderson" kept in North Castle. When Tallmadge saw him, he began to pace back and forth across his cell under Tallmadge's sharp, assessing eyes. "As soon as I saw him walk across the floor, I became impressed with the belief, that he had been *bred to arms,*" Tallmadge wrote later.

This was no ordinary spy.

And Tallmadge was right. On the evening of September 24, "John Anderson" admitted that he was in fact John Andre, adjutant general of the British Army.

Now Andre was pacing back and forth across the floor with the pent-up energy of a panther, and Tallmadge felt even more frantic. It was September 24, and Jameson had sent his report to Arnold September 21. "I knew (the report) must reach Arnold before I could reach West Point," Tallmadge said later.

Sunday, September 25, dawned warm and humid with thundershowers forecast. Washington had sent word he would arrive at the forts the next morning. That evening the muggy air blew out, and Monday displayed a cheerful blue sky, the air clear and cool, making objects stand out sharply and distinctly. Arnold rose early, full of energy, and went down to his office. Peggy was up in the bedroom. Arnold's aide David Varick had a bedroom that was part of the office suite, but that day was in bed sick with a fever. To Arnold it was the start of another week, and he snapped off quick questions to his aide: "Have you answered the letters received from Lieutenant Colonel Jameson? Has Major Tallmadge's letter got answered? Have you written to Governor Clinton enclosing copies of the letters of Colonel Beverly Robinson?"

"No, sir, I am sick and not able to," Varick said. Arnold took Tallmadge's letter off with him, commenting that he would write to Tallmadge himself.

In the meantime, Washington's party, who had set out for breakfast with the Arnolds, stopped briefly to look at some fortifications, prompting the polite and gallant General LaFayette to remark that Mrs. Arnold was waiting the morning meal on them, and was afraid their delay might offend her. Washington thought this oversolicitous. He good-humoredly remarked that almost all his young officers were half in love with her.

Arnold was hard at work in his office when some minutes later, in the buttery, he met an extremely dusty enlisted man and an equally dusty lieutenant, John Allen. They handed him two dispatches from Jameson.

Arnold read them avidly. In the first, Jameson said he was sending a certain "John Anderson" as a prisoner. "John Anderson," Jameson said, had a pass signed in Arnold's name and papers that were "of a very dangerous tendency." Arnold tore open the second letter. Jameson had rescinded his order to send "John Anderson" to Arnold and was keeping him prisoner at his headquarters instead.

Arnold felt his legs start to go soft under him. Surely in his worst nightmares, he could not have believed a catastrophe like this would happen to him. Shoving the papers into his pocket, he excused himself and went quickly up the stairs to his wife. Peggy was sitting in bed. Young officers had gone out and brought her a bunch of peaches, and she was glowing from the satisfaction afforded by the attention when Arnold hobbled in.

The door closed.

Arnold's aide David Franks mounted the stairs and knocked on the door to tell Arnold that Washington was almost there. Arnold burst from the room, a dazed, half-crazed look on his face. He told Allen to please wait, then limped rapidly out into the yard and asked that his horse be saddled. He also sent orders down to the crew of a barge on the Hudson, asking that they stand by. Arnold galloped along the road, suddenly confronted four aides of Washington, greeted them affably, secretly poised to shoot them, but saw they knew nothing and passed on, finally arriving down at the dock. He asked the crew of his barge to pull for Stony Point. They rowed to the British sloop, the *Vulture*. Arnold met his British confederates on board.

Back at the Arnold house, Peggy heard male voices coming up the stairs. She was a traitor, disloyal from first to last, but she also had a good amount of acting talent and never was it more effectively employed. Washington had been perplexed that Arnold had not waited for him, but thought it considerate that his impulsive subordinate had gone to West Point to prepare a suitable reception for his commander-in-chief.

Washington lingered a bit, then left, and it was then that Arnold's aide, Varick, suddenly heard a shrill shriek and bolted up the stairs to see Peggy, raving, distracted, disheveled. With a wildly distressed face, she seized Varick's hand and asked him, "Have you ordered my child to be killed?" Varick tried to calm her, but she burst into tears and became more disordered and distraught. Varick said Arnold would soon be home, and she exclaimed, "No—General Arnold will never return! He is gone! He is gone forever, there! There! There! The spirits have carried him up there; they had put hot irons on my head—" and she pointed in terror up to the ceiling.

Varick was much alarmed. At about four in the afternoon, when the Marquis de Lafayette, one of Washington's party, opened the parlor door, he saw Washington holding Arnold's plans of West Point in his trembling hands, jaw clenched, obviously upset. Washington was finally able to choke out the anguished words, "Arnold has betrayed us. . . . Whom shall we trust now?"

But Peggy's ravings continued with rising intensity.

A doctor begged Varick, "For God's sakes," send for Arnold "or the woman would die." But the aides were not entirely fools. They suspected Arnold had warned his wife and her hysterics were a performance.

Peggy asked to see Washington, and shortly the tall, lean figure in blue and cream entered the room and stood by the bed. Up until then Peggy had been shouting that she had a hot iron on her head and only Washington could take it off. But when he approached to give comfort, Peggy screamed shrilly that the man beside her bed wasn't the commander in chief. Washington sedately assured her that it was, but she persisted in denying that it was he. Instead she accused the general of being the man who was going to assist Varick in the murder of her child, all part of the act.

5

★ ★ ★

THE NEWS OF Benedict Arnold's treachery spread like fire in straw. All across the colonies, on countless village greens in countless cities and towns, enraged citizens surged excitedly to fill the streets solid as effigies of Arnold were paraded and publicly hanged, burned, or otherwise dispatched, the cheers of the populace amid the popping sputter of clouds of firecrackers and the playing of the rogue's march in a countrywide display of utter revulsion and pitiless rage. In Philadelphia, his image was paraded in a wagon with a figure of the devil sitting on a pot of gold.

Peggy Arnold, traveling from West Point back to her family in Philadelphia, witnessed it all, vindictively satisfied to see America's bucolic clods reveal their true character. The intensity of their hatred frightened her, along with gusting rumors that said George Washington had demanded John Andre be traded for Arnold. She halted in her journey across New Jersey at the Paramus home of Mrs. Theodora Prevost, the widow of a British officer. Like a hole poked in the side of a pitcher, all Peggy's disgusted wrath gushed out. She declared that she was heartily sick of the theatrics she had been forced to assume. She had always been an enemy of the patriot cause, she said, adding that it had been "only through great persuasion and unceasing perseverance" that she had finally gotten her husband to agree to abandon the Cause and work for the British.[14]

When she reached her home in Philadelphia, she faced the smug hatred of Joseph Reed and his cohorts. Some of her letters to Andre became public, making clear she had been acting as a cut-out for her husband, and there were those who howled for her head. Reed had her banished from the city, but her influential father intervened and conveyed her to the British lines in New York.

George Washington went to work at once. He was a hard man fighting a hard war. He lost more battles than he won, but it didn't matter. Washington had never thought of beating the British, only of outlasting them, and now his finest fighter and an extremely close friend had defected. The betrayal stung like a slap in the face. Washington may not have been a genius in battle (he had a repeated difficulty in preventing his forces from being outflanked, as at the battle of Long Island), but when it came to being a chief of intelligence and counterintelligence, he has had no peer in American history. (He would only miss capturing Arnold by a hair.) Washington had a gift for intelligence—the singular intensity of purpose, the quick mind, and the streak of mental ruthlessness that the trade required. He was comfortable with kidnapping, psychological warfare, mail openings, and the executions. Washington was also a deft and expert user of codes and agents. His networks included "bright young college graduates, respectable businessmen, state governors, tavern-keepers, semiliterate farmers, barmaids, dear old ladies in Quaker bonnets who carried vegetables to the enemy, young boys who could wriggle past the enemy lines, the American lady who owned the waxworks museum in London, several of Sir Henry Clinton's trusted agents, Lord Cornwallis's valet, and one of Lord North's diplomatic emissaries."[15] It was only until the last century that many of the identities of Washington's spies were finally made known; Washington had such an abiding and vivid obsession with secrecy.

Washington's mind had hardened early. When he was a colonel and a commander of Virginia Forces in the French and Indian War, he wrote to a superior, "Your honor has had the advice of two spies, taken at Fort Cumberland; one of whom they quickly hung up as his just reward."

Washington would extract intelligence by any means. In one incident, the stolid, unemotional spymaster even used a chaplain as the instrument of interrogation. Two convicted spies were about to hang, and Washington's instructions are chilling: the chaplain was to get from them vital information at all costs. While the chaplain's prayers were helping to "prepare them for the other world, it will naturally lead to the intelligence we want in your inquiries into the condition of their spiritual concerns. You will therefore be pleased to take charge of this matter upon yourself, and when you have collected in the course of your attendance such information as they can give, you will transmit the whole to me."[16] In fact, Washington's coldness reached such depths that when Alexander Hamilton watched Washington's calm pitilessness in disposing of Andre, it prompted him to say that his commander-in-chief suffered from "a deficit of feeling." But as swift, lethal, and rigorous as Washington's countermoves against Arnold were, they produced no results and Washington might as well have saved his exertions. Arnold's defection would more than prove to be its own punishment.

The famed American's appearance among the British in New York at first stirred up a hornet's nest of excitement. The mere personality of the man attracted a fascinated attention, but this mood did not last. How could it? Arnold had been recruited and paid to turn over the most strategic chain of forts in America. Instead, he had brought nothing with him—no forts, no body of armed and well-drilled men—only his talents for command and fighting, and he was profoundly shocked to find these were not held to be worth much by the British. The caste-conscious British declined to give Arnold an important command. They were in no way willing to serve under the authority of a low-born American, no matter how able. To British eyes, Arnold was a damaged quantity, a man who was a traitor twice over. He had first betrayed the Crown by rebelling, and now betrayed the colonial cause by switching back. True, Arnold was installed in a comfortable house in New York at 3 Broadway, but when he met British officers, there was courtesy but no warmth. Sir Henry Clinton was not the kind of man to whom friendship came easily. But there had been one person to whom he had grown close, and that was John Andre. Clinton came to look upon Andre as a son, and there is even speculation that the two men had been lovers. Clinton's feelings for Arnold were correct, but inwardly he could not look upon Arnold without experiencing the deepest feelings of aversion.

The insurmountable problem for Arnold among most of the British officers rested on the fact that Andre had been an enormously likeable man, full of toughness and grace, sensitive yet brave. All who knew him loved him for his learning, his wit, his broad range of interests, and his kind and affectionate nature. The frost settled on the British at the sight of Arnold because they suspected he had been careless of Andre's security. Had it really been essential to have a British major travel behind American lines, as Arnold had insisted? Was this revenge for Andre's earlier insolent and offhanded replies to Arnold's offers to spy for the British? Plus after meeting Andre face to face, Arnold had let Joshua Smith attend to the security of Andre's trip. It was because of Arnold that Andre could not return to the *Vulture* and had to go by land. Arnold had given Andre a pass, but it was Arnold's advice for Andre to dress in a civilian coat. Why urge a man to dress in a civilian disguise, and carry plans in his stocking? Clearly, it was all unsound procedure. Andre apparently had lost his head, and, as a result, lost his life. Andre was hanged, in spite of pleas and appeals from men like Hamilton to a Washington who would not soften in the least.

Certainly for Arnold, there was no going back. When Arnold asked a captured American what his country would do with him, the man told Arnold that if they caught him, they would cut off the lame leg wounded in the cause of honor and freedom and bury it with the honors of war. Then they would take the rest of Arnold's body and "hang it on the gibbets, high."

The British paid Arnold handsomely. Clinton made him a temporary brigadier general, and Arnold was given an immediate cash settlement of 6,315 British pounds. In addition to cash, he was awarded half-pay for life, and his wife and children received King's pensions called "king's commissions." The Arnolds and their children would be paid, in total, about 50,000 pounds from the British government over the next sixty-seven years.[17] He was also given 13,400 acres of land the Crown had reserved from among its holdings in Canada for American Tories. But what Arnold received was far, far less than the property he had lost, the back pay owed him by the colonial government, and the huge debt he had been forced to write off.

But if Arnold thought he had regained the prominence and authority he had lost and had stepped once again into the glare of center stage, he had in fact sunk into the shadows of insignificance. Arnold's loyalties soon displayed their customary flexibility. He possessed no more patience than he had before, and when a superior did not do things to his liking, he contrived to have the man removed. Even though Clinton had outwardly flattered him at first, Arnold disliked his commander and intrigued against him, quietly attempting to convince Lord George Germain to bestow Clinton's post on himself. Unfaithful to his commander, Arnold was soon unfaithful to his wife. Within five years, he would take a mistress by whom he would have an illegitimate child.

Even among his new mates, Arnold was soon quarreling over what he felt was his righteous portion. Only four months after receiving his new commission, Arnold was locked in bitter dispute with the British Navy over a division of loot from raids, saying the navy had violated a verbal agreement on the division of the spoils and that he would "bring the matter to the attention of the Commander in Chief."

But that lay in the future.

What Arnold had most to fear at the moment was Washington, who had put a price on his head. Washington would even send a fake deserter to kidnap Arnold in New York, but the plot fell flat. But Washington's standing order was that Arnold was to be "summarily executed" if captured, illustrating that once you were in Washington's bad books, you tended to stay there with no hope of change.

Arnold had written pieces of propaganda designed to inspire desertions on the American side, but none had come, deepening the British distrust and disappointment. Considering Arnold low-born and dishonorable, it was only after much behind-the-scenes pleading and agitation that Clinton finally allowed Arnold to take the field in command of a group of 1,700 American defectors called "the American Legion." They engaged in bloody skirmishes and battles, including a savage raid in the winter of 1780 to 1781 that captured Richmond and came within a whisper of capturing Thomas Jefferson, the governor of Virginia. Lieutenant Colonel Simcoe, who served with Arnold, noted that the troops were "in great spirits, full of confidence in the daring courage of General Arnold."[18] Next September came an attack on New London in which the town was burnt and there was much bloodshed.

But Arnold's bright, great days as a battlefield warrior were sinking out of sight. He had suffered bad losses and would never be given another command.

In December 1781, he left for England with his family, and now began a long chronicle of unbecoming squabbles, wasted efforts, balked talents, stillborn projects, and scorned and unappreciated powers. Arnold had underestimated British snobbery and had not in the least understood its mazelike British class system. Since he was not a member of the upper class, not only was Arnold unable to obtain a command, but he didn't have enough money to live as he wanted to live. Financial pressure redoubled when peace came, and Arnold was retired on a colonel's half-pay. In London, Peggy was as insistent as ever on keeping up appearances and required expensive wines, a fine house, and a luxurious coach with splendid horses and footmen, just as she had in Philadelphia. But for all his exertions, Arnold came no closer in London to amassing the fortune he craved. His standing among the British remained very low. He was attacked in the Whig press and hissed at when he went to the theater. Perhaps the darkest point of Arnold's life there occurred when he ran into Johnny Burgoyne at a routine social occasion. The British general who had never gotten another command and yet who had been effusively generous about Arnold's battlefield talents curtly turned on his heel and walked away.

Arnold's inability to gain sound financial footing inflicted on his wife the same dismal shame his father had inflicted on his wife: Peggy was pitied for the man she had married. In his forty-fifth year, at last seeing clearly that what he had sought in London wasn't to be found there, Arnold sailed away on a merchant ship to become a businessman in a Loyalist colony of St. John in New Brunswick, Nova Scotia. The year was 1785. Exiles, failures, and losers from the wrong side of the war inhabited St. John. Arnold, still nursing his upper-class pretensions, soon installed himself in grand houses elegantly outfitted with furnishings from England. But to the colonists, Arnold was an outsider: greedy, disagreeable, and despised. Arnold had moved there solely to make money, and he ran foursquare into an elite who did not admit him as a member and who viewed St. John as a place where "the common people would be their grateful and obedient subjects."[19]

Soon Arnold had set up a store three stories high with a site for a wharf where imports could be unloaded. Peggy arrived, and Arnold lived richly. He appeared to have seized success, except his life was marred by constant business quarrels. He was extremely generous in lending people money because money was scarce and the colonists lived on credit. Unfortunately, many of these people were often unable to pay, and just as he had showed no hesitation in helping them, Arnold showed no hesitation in hauling the people he had helped off to court. But even when the judgments were in his favor, they often produced little income and they placed his name under a cloud. In 1788, a dispute with a corrupt business partner named Hayt acted to eclipse Arnold's reputation in the town. Even though Arnold was right and Hayt wrong, the public had turned up its nose and began avoiding his store, and by then Arnold knew "the sad fact that he really had no safe haven where he would be welcomed as a hero." A year later, in 1791, he went back to England, glad to escape. At fifty, the lights were dimming on the stage that was his life, the auditorium emptying. Within two years, his career had begun its final decline. Isolation spread around him. Investments he had made were bringing in no return. His money troubles deepened and his health got worse, and he began drinking heavily. He had legs fatly swollen as big as barrels and difficulty breathing. His money troubles were felt deeply by the family. At one point, his wife, struggling like a swimmer trying to stay afloat at sea, was heard to comment bitterly, "Marriage is a lottery."

On June 14, 1891, at half past six in the morning, he died without a groan. Peggy wrote that "as the disappointment of all his (pecuniary) expeditions and the numerous vexations and mortifications he endured, had so broken his spirits that he has for a long time past been incapable of the smallest enjoyment."

In Nova Scotia his death was reported in a paragraph. No mention was made of his overcoming incredible obstacles, facing insuperable odds, or carrying overwhelming responsibilities all the while in perpetual danger of defeat, mutilation, or death.

Peggy herself would die of cancer at the age of forty-four, after paying off the family debt.

So concluded the career of America's Coriolanus, the American Hannibal, the tireless, dauntless fighter the Indians called "Dark Eagle."[20] Aaron Burr had said of Arnold that Arnold was a man of no moral principle, but Arnold's was a deeper tragedy, one that Goethe touches on when he describes the poet Byron as a man "totally in the dark about himself," a man destroyed by his own "unbridled temperament," and by his rebellious, inborn impatience with limits and restraints of any kind. Arnold came from the same unhappy mold. He was a man whose ardent and heroic energies led him to the great test and adventure of war—an area in which Arnold's deeds shone with the glory of a fixed star. They still do.

By contrast, Arnold's inner life seems to have been of the most coarse and primitive kind. Goethe said of Bryon that he lived "impetuously from day to day, and neither knew or thought of what he was doing." Arnold was the same. The drive for gain, the grim, relentless will to get ahead, permeates every fiber of his nature the way a heavy dye stains a fabric. Morality is only a kind of inner energy and a certain responsiveness to the abstract, and Arnold lacked it. He was incapable of moral ideals, incapable of loving something above his own happiness or that of the others on which it depended. Happiness for Arnold too often was no more than the ratio between what he had demanded and what he had received. Plus he had a fatal, morbid fascination with money. Napoleon remarked that "contempt for riches" had been key to the rise of powers such as Sparta, Cretonia, Persia, and Rome. But Arnold was incapable of such contempt. He had a streak of shallowness in him and seemed to judge the value of things by their expensiveness, which is on the level with thinking a thing superior merely because it is popular. Arnold was missing something in his makeup and did not understand that social standing and wealth could not put in a man's character what God had left out. Headstrong and brutal, always seeing the faults of others but detecting none in himself, Arnold never reined himself in, never accorded to the interests and egos of others the respect and precedence he gave his own. Always in the right, always smelling conspiracy where there was only opposition, he never deeply questioned the consequences of his actions or decisions, but pressed on to his ruin, heeding no one's voice. Arnold died morally blind, never seeming to understand where his true gifts lay or the meaning of the great and noble glory he had gotten by their use.

Yet whatever his faults, Arnold was a superb, dauntless battlefield warrior. Once in battle, the dross in his character fell away. Setbacks, obstacles, discouragement, fatigue, and strain beyond telling meant nothing to him. His uncertain character, in peacetime so wildly responsive to others, was replaced by untiring energy and sangfroid, by balance and sense, and he pushed into his enemies with unfaltering will, endurance, incredible tenacity, and a power of resolution that simply refuses to perish until it succeeds. In whose name did he really fight? We don't know. But he was a man of gigantic dimensions. The spies who follow him are no more his size than the fleas on a bear.

The Traitor as Assassin:
JOHN WILKES BOOTH

I am gall, I am heartburn. God's most deep decree
Bitter would have me taste: my taste was me.

—G. M. HOPKINS

1

★ ★ ★

LOCATED IN SOUTHERN Maryland, the town of Surrattsville was a snug collection of modest frame houses. The normal travel time on horseback from Washington across the Anacostia River southeast to Surrattsville was two hours. But the night of April 14, 1865, Good Friday, two riders were heading for it, pushing their horses hard, spattering through water pooled in the hollows on the road, and cutting the time in half. Their horses lathered, the mounted riders turned off the road and went at a walking pace down a dirt lane that led to a tavern located in a large frame house, with its door on the side porch. The place was owned by John Surratt and tended by a man named Lloyd. One of the mounted men slid down and walked to the door. His name was David Herold, and he was in his twenties, slender, lightly built, with a weakly handsome face. He pounded on the door, thundering, one, two, three times.

Lloyd, who was sitting slumped inside, stupefied by whiskey, woke up. He crossed the floor and opened the door. As he did, Herold brusquely pushed past him and seized from the bar a bottle of whiskey. Herold filled a glass for himself, then snapped out, "Lloyd, for God's sake, make haste and get those things." Herold pushed past Lloyd again and went out to the man who had remained mounted and handed the bottle to him. The black shape of the mounted man shook its head, no. He was using both hands to hold fast to the saddle. Lloyd promptly brought out two carbines, ammunition, and a pair of French field glasses. The mounted man slung the field glass over his shoulder. Herold remounted, and both men wheeled about and headed at a gallop back out to the road.

A large, low moon lit up the deep velvety blue of the night sky. The moon's light silvered the surfaces of things, and objects were outlined in its weak luster. Dawn was only an hour away when the two riders finally walked their horses up the dirt road that led to the large, three-part frame house of Dr. Samuel Mudd. The doctor, thirty-two, was a distinguished looking man, with a rounded head bald as a stone, except for fringes of curly hair at the sides by the ears, and a down-curving mustache that ran into a bushy pointed goatee. His eyes were small, hard, and ungiving.

Herold spoke to the doctor. His companion was injured in the leg and needed medical attention. Standing outside, Mudd raised his eyes to see a dark, bearded figure in a shawl sitting astride his horse.

Mudd invited the men inside.

As the lamplight fell on the bearded man's face, Mudd beheld a young man of thirty-five and weighing one-hundred-fifty pounds. The patient had black hair worn long that seemed inclined to curl, a full forehead, and skin that was fair but very pale, which indicated he led an indoor, not an outdoor, life. The man had a mustache and a full beard.

The doctor set to work, first cutting open the boot and then removing it with great care. Clearly the left leg was broken, about an inch above the ankle. Mudd was an ingenious man, so he broke apart a hatbox and used long, slender pieces from it to splint the shattered leg. After he had bandaged the leg, he put the patient to bed. When morning came, Mudd went about his usual business, riding into Bryantown to buy some sundries. Later he'd say that it was in town that he first heard that President Abraham Lincoln had been murdered. This would not be true.

Upon returning home, Mudd saw the men were about to leave. They asked for directions about how best to head west, for they were in search of waiting friends. They rode off, having spent over twelve hours at the doctor's house.

But the wife had something disturbing to tell the doctor. The man with the broken leg had a false beard. As he'd been struggling down the stairs to leave, she said a portion of the beard had pulled loose. The couple talked over what actions they should take, but dithered and did nothing.

The pair of men kept heading south and finally pulled up before a house. It was now one o'clock Easter morning, and the weather was clear. The constant, throbbing pain from the break in the wounded rider's leg had worn him down. He sat dully astride his horse, the broken leg hanging free of the stirrup. The house belonged to "Captain" Samuel Cox, a Confederate sympathizer and major landowner who was much feared by local blacks. Cox had a close-cropped beard running from ear to ear on his round, heavy face. He invited the men to come inside, and they did, resting for five hours.

When they had recovered their spirits, Cox had his father's overseer, Frank Roby, take them to a small pine thicket to hide, providing them with blankets and bedclothes. Federal patrols were starting to comb the country, looking for Lincoln's murderer, and Herold and his partner remained in the thicket for several days while Cox's man came back every day to give them food and newspapers, which the wounded man read avidly, with the recklessness of starvation.

The wounded man was none other than John Wilkes Booth, and as he spread open the pages of columned print and let his eyes fall upon the accounts, he finally got a chance to see the public reception being given his great and redemptive deed of assassination. He could not believe what he saw. He ransacked the crackling pages of the *National Intelligencer*, looking for the letter he had written explaining why he had killed Lincoln. It wasn't there. The *Baltimore Clipper* spoke of "fiendish acts . . . cowardly . . . vile . . . utter madness . . . an atrocity." Booth was utterly dazed. But that was not the way it was. In a memorandum book he carried, Booth wrote furiously, "I struck boldly, and not as the papers say. I walked with firm step through a thousand of his friends, was stopped, but pushed on. A (major) was at his side. I shouted Sic Semper before I fired. In jumping broke my leg. I passed all his pickets. Rode sixty miles that night with the bone of my leg tearing the flesh at every jump."

To Booth's eyes and estimate, his act was bold, decisive, great, an attempt to rid the country of a diseased tyrant of unprecedented destructive ferocity. Yet all he had reaped on all sides were contemptuous jeers. In profound distress, he wrote, "Every man's hand is against me. I am here in despair. For doing what Brutus was honored for, what made (William) Tell a hero.[1] And yet I am striking down a greater tyrant than they ever knew and looked upon as a common cutthroat."

It was all bitter, vain, futile, absurd.

Cox, who, fearful of reprisal, wanted Booth off his land, had sent his son to Thomas Jones, his foster brother. Jones was a trusted Confederate secret agent who smuggled secret messages, contraband, and secret agents through Charles County across the Potomac River. Jones had known of an 1864 plot that involved kidnapping Abraham Lincoln by force.

Jones showed up at the thicket, causing a nervous Herold to emerge with a cradled rifle. Jones froze quite still, as if waiting for strangers to be able to see who he was.

"Who are you and what do you want?" said Herold.

Booth was lying on the ground, his head in his hand, his carbine, pistols, and knife close beside him, a blanket partly covering his body.

"I'm come from Cox. He told me where to find you. I am a friend. You have nothing to fear from me."

With Jones leading, the three men headed south and west, and finally reached the east bank of the Potomac River. Their horses wound down a long descent, steep and narrow in spots, reaching a flat-bottomed skiff beached on the pebbly shore. "Wait a minute old fellow," said Booth as Jones started to push out the boat. Booth took out a roll of bills, but Jones counted out carefully only $18, which was what the boat cost.

"God bless you," said Booth as Jones pushed the boat out into the water.

The first try at a crossing was a failure, but a second, made the next day, was successful. When the pair reached the opposite shore and beached the boat, they met a bearded, intense man named Thomas Harbin, also a dedicated Confederate agent, who gave them help. By three o'clock in the afternoon, April 24, Booth and Herold finally made it to Garrett's farm.

Morale is often only a matter of a certain level of energy, and once inside the shelter of the farm, Booth had regained his spirits, especially once he found himself the center of interest. He spoke entertainingly and with warmth of charm to the Garretts and Miss Lucinda Halloway, Mrs. Garrett's sister. Making use of a pillow for resting his leg, Booth had slept for several hours and woke a new man. The throbbing in his leg had eased.

"I have too great a soul to die like a common criminal," Booth had scribbled in his little memo book.

Meanwhile, Herold had left Booth back at the Garrett farm, going off in the company of three men and stopping at a small log building just before a rustic speck of a place called Bowling Green. Inside the log hut was a woman named Carter and her four daughters. At the sight of them, Herold and three men felt their blood quicken. After the four had chatted and charmed the women, they left, feeling happily satisfied with themselves, the company, and the afternoon.

Tuesday morning showed a sunny spring day with a cheerful air of balmy freshness. Deep pink blossoms covered the redbud trees, and the sarvis trees had erupted with delicate, pretty white sprays. Booth and Herold were snug and secure inside the tall barn of the Garrett farm while outside things were happening that would end by bringing death to both.

The Federal cavalry, the 16th New York, had arrived in the area, and by talking to people and tracing leads, quickly heard of the four men who had been entertaining Carter and her daughters. When the Federals asked the women for information, they were glum and did not reply. After all, their hearts were loyal to the South. But then one resourceful questioner changed his tack, claiming the men were not wanted for anything to do with the war, but for raping a young woman.

The young ladies started talking at once. Soon after, the convoy of cavalry headed out to the Garrett farm, pulling up short at a distance from the farmhouse. They wanted no loud noises to alert Booth. A man named Doherty dismounted from his horse and headed to the farmhouse, climbing the steps to knock on the door. Old man Garrett peered through a crack in the door, dressed only in a nightshirt. What did he want?

"Where are the men who were here today?"

They were gone, said the flustered old man.

"Liar," said someone. "Where are they?"

As the troopers were about to hang the old man, his desperate son, Jack, appeared to plead for his father's life. "Wait!" he yelled. "I'll tell you what you want to know." The men they sought were in the barn, he said.

Baker, the cavalry commander told Garrett to get into the barn and get the men to give up their arms. The cavalry waited. Suddenly as fast as a crab, a visibly shaken Garrett came out. Booth had ordered him out at gunpoint.

By now the cavalry, eager for action, completely ringed the barn. Booth tried to engage Baker in conversation, but Baker cut Booth off, telling him to surrender or they would fire the barn. "Captain, that's rather rough," replied Booth smoothly. "I am nothing but a cripple. I have but one leg, and you ought to give me a chance for a fair fight."

Baker was impressed by the man's pluck and relented. He gave Booth five minutes to come out.

But inside the barn, Herold's weak nerve suddenly gave way like a wall. He had never been a man with much iron in him. He decided to surrender. As the troopers dragged him off, he was whining and crying, whimpering so pitiably that the troopers got impatient and roughly gagged his mouth with a rag.

Meanwhile, Booth said, "Throw open the door, draw your men in a line, and let's have a fair fight," an audience giving him new confidence and a fresh sense of having a final role still to play.

A man named Conger answered by impatiently setting afire a fistful of straw and thrusting it brutally into a pile of brush leaning against the wood of the barn wall. By peering through the barn slat, the soldiers could see Booth, a revolver in one hand, a rifle in another, about ten feet from the door. A shot cracked out. Booth grabbed blindly at his neck, then fell. The soldiers all stood as if turned to stone. Then Baker and his men rushed the barn, broke in, and stood over the stricken figure on the floor. A flood of other noisy figures swarmed in from behind.

The soldiers dragged Booth out of the burning barn and had him taken and laid on the front porch of the farmhouse. Someone gave him some water, which quickly revived him. The ball had made a hole in his neck and cut part of his spinal cord as it came out. He felt no pain. Several times, he muttered weakly to the men around him, "Kill me. Kill me. . . ." Baker gave quick orders to get medical attention, and the messengers sped away. But the eager flame of Booth's life was beginning to flicker very low. His eyes were closed. His lungs were paralyzed, but he was a fit man, able to breathe by exerting great work on his diaphragm. Suddenly he opened his eyes. His lip quivered slightly. He faltered out, with great tortured pauses in between the gasps: "Tell . . . my mother . . . I . . . die . . . for . . . my . . . country." Conger, a cavalryman, knelt close to Booth's whispering lips. He repeated the words to ensure they were what Booth had said. Booth gasped, "Yes."

Death was already deep in him, busy at work, but Booth lingered a little more. Amid terrible bucking gasps, he brought out, "I thought I did for the best." A doctor finally arrived, but it was too late. Booth then asked that his hands be raised so that he could look at them. This was done. As he gazed dully at his hands, he muttered hoarsely, "Useless, useless."[2]

Suddenly his jaw pulled down, his eyeballs bulged, he gurgled, and, throwing back his head, died.

It was exactly twelve days after he had entered Lincoln's box at Ford's Theater, a gun and knife in his hands.

2

★ ★ ★

THE ASSASSINATION OF President Abraham Lincoln by John Wilkes Booth brings us abruptly to the lethal ferocities of the modern age.

Instead of a single act by a single, sick, fixated man, the killing of Lincoln was a carefully planned intelligence operation that included an attempt at mass arson, the first incidence in American history of an attempt to inflict huge and indiscriminate casualties on the public by means of germ warfare, and even an attempt to murder the entire upper echelon of a country's leadership by blowing up the West Wing of the White House to kill Lincoln and all his Cabinet.

In peacetime, when the distribution of forces is in harmony, the beasts that slumber in human nature are dormant and stay out of sight so that we tend to forget they are there. Peace acts on people like the policeman on the corner: his presence doesn't reduce the willfulness, the evil, the impatient tyrannies of human nature, but his being there, backed by the brute force of law, reduces the number of occasions on which those things can make themselves manifest without penalty.

But a war lets the beasts slip loose. Any war's first casualties are moderation, truthfulness, and moral balance, which is why all wars are morally ugly. Its participants see the most complex of human situations as a simpleminded melodrama in which all that is good and fine is threatened by extinction by all that is squalid, corrupted, worthless, vicious, and deadly in the world. To save the innocent good of one side, any evil can be resorted to, any lie can be told, any crime can be committed, and any heartlessness indulged in without fearing the menace of any sufferings of conscience to follow.

The beginnings of the assassination of Lincoln appear to have their root in an early 1864 cavalry raid by the North whose ostensible purpose was to free Union prisoners, but, in the end, was a failure.

It was called the Dahlgren Raid.

Ulrich Dahlgren was only twenty-one, a tall, lean, Scandinavian with a tawny beard and a warm, winning courtly grace of manner. Someone once said his manners were "as soft as a cat's." But besides his youth and grace, he had other things: a colonel's commission in the army, unbounded courage, and a wooden leg as proof of it. After a boyhood in Pennsylvania, he had grown up in the Washington Navy Yard, the son of Rear Admiral John A. Dahlgren, a crusty, tenacious, square-jawed man who many considered the father of modern naval gunnery, as he was a world authority on cannons and the inventor of the fabled Dahlgren gun who had a protector in Lincoln.

Ulrich Dahlgren, like most young men, was driven by those urgent dreams of glory that promise a young man that his best qualities will find their fullest use and fulfillment in an action that will take the world by the throat. In a cavalry raid on Fredericksburg in 1862, he got himself talked about for his leadership, fearless verve, and liking of danger. At the Battle of Gettysburg, he would display the same audacity and exhilaration in the face of risk by taking a dozen men and stealthily prowling about in the rear of General Robert E. Lee's forces, which was very dicey work that he did extremely well.

It was only a few days after the Battle of Gettysburg, while in Boonsboro, Maryland, that Dahlgren got in a fight with rebel cavalry, so badly mauling his leg that a surgeon was forced to remove it. He spent months of lethargic torpor at his father's house, but then gradually improved, got an artificial limb, and, returning to service, was awarded his commission as colonel. It would be early 1864 in Washington that he heard that there was a secret mission afoot.

Intelligence reports revealed that Richmond, the confederate capital, lay in a feeble and undefended condition. This was important because several thousand Union prisoners were kept at two sites in the city—at Libby

Prison and Bell Isle. The inmates of both places were festering in squalor, living in a state of the most dismal hopelessness and spiritual dejection, starving, and dying from disease. If a column of cavalry could head south, slip through Lee's lines, and get to those men and release them, then everlasting fame would crown the liberator's name.

Commanding the mission that formed around this ambition was Brigadier General Judson Kilpatrick of the 3rd Division of the Cavalry Corps. Only in his mid-twenties, Kilpatrick was a wiry, small, nervous, incessantly active man who had a personal flair that attracted admiring attention. With his hard, expressionless eyes, he was afraid of nothing, living or dead, and, like Benedict Arnold, was afire to make his mark, his scratch on the face of anonymity. William Tecumseh Sherman, the capturer of Atlanta and the commander of the Union Army's vastly destructive march across the Confederacy to the sea, once called Kilpatrick "a hell of a damned fool," but Kilpatrick had once almost gotten into Richmond, and Sherman added that he wanted Kilpatrick to command his cavalry.

Kilpatrick's plan was simple and deceptive and for that reason was thought likely to succeed. Kilpatrick would take his column and make a lunge toward the right, as if menacing the Orange and Alexandria railroad. While the Confederates congregated there to block his way, another smaller column, led by Dahlgren, would go knifing left behind the enemy's rear, heading for Richmond and the pest holes that were thronged with abused and miserable prisoners.

What now occurred was to have the most profound effect on the ultimate fate of Lincoln.

The raid left on February 6, 1864, amid the cheerless, gray austerity of winter. Dahlgren's men had peeled away from the main group, which kept on south. Kilpatrick's column met chilly winds, cold mud, twisting dirt paths winding between the tall, bleak walls of silent winter woods. They had stolen past Lee's right flank, but the weather worsened, the cold wind driving bitter sheets of rain into soldiers' faces, and the rain turning the ground sodden, soaking the exhausted men, and causing steam to rise from the wet black horses.

Time passed. Suddenly there was the crack and flash of a shot. A puff of smoke appeared as more flashes peeped and winked among the dim, mist-shrouded trees. Men toppled over. The column was struck with such fury and force, that Kilpatrick's men grudgingly gave ground. As time passed, Kilpatrick began to feel things weren't going well. Facing him was not a force of file clerks from Richmond, as he'd been told, but seasoned, experienced fighters out to destroy his force.

Still, he remained a man who didn't like a difficulty to get the better of him, so Kilpatrick took thought, mustered his stores of nerve, and made one last try to force a way in. It came to nothing. Kilpatrick's force finally faded back, still fighting. They found a way out, broke off, and stopped to make camp some miles from Richmond, exhausted, cold, and wet through. The soldiers were in camp warming coffee, when three hundred of Dahlgren's men suddenly materialized out of the woods, half their number gone and their leader missing.

The story they told was grim. Dahlgren had made it to the James River; he had even made it to the home of James A. Seddon, Confederate secretary of war. Dahlgren being Dahlgren had even stopped to charm Seddon's wife who had once been courted by Dahlgren's father. But when Dahlgren's troopers rode off and finally arrived at the riverbank of the James, determined to plunge ahead, everything turned ugly.

The guide of the small group was a young African American that Dahlgren had picked up along the way, except when Dahlgren's force reached the place where they were supposed to ford the James, they found instead steep banks and an angry river, the wind whipping the surface to white-caps, the swift current wildly sliding the sheet of water past them. Dahlgren's column found stark failure staring them in the face. The young colonel's charm vanished in an instant. Suspecting treachery, he turned and hanged his young black guide in a fit of furious, cold, vindictive rage while his tough-faced men looked on, stonily.

But the clock was ticking. Dahlgren hastened along the north bank, eyes peeled for a ford, but none was to be found, and the specter of disaster grew larger and larger with each hour. Finally Dahlgren and his troops turned to go east and skirt Richmond, escaping in a driving storm of sleet, ice pellets flying and gusting in lateral sheets. On they went, saddles creaking with frozen ice, trees along the way slivered with coats of sleet, branches clicking like knitting needles in the wind. But in the dark, the fear, and the confusion, Dahlgren's column broke in two.

As would be learned later, the remnant of Dahlgren's column, 200 men, had gone off to the northeast. Dahlgren was in the lead, riding his horse like a patriarch, when, instead of safety and escape, he ran straight into an ambush and his doom. As his horses trod the narrow, cut-up for-

est track, Dahlgren saw the gray-clad figures rise up, and Dahlgren, all audacity, shouted, lifting his gun, "Surrender, you damned rebels or I'll shoot
you!" Multiple bullets thudded into him, tumbling him dead from his saddle. As a ring formed around his body, Confederate troopers swarmed
over his tiny force.

They were in a mean mood. Some Confederate soldier hacked off
Dahlgren's finger to get the ring he was wearing. Even his artificial leg became some soldier's souvenir. The Rebels took his clothing and his watch,
and displayed his mutilated, muddy, sodden corpse in an open pine box
paraded through the streets of Richmond to the railway station amid the
savage jeers of the infuriated, indignant mob.

A public relations disaster was to come because of the exposure of papers carried by Dahlgren in a pouch. They outlined the objectives of his
mission, and they did not make for comfortable reading. According to a
document titled "Headquarters: Third Cavalry Corps," after freeing the
prisoners at Bell Isle, Dahlgren's troops were to enter Richmond, burn the
city, and capture Confederate President Jefferson Davis and his Cabinet.
But there was also a second, more sinister document that said, "The men
must be kept together and well in hand, and once in the city, it must be destroyed and Jeff Davis and the cabinet killed."[3] Till then, the war had been
fought full out, tooth and claw, but savagery had so far been confined to
the battlefield. The Dahlgren plan was different—something called "black
flag war," the term derived from the black pirate's banner with its death's
head. Lincoln, the South believed, had raised the black flag first.

The Confederate newspapers had a day, trumpeting the alarm that the
North was now waging a "war of extermination" and that Southerners
were no more "than barbarians in the eyes of our enemies." Propagandists
were busy weaving at their looms of righteous wind. A worried Lee sent
the Dahlgren papers under flag of truce to General George Gordon
Meade, with a note asking if this was "the kind of war the North was going to be fighting from now on?"[4]

Bruce Catton, the preeminent genius of the Civil War historians, had
suggested the papers had been tampered with, but modern research says
otherwise.[5] There is no doubt that a unit of Dahlgren's group called the
"Pioneers," armed with turpentine, oakum, and torpedoes, had been ordered to burn the city. And the documents talking of killing Davis and the
Cabinet were even harder to explain. As proof against tampering, the
Confederates made photographic copies of the orders, and it is now con-

ceded that Lincoln had to know of the plan, for Meade had approved it and would not have done so without Lincoln's knowledge.

It isn't a real surprise to discover that Lincoln had a ruthless aspect to his will. It is manifested in General Orders 252, which declared that for every Union prisoner killed by the Confederates, one Rebel prisoner would be killed by the Northerners, and for every Negro Union soldier enslaved, one Southerner would be put to hard labor.[6] Some of this is mere inference, but it is persuasive. Hearts on both sides of the conflict had reached a new level of hardness. The conduct of the war had placed great, almost unlimited powers in Lincoln's hand—all except the power of being an unhated man. At first, he had fought the war only to restore the authority of the Constitution and the union. He was initially not fighting to suppress slavery, chiefly because the average Union soldier was not going to fight for the freedom of the black race, which was seen, even at times by Lincoln, as unequal to the white. In a speech in Charleston, September 18, 1858, Lincoln said, "I will say, then, that I am not nor ever have been, in favor of bringing about in any way, the social and political equality of the white and black races."[7] But if slavery was to be touched at all by the war, it was to be touched only gently—that had been the keynote of Lincoln's first year and a half in office, that he was fighting the war neither to save or destroy slavery, but to save the union.

But the savagery was growing with each battle, and the qualities that would win the war would be cunning, ruthlessness, dogged persistence, iron will, and the endurance that can persist in the face of stubborn obstacles no matter what the cost, and Lincoln began to harden like the rest. "I shall not surrender this game leaving any unavailable card unplayed," he said in 1862. What would people do? He asked in annoyance, "Prosecute (the war) in the future with elderstalk squirts charged with rosewater?"

Lincoln's plan was to wait for a victory in the late summer of 1862 and unleash a blow aimed at toppling the very foundations and framework of the South. The moment came in September, when Lee ventured across the Potomac with an army that had never known defeat. Lee would finally confront Union General George McClellan at Antietam Creek, a small town in Maryland. Lee was fearfully overmatched, but the next day his army stood and fought to the utmost limit of its force and endurance, and the battle of Antietam would kill or wound more Americans than any single day of battle throughout the war. Lee was stopped cold.

For McClellan it wasn't much of a victory, but it wasn't an actual defeat, and on September 22, three days after Lee withdrew his troops back over the Potomac, Lincoln issued his Emancipation Proclamation. Its terms were simple: beginning on the first day of January 1863, all persons held as slaves in states where the constitutional authority of the United States was not "practically recognized, submitted to and maintained" were to be free men.

The proclamation lacked logic: slaves would be freed only in the Confederate states that were fighting against Washington but would not be freed in slave states like Maryland or Kentucky who were still in the Union. In other words, freedom for slaves was proclaimed in states where the U.S. Constitution had no authority and no power to enforce its authority. This prompted H. L. Mencken to say later that the proclamation had all the "moral grandeur of a bill of lading." The South, however, saw the proclamation for what it was: a dagger thrust whose purpose was to disembowel the South.

Until the proclamation, the underlying hope had been that the South would come back into the Union, slavery or no slavery, and now Lincoln had said there could be no reunion without slavery's destruction, making reunion under *status quo ante* terms impossible. There could be no fighting a slave power without in the end fighting slavery. The dream of some sort of reconciliation, of a softer war, was ended forever, and if some did not see it, almost all did. Something ugly, vengeful, and poisonous had entered the conflict, deflecting it from decency and restraints and pushing it into new wastelands of savagery.

Within a month of Dahlgren's Raid, the Confederacy had come up with its diabolic form of retaliation. It was the brainchild of a Kentucky physician whom Jefferson Davis had made one of his top agents in Canada, Luke Pryor Blackburn, a recognized authority on yellow fever. In March 1864, Davis had given his agents the general assignment of wreaking as much chaos on Union war operations as possible while working to engineer the defeat of Lincoln in the election to be held next fall. The Confederate ring assigned those tasks began to be active that spring. Clement Clay and Jacob Thompson were personally selected by Davis to oversee these operations and were given a million dollars in gold to take to Canada. Blackburn joined them, but added a rather startling proposal: it was for waging germ warfare. It seemed an odd plan for a man who had taken the Hippocratic oath of "First, do no harm," but Blackburn was in earnest. He had been born in Kentucky of an upper-class family, and his plot appears the first instance in American history of a plan to use viral disease as a weapon of terror.[8]

Yellow fever was a hideous, lethal disease. In mild cases, it had symptoms like the flu, including headache, nausea, and fever. In severe cases, the patient suffered searing headaches, raging fever, vomiting, severe epigastric pain, and jaundice, where the skin turned a sickly bronze or yellow in hue. In its final stage, there was "black vomit," resulting from chronic bleeding into the stomach, which always killed the patient through shock.

The disease was predominant in the southern areas of the country. In fact, an 1801 outbreak was so dreadful it helped to prompt Napoleon to sell Louisiana to the United States a year later. But the idea of any party intentionally inflicting the catastrophe on huge segments of people sends a shudder down the spine.

But Blackburn was made of merciless stuff. In April 1864, when a major yellow fever epidemic erupted in Bermuda, Blackburn saw his chance. He left Halifax, Nova Scotia, where he lived, and arrived in Bermuda as the fever raged at its fiercest to offer his medical skills in caring for the sick. But a more sinister purpose underlay the apparent one. While he treated the dying, Blackburn also carefully collected their bedding and clothing. These he carefully packed into eight large trunks, which were shipped back to Nova Scotia.

Back home, Blackburn hired a sub-agent, Godfrey Joseph Hyams, to guard the trunks. Hyams was a slight, frail, weak creature with crossed eyes and a dark complexion—not likely to be noticed by most, or, if noticed, dismissed. Blackburn tasked Hyams with taking the trunks and finding a way to import them back into the Union, where he was to sell their contents at auction in cities like Washington, Norfolk, and New Bern to assure the greatest and speediest spread of the disease.

Blackburn and Hyams had one more target in mind: Lincoln.

A small valise packed with expensive dress shirts would accompany the trunks from Nova Scotia. The shirts had been worn by the dead and the stains of black vomit removed. Blackburn told Hyams to write a letter and take it and the valise and present them at the White House as a gift to Lincoln from an anonymous benefactor.

But Hyams balked and refused to go to the White House. It was too risky. He would, however, take the trunks under his care, and, using the alias of J. W. Harris, Hyams headed south, bribing a corrupt ship's captain to carry five of the trunks through Boston and down to Washington where they ended up at the auction house of W. L. Wall. Hyams transported the other three trunks to their destinations.

In the meantime, Blackburn had returned to Bermuda, and was once again offering his medical services to the government there, at the same time diligently filling three more trunks with what he thought was deadly contagion. Unknown to Blackburn, yellow fever was a virus, highly infectious to be sure, but incapable of spreading among individuals without the help of an intermediate host—in this case mosquitoes that bred in pools of stagnant water near human habitations. Once the disease had taken root in a victim and was circulating through the victim's bloodstream, the bite of the mosquito, sucking up the infected blood, provided the trigger to an epidemic. Alas, the clothes were not in the least contagious.

Blackburn's tightfistedness toward his own agent caused the plan to collapse. A Roman philosopher Junius once said that men will forgive injuries, but insults, never. Blackburn had not paid Hyams any money for his work beyond a minimal sum to bribe the ship captain to carry the trunks south. Hyams kept asking Blackburn for more money, but whenever he asked, Blackburn found he was not in a giving vein. Hyams grew disgruntled. In April 1865, he walked into the U.S. consul's office in Toronto and told them everything he knew about the plot. He also compromised several secret Confederate operations, including a plan to disrupt Union fishing off the Canadian coast, and pointed out a house in Toronto where bombs were being made. These two revelations convinced the Federals of Hyams's authenticity, and they granted his demands: back pay and a pardon in exchange for his cooperation. On April 12, Hyams gave a full statement about Rebel plans for biological warfare. A tip identifying the man in Bermuda holding Blackburn's trunks added further confirmation of the scheme. Blackburn would be arrested on May 19, 1865, in Canada, and placed on $4,000 bail, and Hyams would be the primary witness at his trial, proving once again that the capacity of human beings to bitterly resent any slight or humiliation is one of the most active capacities, and dangerous for those wielding power over people to overlook.

That Davis knew of Blackburn's plans came to light when a 1864 letter was discovered, written by a Confederate agent, Reverend Kensey Johns Stewart, that rebuked Davis for allowing Hyams to convey and cause "to be sold in the city of Washington at auction, boxes of small pox clothing."[9] But Blackburn's was not the only plot. There was another, just as sinister, which also targeted the Union president. In fall 1864, Confederate agent Thomas Nelson Conrad, a cavalry scout seconded to do missions for the Confederate secret service, was tasked with reconnoitering the White House and observing the president's "customary movements," especially his comings and goings to and from the White House. Lincoln had his summer residence to the left side of the bulky main building at the Soldiers' Home. Conrad, who knew the city of Washington very well, would note in a memoir that such men as himself "were frequently sent by President Davis and our general officers into Washington and sometimes into Canada." Since Lincoln traveled to and from the Soldiers' Home by carriage, the Confederates planned to capture him in it, move him through Maryland by means of preprepared escape routes to the lower Potomac, then deliver him to Confederate Lieutenant Colonel John S. Mosby's Rangers, a sheltering guerrilla force, for transportation to Richmond.

Mosby is almost a storybook figure. He was a tactical genius as a battlefield commander, much given to picturesque and heroic exploits, a bold, intrepid taker of chances, and a man of haughty daring who loved to defy risk and poor odds. The bronzed, weathered, bearded wide-mouthed face that stares out of a photograph of him is a tough face, made tough from his having endured and defied hardship by virtue of his determination, intelligent resolve, and ability to suffer.

But Mosby was no mindless, adventuring thug. He had a voracious appetite for reading, a breadth of cultural knowledge, and a desire to increase that knowledge that is truly astonishing. In twenty-one pages of his autobiography, he quotes from writers Sterne, Byron, Homer, Virgil, Gibbon, Longfellow, Moore, and Macaulay.

Always on the move, never settled at a camp, Mosby somehow managed to keep the classics with him at all times. A good example of his tastes can be seen in a letter to his wife in which he asks for Shakespeare, Bryon, Hazlett's *Life of Napoleon*, Plutarch, and Scott's *Poems*.

Yet for all of his elegance of mind, there was none of the chivalric knight about Mosby. Accused of not fighting fair, he admits the charge: "I fought for success, and not for display." No man, he said, had a more practical view of war than did he.

Mosby also had the stomach to meet ruthlessness with ruthlessness. Grant had given the order that when any of Mosby's guerrillas were caught, they were to be hanged without any trial. In Fall 1864, General George Custer had executed six of Mosby's followers. Two were shot and three were hanged. A seventeen-year-old boy, who had borrowed a mount to join Mosby, was dragged by two horses through the street and killed in the presence of his distraught mother, who was begging that he be made a prisoner of war. In retaliation, Mosby picked out seven men of Grant's by lot and hanged them, justifying it later because he claimed it stopped the hanging of prisoners without trial.

He once came within a hair of capturing a train that was carrying Grant. New research discloses that Mosby was something more than a devil-may-care adventurer, however. He was at the center of some highly sensitive Confederation espionage and black flag operations. For example, Mosby was key to running communications between Confederate agents in Washington and the Army of Northern Virginia. Washington was a major transportation juncture, the Union national command center and a city with a large population of troops. Much intelligence of importance to Lee's army was to be had from it, and Mosby was an irreplaceable resource.

That Mosby was involved in Conrad's operation there appears to be of little doubt. On September 15, 1864, Seddon, the Confederate secretary of war, gave Conrad a piece of paper that read, "Lt. Col. Mosby and Lt. Cawood are hereby directed to aid and facilitate the movements of Captain Conrad"[10]—evidence that the operation had the highest backing of the Confederate government. Lieutenant Cawood managed a station on the Confederate Secret Line that sent signals from Washington in to Virginia through the war. Conrad is known to have stopped at Cawood's station on September 22 or 23, only a day before another Confederate agent involved in another plot to kidnap a Union official had been there.

Conrad's plan was simple. He was going to use four men. Conrad's half-breed servant, who was six feet tall, strong, athletic, and full of unfazed, icy nerve, would climb up next to the driver and force him to divert the carriage along the route of escape. Conrad would lead the carriage while a friend, Daniel Montjoy Cloud, covered the rear. A rogue named John "Bull" Frizzel, who had allegedly been in Harpers Ferry for the capture of John Brown and who claimed to have cut off one of Brown's ears, would climb inside the carriage and subdue Lincoln. This may have proved more difficult than was thought. Lincoln, at six feet four, weighed only 180 pounds, but he had long, muscular arms and was tremendously strong. His law partner William Hearndon said Lincoln once lifted 400 pounds with ease and on another occasion lifted 600 pounds. When Lincoln was lying dying in a room across from Ford's Theater, Secretary of the Navy Gideon Welles remarked, "His large arms . . . were of a size one would scarcely have expected from his spare appearance."[11] In any case, the group would cross over the eastern Potomac into the southern Maryland Confederate line of escape used successfully by Dixie agents throughout the war.

But the dead weight of time was pressing on Conrad and his men. No moment ever seemed to be quite right for the plot's execution. With mounting anxiety, the plotters would station themselves in Lafayette Park across the street from the White House, watching Lincoln as he took his daily rides to and from the Soldiers' Home. The conspirators knew the cold weather was coming and that the Lincoln family would return to winter in the White House, and that any chances of seizing him would then be lost. They waited, poised, to make their attempt, when, to their utter dismay, they discovered that Lincoln's carriage was now being escorted by a troop of Union cavalry. The knowledge left them in a stupor of distress. What did it mean? How long would the escort last? Had their plans and movements somehow been betrayed?

Conrad kept up his scrutiny, but the cavalry remained, and the agent came to a strange conclusion—that another group, with the same mission as his own, must have tipped their hand and put Lincoln on alert.

Conrad was wrong. There was another plot afoot, but neither Lincoln nor the War Department nor the National Police were aware of it.

Besides, a new actor had stepped upon the stage. His name was John Wilkes Booth.

3

JOHN WILKES BOOTH was born on a 200-acre wooded farm about twenty-five miles from Baltimore, one of ten children of Junius Brutus Booth, a great Shakespearean actor who was intermittently mad. Junius felt that the glass was a good man's failing, and drank often and drank hard and, when the inner darkness came down, was nursed by his devoted wife. His daughter, Asia, would later write that such attacks were looked on "with awe and reverence" by members of the family.

Junius had a mind packed with incoherencies and filled to the brim with the vivid force of utter inconsistency. He was a man who, not entirely certain of what or who he was, seemed to imagine he was everything. He was brought up an Episcopalian, but liked to keep the Muslim holidays mandated by the Koran. Catholics thought him a Catholic, but he could speak fluent Hebrew so that others thought him a Jew. It's only fitting that he would be buried in a Baptist Church by Masons.

John Wilkes Booth was a dashing and physically favored man, with the splendor and grace of a virile animal. Named after the English political agitator and reformer, John Wilkes, Booth also had that disposition that is full of flair and style and the kind of confident swagger that conquers women and makes admirers of lesser men. In a photo, he appears broad shouldered, wearing a dark suit with a white shirt and dark bow tie.

He is looking off to his right, the tip of a cane handle climbing into the air above his right hand, the attractive hair dark and wavy, the eyes intense and intelligent, the mustache wide and drooping at the ends, and the face oval and good looking, almost noble, with nothing coarse or gross about its aspect.

As a boy on the farm, his bedroom had an oak floor and faced east. As the morning came, he could lie in bed and see the sun red behind the horizon and the dense screen of broad, untrimmed trees. Daggers, deer antlers, swords, and pistols adorned the walls, and his bookcase bulged fatly with Shakespeare, Byron, Bulwer, Marryat. Wilkes Booth was from the first a child the women of the house took to and pampered, humoring his whims and caprices, letting him get his way, allowing him to surrender to whatever impulses gained the supreme claim to his nature at the moment. The result was he lacked powers of steady application, and was an indifferent student, attending several private schools including St. Timothy Hall in Catonsville, Maryland, where he made friendships with two men he would recruit as Confederate spies.

But in spite of a mother and sisters who believed in the wonders he would make of his life, Booth had a spiteful, limited intelligence that made of him a racist and a snob. To him, worthiness was a matter of class. For example, it was the custom of the family to eat with the white men who had been hired as hands to work the harvest. Booth was too haughty to condescend to sit at the same table with them. He looked down on foreigners too, especially Irishmen, seeing them mainly as ignorant menials. Part of the reason he despised Lincoln to the fervid degree he did was due to Booth's sniffy arrogance about Abraham Lincoln's day-laborer background (a fact of Lincoln's life that the American public has never much liked or acknowledged). Booth also secretly attended meetings of the anti-foreign, anti-black Know-Nothing Party. In Booth's eyes, blacks especially were not worthy of respect, confidence, or decent human treatment. As a white supremacist, he tended to endorse and side with those who saw African Americans as lacking any worthwhile qualities or in any way sharing a common human nature with the whites. "The country was formed for the white, not for the black man," he said.

In sum, Booth's character manifested serious streaks of weakness: a lack of hardness toward himself, a lack of conscientiousness of small things, a style of life that centered too much on personal indulgence, a taking and absorption of things only for pleasure, and an avoidance of the stress of continual effort. Instead, Booth thought "big." He liked the dramatic, the breathtaking, the stunning, the spectacular, the heart-stopping singular act that only one exceptional man could successfully bring off. He wanted to astonish, startle, and be pointed out by people. Audacious acts to him seemed to pose the most authentic test of character, distinguishing the weak from the strong and the real hero from the fake. He had an ideal image of himself that wanted to stand up to things, to be effective in them, perhaps even to lead in them, but almost until the last of his life, it remained only a wishful dream.

In 1859, as a lieutenant in the Richmond Grays, he went to watch the hanging of John Brown, and although, as a racist, he abominated Brown's attempts to give liberty to the slaves, the lonely, unsupported audacity of Brown was a quality he sought to embody in himself. Like Brown, he liked grand, florid, attention-getting gestures.

Given his father's background, acting was a natural way for Booth to earn his bread. He had a strong liking for make-believe, combined with that need for an audience that acts to establish and strengthen a sense of self. It is no accident that his first great theatric successes occurred in southern cities. Critics noted Booth was a trifle too short for heroic roles, and critics called his acting technique a bit crude, resembling a kind of "boisterous declamation," according to one. His father's fame made for critical tolerance, and he improved with practice and repetition. By 1862, the *New York World* called him "an emerging star of real magnitude, and singular, though fitful brilliancy." He was a "star," earning $2,000 a year or the equivalent of a quarter of a million dollars today. And he was a wonderful athlete on stage, addicted to spectacular leaps and to the most energetic duels that sometimes pitched opponents into the orchestra pit or left them with cuts from the fake swords. He had great strength of leg. A friend W. J. Ferguson saw Booth leap over a piece of stage scenery five feet high "with little effort." Like other psychopaths like John Walker and Aldrich Ames, Booth liked practical jokes. When two men were quarreling in a bar room, Ferguson saw Booth deftly hurl a heavy book that hit a man with a thud in the back. The man turned, enraged, accused an innocent onlooker, and started a huge brawl. The lights went off, and Booth left, not caring a curse.

He captivated all who crossed his path. Friends praised his erect carriage, his remarkable powers of conversation, his extraordinary presence and magnetism. Women idolized him. "Women," said a friend, would "rave of him, his voice, his hair, his eyes." Actresses, mistresses, wayward wives, theater groupies—women of all conditions and kinds thronged his life. One even tried to kill him. Booth was starring in Albany with a stock company when his leading lady, Miss Henrietta Irving, rushed into his room and stabbed him, able only to inflict a small cut on his cheek.[12]

By 1863, his career as an actor had reached its peak. In early 1864, plagued by throat problems, his voice had started to fail, and he turned his interest to the booming oil business in Pennsylvania. Partnering with three men, he used his stage earnings to help the quartet purchase oil in Venango County near the town of Franklin. Unfortunately, the venture quickly went sour, and by the time he sold his holdings, Booth had lost $6,000, a fair amount of money for the time.

But making money and gaining fame on stage had begun to pale in importance. Booth's horizon of accomplishment had changed. During the summer of 1864 came the terrible battles between Grant and Lee, Grant choking, crewing, and finally penning Lee up near Richmond, never again to exercise the initiative in a battle. On September 2, Sherman took Atlanta, and the Union strategy to neutralize Lee and allow Sherman free rein to ferociously plunder and rummage through the South was at last taking hold.

The Confederacy was dying and Booth, seized by fury, despair, and vengefulness, found he had arrived at a key moment—a turn in his life's road that seemed critical for his future and his character. He was twenty-six.

Booth's loathing of Lincoln was rancid, personal, and unappeasable, but it must be remembered that Lincoln was widely hated in the North and the South. It was a venomous, irrational incessant excoriation similar to that directed at Franklin D. Roosevelt when the latter had first been president. First, there was Lincoln's poor physical appearance. There was no aura of eminence about Lincoln. He was a very tall, spare, lank person who moved awkwardly and slowly as if his frame "needed oiling," according to his law partner William Hearndon. He had a nasal, grating, high-pitched voice, marred by a distinct frontier accent that would pronounce, "I heard" as "I heeeerd." He reportedly preferred to blow his nose, not by using a handkerchief, but by using his thumb and fingers, frontier style. George Templeton Strong, a proadministration diarist who was scandalized by Lincoln's lack of social finish, called him "a barbarian, Scythian, yahoo, or gorilla." A New York matron said she would only admit to her drawing room Secretary of State William Seward and Secretary of Treasury Salmon Chase, not Lincoln or the rest. One hostile visitor to the White House found Lincoln, "seated, in shirt sleeves, his feet on the mantelpiece, his hat on his head, amusing himself by making huge semicircles with tobacco juice that he squeezed out his quid."[13] "Can our countrymen be so blind," asked Mary Daly of New York, "as again to place such a clod . . . in the Presidential chair?"

Then there were his politics. Confederates and Northerners hated him for using force to maintain the Union, and for abridging or suspending cherished civil rights like the right of habeas corpus. Others feared that his resolve to free the slaves would Africanize America, making a country of racial degenerates, a belief that Booth shared.

For Booth, the fatal bacillus of revenge had finally entered his thought. It was almost as if Lincoln's policies represented a personal injury done specifically to him. One senses Booth had no glimmering of Lincoln's immense superiority to himself as a person, as a center of life, and as having the highest human responsibility. That Lincoln was a genius—a man of first-rate and astounding mental capacities who saw "all things through a perfect mental lens," as his law partner Hearndon said—was beyond the power of Booth to conceive. Booth was more apt to imagine the ideal man as closely resembling himself. One also suspects that his hatred of Lincoln was fed by factors of which Booth was hardly aware. There were first the personal, physical differences between the two—the one abnormally tall, the other one short. But there were others. One possessed vast, dominating power over a whole nation of people, the other craved power beyond the narrow world of the stage, but such mastery always remained just out of reach. But one also wonders if it bothered Booth that the profession he had chosen really came down to pretending to be someone else, other people, characters and personalities often possessed of a size and dimension richer and fuller than himself. Whatever the part he played, Booth remained a mere impersonator. But Lincoln, the person destroying piecemeal the South that Booth loved, had a personality that reposed broad and majestic on its own resources and exerted its lethal strength without much show.

And one has to wonder if there were other dissatisfying misgivings that preyed on Booth's mind. He certainly appears a man anxious to judge the political currents of his time to discover who was responsible for them and the guilty parties behind them. Yet did his style of life—his staying out of the fighting while so many other and better men had already died—act to sharpen his dissatisfaction with himself and require him to find a diverting scapegoat? It does seem strange that such a fiery backer of the Southern cause, as Booth clearly was, did not ever fight for it. When a man asked him why he had not fought for the Confederacy, Booth answered lamely that he had promised his mother not to. Did this lead him to embrace a compensating conviction that one act for the South was equal to many acts of service and that excess in action was only a reprove to those who had no right to it?

We can infer from records that within the inner recesses of Booth there moved about dark, insatiable dragons of vanity and vindictiveness—what Lincoln biographer, poet Carl Sandburg called "projects and purposes vast with a sick desire, dizzy with ego." At first look he appears to match the classic description of a regicide formulated by French alienist Dr. Emanuel Regis, who in 1890 noted that the regicide is given to much solitude and thinking, and concluded that "whatever sane reason he may have possessed gives way to a sickly fixation that he is called on to deal a great blow, sacrifice his life to a just cause and kill a monarch in the name of God, Country, Liberty, Anarchy or some analogous principle."[14] Such an assassin is proud of his mission and acts in public and in the focus of maximum glare. He uses a technique that demands personal violence, and he doesn't seek to escape but wants to exhibit his deed as reflecting pride and accomplishment. He works alone.

But there is another, and extremely critical, fact that must be taken into account in evaluating Booth's conduct. Booth was not a loner; he was an official Confederate secret agent, with an action team, who was on a mission sanctioned by the Confederate government.[15] That part was still to come, but come it would. Up until the bloody summer of 1864 with a presidential election approaching, Booth had been simply a Confederate sympathizer and a sometime-smuggler of high-grade quinine to the South. It was in August that Booth changed. All of a sudden, he seemed to move dully in a daze of listless discontent and waywardness, but the beginnings of most things are awkward. In fact, what was taking shape in his mind was a frightening design.

That month, he traveled to Philadelphia with his older brother Junius, then moved back to Baltimore, asking two old friends—former schoolmates of St. Timothy Hall, Samuel Arnold and Michael O'Laughlen, who were untidy-looking characters and both former Confederate soldiers—to join him at Barnum's City Hotel. When the three friends found themselves in Booth's room, drinking, Arnold heard Booth fluently and wrathfully unburden himself about Lincoln's destructive malevolence with the same insane animus he always displayed, ending with the declaration that he, Booth, intended to abduct Lincoln, take him to Richmond, and have him held as a hostage, using the president's captivity to bring about a prisoner exchange. It would be, as Arnold remembered Booth's words, "an act of honorable purpose, humanity and patriotism." Like Confederate agent Thomas Nelson Conrad, Booth saw instantly that Lincoln would be most vulnerable to capture while coming in his coach to the Soldiers' Home.

But Booth's powers of will were nothing if not intermittent. He fell ill for a while, had a love affair, and nothing of the plan moved forward. Yet inwardly, the seducing design of Lincoln's capture was coming to fasten an iron hold upon his mind. An old friend of Booth's, one of his partners in the oil venture, observed the change in him right away and wrote to him, "I hardly know what to make of you . . . so different from your usual self. Have you lost all your ambition or what is the matter?"

Booth was officially recruited as a Confederate secret agent in Montreal in October. The South at the time was very active in building assets and expanding its apparatus, and perhaps it was the fact that Booth shared sympathy for its goals that led his recruiters to believe he would be willing to spy on the North. Perhaps his recruiters saw in him some vulnerability that would make him susceptible to the intrigues and deceptions of espionage life, or perhaps the vulnerability were Booth's views themselves, a virulent Confederate positioned in the North. One thing was certain: his occupation provided a perfect cover for an agent. As an actor, Booth could meet and mix with all kinds of prominent people and travel anywhere to collect secret information without causing suspicions to be raised. He could go to places without attracting undue attention, and his fame and name could act as a pass to get him access denied others. Fame also acts to make others anxious to oblige and please, another advantage for an agent. These advantages alone may have decided on his selection.

In any case, Booth stayed at Lawrence Hall, a known gathering place for top Confederate agents. Soon after his arrival "Mr. Davis," an alias for Confederate money handler Patrick Charles Martin, the principal Confederate secret service agent in Montreal, gave him $300. Booth went and opened a bank account with it. This has been verified.[16]

Booth also spent time with George Sanders, a Confederate agent who advocated assassination as a tactic. On October 19, a group of Confederates under the command of Lieutenant Bennett H. Young raided St. Albans, Vermont, as part of a Confederate program of terrorism and irregular warfare that included setting fire to several New York hotels.[17] The raiders escaped to Canada but Canadian authorities questioned some. One was Caleb Wallace, who sent a telegram to Sanders asking his help. But when Sanders returned, he stayed at St. Lawrence Hall in a room near Booth's and witnesses saw the two men frequently together.

Sanders was a pouchy little man with sweptback hair, plump face, goatee, mustache and thick-browed eyes that had a dark, glinty look to them. Sanders had the true temper of the desperado—energetic and shameless. In the words of one former U.S. intelligence agent, Brigadier Gen. William Tidwell, it was probably Sanders who made assassination seem acceptable political action to John Wilkes Booth.

In 1848, Europe was in ferment, and Sanders went there to furnish arms to those rebelling against authoritarian governments. The revolutions were bloodily put down and many of the leading liberal intellectuals fled to London in exile. In 1854, thanks to connections to Franklin Pierce, Sanders was U.S. Consul in London, and that year he wrote a letter to the people of France urging them to rid themselves of Napoleon the Third and restore democracy.

But for the moment, Martin was the more important contact for Booth than Sanders. Martin was a native New Yorker who had recently been a Baltimore liquor dealer. He had also had an extensive career as a sea captain and had successfully run the Yankee blockade of the Southern coast. Martin was a man of pluck, courage and imagination who had already drafted several schemes to use captured Union ships to free Confederate prisoners.

In Montreal, called "Little Richmond," Martin introduced to Booth an actual plan afoot to capture Lincoln. Grant had understood the brutal nature of a war of attrition. He knew that the North's greater manpower reserves meant he could more readily replace his losses than could General Lee, and Grant quickly acted to put an end to prisoner exchange. The tactic worked wonderfully well: soon the South was suffering from a shortage of soldiers so severe that Davis' government was contemplating drafting slaves into the Confederate Army. Martin meant to capture Lincoln and trade him for Confederate men being held prisoner.

4

★ ★ ★

IT ISN'T KNOWN just how many of the details of the plot were disclosed to John Wilkes Booth, or what his reactions to it were, but the encounter was decisive. We do know from Confederate records that Booth, who had come to Montreal with his theatrical wardrobe, agreed to ship it in a trunk to a southern port aboard one of Martin's blockade-runners, the *Marie Victoria*. Martin also gave Booth a letter of introduction to two of Charles County's most prominent Confederate sympathizers, Dr. Samuel Mudd and Dr. William Queen.

Mudd, like Booth, was a racist. As a former owner of slaves and a man who had helped to recapture them, Mudd had a bad time, when, after the capture of Booth, the 161st New York Cavalry was replaced by the 82nd United States Colored Troops. The change affronted Mudd without end. "To be lorded over by a set of ignorant, prejudiced and irresponsible human beings of unbleached humanity was more than I could submit to," he wrote to his wife.[18]

Booth, carrying Martin's letter of introduction, first met Mudd in November 1864 in Charles County, Maryland, and they would meet there again very soon. Mudd would say later that the pretext of Booth's travel for the second meeting was that the actor wanted to buy a piece of land from Mudd. In fact, Booth had gone to Charles County to meet another

Confederate agent by the name of Thomas Harbin who maintained a signal camp at King George County on the western side of the Potomac, passing messages to the Confederates, and who had met with Walter Bowie, the Confederate agent and would-be kidnapper of the Union governor of Maryland in September. Harbin had "mail agents" who took smuggled letters from the South to Harbin who turned them over to trusted operatives in one of the South-sympathizing post offices to ensure they received proper handling and postage. The mail would then be reinserted into the Federal mail system for delivery to addresses across the Union. Two of Harbin's mail agents were Mudd and John Surratt, the owner of the tavern in Surrattsville.

Mudd arranged another meeting for Booth with Harbin on December 18 at the Bryantown tavern. Harbin in a newspaper interview many years later would comment that Booth had outlined a scheme for "seizing Lincoln and delivering him up to Virginia."[19] The reporter went on to say, "Harbin was a cool man who had seen many liars and rogues go to and fro in that illegal border, and he set down that Booth was a crazy fellow, but at the same time said he would give him cooperation."

As we've seen, Harbin would help Booth in Virginia after he came across the Potomac River with Herold.

After his meeting with Harbin, Mudd and Booth rode over to George Gardiner's farm where Booth purchased a horse that had lost one eye. That horse would be found the day after Lincoln's assassination, ridden hard the night before by Lewis Powell, the man who had almost killed Secretary of State William Seward.

Mudd met Booth again on December 23 at the National Hotel in Washington. Mudd and Booth had run into Surratt in the street, and Surratt agreed to join Booth's ring. Surratt was one of the South's most competent agents, running the tavern at Surrattsville as a Confederate safe house where Thomas Nelson Conrad and other top Confederate secret agents often stopped. Surratt's mother, Mary, owned a boardinghouse in Washington where the Booth ring would stay and find refuge.

Surratt would bring in Booth's next recruit, George David Atzerodt, an alcoholic, born in Prussia twenty-nine years before. Atzerodt was a seedy-looking fellow, with long hair worn parted, a mustache and goatee, and a face with a brief chin. What Atzerodt brought to the ring was detailed knowledge of the people and towns through which the conspirators in the ring would later try to escape.

Booth now had five men: Samuel Arnold, Michael O'Laughlen, John Surratt, David Atzerodt, and Thomas Harbin. Note that Dr. Mudd and the others were "enablers," not part of the actual "action team."

Surratt then brought Booth another man, David Herold, a twenty-two-year-old, who lived with his mother and sisters near the Washington Navy Yard Pharmacy where he was employed. Herold had access to drugs such as chloroform that could be used to render unconscious a president resisting his kidnappers.

The last recruit for Booth's ring was Lewis Thornton Powell. Powell, a Confederate soldier, had served most recently with Lieutenant Colonel John S. Mosby's Rangers, the group that was intimately connected with Confederate covert operations. He was an extraordinarily handsome, intense man, with dark hair, a strong jaw, and massive physical robustness and power. For example, in attempting to stab to death Seward, who had been injured in a carriage accident and whose neck brace saved his life from Powell's frenzied slashings, Powell would injure five people of Seward's household, putting three into critical condition.[20] He and Bowie were described by their organization as "first class men, always ready for any duty, and game."[21]

Powell had served with the Army of Northern Virginia, until, having been shot through the right wrist, he had been taken prisoner at Gettysburg. He had worked as a POW nurse and met a woman named Margaret Branson from Baltimore and, through her, John Surratt. Powell escaped from the Union hospital and made his way back to Mosby's 43rd Battalion of Virginia Cavalry. Powell served with this unit in 1863 and 1864, but on January 13, 1865, in a mystifying move, he rode into a Union encampment at Fairfax County Courthouse in Virginia, retailed a cover story, and was allowed to proceed to Alexandria. He was now using the alias "Lewis Paine." As Paine, he took the oath of allegiance, and was released from further custody.

On January 14, as Powell was on his way to Baltimore, Surratt met with Harbin and procured a boat, which both men gave to Atzerodt for safekeeping. Surratt then went on to Washington to his mother's boardinghouse. He picked up Louis Wiechmann, a Confederate sympathizer, and both went on to Baltimore where they checked into a hotel.

At his trial in 1867, Wiechmann told of Surratt's having $300 in cash and telling Wiechmann he had to see another man in private. That man was Lewis Powell, and the $300 was to give Powell living expenses until he was called to Washington, where within three weeks he turned up. Powell was soon at Mary Surratt's boardinghouse using the alias of "Reverend Wood," and had become a full member of the ring.

Booth now convened his full team. They first went to Ford's Theater to see a play, *Jane Shore,* in order to case the place. They then chose a midnight dinner at Gautiers, a fashionable restaurant in Washington on Pennsylvania Avenue near Ford's Theater. The meeting was raucous and dissensions divided the men. Arnold and O'Laughlen wanted action taken soon or they wanted out of the team. Many drinks were downed, dark, bitter words flew back and forth, and tempers blazed up. Booth got the group calmed and its members talked. He wanted to kidnap Lincoln from Ford's Theater. The team would seize Lincoln in his box, handcuff him, lower him to the stage, then slip him out a side door. Booth was dealing with sensible men, and this was not a sensible plan. Their sneering opposition was unanimous. The meeting broke up at five o'clock in the morning.

Two days later, Booth paid a personal visit to the theater. Booth's home was wherever he set down his hat, and he had his fan mail steadily accumulating at the theater. While at the theater talking to cronies, Booth was electrified to learn that Lincoln was scheduled to visit a group of convalescing soldiers at Campbell Hospital on Seventh Street, quite close to the District line. Few travelers used the rural road leading to the hospital. The Eastern Branch River Bridge, leading south, was close by. Within minutes of grabbing Lincoln, the group could be in Maryland.

Booth prepared. He sent Herold rattling off in his buggy to the Surrattsville Tavern with the gear needed to take Lincoln south. This included a length of rope, two double-barreled shotguns, a knife, a pistol, ammunition, and a monkey wrench. The rope would be used to string across the road to unseat pursuing Union cavalry. The wrench was there to remove the wheels of Lincoln's carriage so it could be compactly ferried on a boat across the Potomac. Booth had already sent food and whiskey ahead to the tavern by means of Mudd.

As Surratt would say later, "We were instantly in our saddles on the way to the hospital. This was between one and two o'clock in the afternoon. Our intention was to seize the carriage, which was drawn by a team of splendid horses, and to have one of the men mount the box and drive directly for southern Maryland via Benning's bridge." The team had decided to abandon the carriage to transport Lincoln and use horses instead.

"By the time the alarm could have been given and the horses saddled, we would have been on our way through southern Maryland towards the Potomac River."[22]

The hour drew near. Everyone was somber, nervous. No Lincoln. The group waited, passing through every possible stage of expectation. No Lincoln. In the grip of feverish frustration, Booth approached a staff member of the hospital, an old friend named Davenport. What was happening? Where was Lincoln? asked Booth. Davenport looked at Booth. Why, hadn't Booth heard? The president had changed his plans at the last minute and wasn't going to show.

The heart of steadfast purpose went out of them. Even more infuriating than the flat fizzle of the plan was that fact that Lincoln at that very moment was at the very hotel where Booth was staying, the National, presenting a battle flag to the governor of Indiana and making a speech, an event well publicized in the city's morning's paper. Vexed, despising themselves, assailed by feelings of failure, feeling angry and downcast, the group disbanded. Surratt went to Richmond to talk to Confederate Secretary of State Judah P. Benjamin, his case officer. Arnold and O'Laughlen went to Baltimore, Herold and Atzerodt stayed in the city. Booth went to Ford's Theater the next day to watch a friend perform, and then on the twenty-first, made a strange and mysterious trip to New York.

New York was a critical gathering place for clandestine Confederate activity in the East. Atzerodt told a Maryland provost marshal after his capture that Booth told him that he had met "a party in N. York who would get the Prest. (president), certain. They were going to mine the end of the Pres (president's). House, next to War Dept. They knew an entrance to accomplish it through. Spoke about getting friends of the Prest. (president) to get up an entertainment & they would mix in it, have a serenade & thus get the Prest. (president) and party. These were understood to be projects. Booth said if he did not get him quick, the N. York crowd would. Booth knew the New York party apparently by a sign. He saw Booth give some kind of sign to two parties on the Avenue who said they were from New York."[23]

Coincidences in espionage are never insignificant. They cannot prove anything—nothing is harder to prove in court than conspiracy—but for historians, coincidences act to uncover connections, meaningful chains of contacts. What is significant about Atzerodt's story is that, while Surratt was in Richmond to report on the failure of the kidnapping attempt, the

Confederate government had already decided to give up on plans to kidnap Lincoln, deciding instead to attack and annihilate the whole top echelon of the Lincoln government. In our day, during the Cold War, this was called the doctrine of "nuclear decapitation"—killing the whole Soviet leadership or American leadership with a single salvo of missiles. It works along the principle that if you have one shot at an enemy, you shoot at his brain, not his body. If you paralyze the central command, then you may also disrupt and paralyze what that command controls. At a single, terrible stroke, the South would kill the president, vice president, secretary of state, and secretary of war, thus decapitating the leadership and fatally crippling the North's ability to prosecute the war.

The South already had just such a "decapitation" mission in the works. Its enabler was Thomas Harney, employed by the Confederate Torpedo Bureau, commanded by Brigadier General Gabriel Rains. The bureau's task was like that of Hamas or Hizballah in our day—to develop a variety of explosive devices for sea and land use. Rains had already had some success. In August 1864, he had put a time bomb aboard a Union supply barge at City Point, Virginia, and blown up a part of Grant's major supply base in a single, devastating instant, killing fifty-four people and wounding another 126.

Jefferson Davis knew and approved of such missions. In a letter of May 15, 1864, talking about such an action, A. L. Rives, a colonel in the Confederate Engineer Bureau, said, "His excellency the Presdt. (president) (Davis) thinks the (explosives) should be planted in front of the work called by your name Ft. Stevens, say within musket range of the slope of the hill. The (president) counts on producing by this explosion a great demoralizing effect on the enemy."[24]

On April 2, 1865, Harney, "under orders to blow up the White House" and carrying a special cache of explosives, had joined Mosby's Rangers who were operating in Farquier County, Virginia. On his way to Washington, Harney and Mosby ran into Union cavalry, and in the ensuring skirmish, Harney was captured and taken to the old Capitol Prison. A Mosby officer wrote that Harney's loss was "irretrievable."[25]

But to what? Harney was the explosives expert essential to successfully executing the plot.

The Torpedo Bureau, under Rains, had evacuated Richmond in January 1865, leaving a remnant behind under Captain Samuel Leitch who soon appointed an enlisted man, William H. Snyder, to the bureau. Richmond fell and was evacuated on April 2. On April 4, Union Colonel Edwards Hasting Ripley, commanding the 9th Vermont Infantry, had set up his headquarters not far from the captured Torpedo Bureau when a Confederate enlisted man asked to see him. It was Snyder. He said he wanted to alert Ripley and his superiors to a plan that filled Snyder with anxious unrest and dread—a party of men had been dispatched on a secret mission that he vaguely understood to be aimed at the head of the Yankee government, and he wished to put Lincoln on his guard and have impressed upon Lincoln that he, Snyder, believed him to be in the greatest danger of violence and should take better care of himself.[26] The information was compartmentalized, and Snyder could have no names and particulars, only a general warning.

Were Synder and Atzerodt talking of Harney's plot? Modern historians such as William A. Tidwell and Edward Steers, Jr. and other experts on the period believe that he was. Others dismiss the theory as too speculative. But Tidwell and Steers also believe that with Harney captured, Booth took up the Harney plan or was assigned to take it up. There is no solid evidence of this, but as a suggestion, it helps to explain ensuing facts.

After the collapse of the kidnapping, a deep gloom had settled on Booth's spirits. Booth knew the failure made him a ridiculous figure both in his own eyes and in the eyes of his men. He was no longer a man full of resources, full of confidence in himself, ready to take chances and risks of every sort. All his buoyant, hard energy had come from a sense of having an authorized mission, but his most determined and energetic efforts had failed in utter fiasco.

On March 27, Booth sent a telegram to O'Laughlen telling him to come to Washington. There was no reply. Booth had clearly lost any personal ascendancy he had previously enjoyed. Booth's spirits sank, and despair closed over him like water. He began drinking heavily. Perhaps the real face of such pleasure is utter despair, or perhaps the drinking was a desperate attempt to numb his nerves or an attempt at artificial strengthening, to reassemble and reassert his inner forces. After its capture, Richmond had been quick to collapse, and shortly after it was evacuated, the old city began to burn. Within twenty-four hours, 700 of its structures blazed up to die out into empty, gutted, smoldering shells. Lincoln, who traveled by carriage through the city, the streets heavily covered by debris, saw acre upon acre of gutted shells, heaps of smoking rubble, a naked forest of blackened chimneys.

When asked by a friend if he planned to go to Richmond, where he had once enjoyed popularity, Booth said morosely, "I will never go to Richmond again." He paused, and then said, "I will never go to Richmond again." To see the city swarming with Union soldiers would be too painful a sight, he said.

The previous fall Booth had at last realized that his was a fitful, inconsistent life full of starts and stops, of brief flights and long rests, of this allurement or that petty pleasure getting the upper hand for a time, only to be followed by another just as worthless and fleeting. In his letter to his mother he mentioned his four years of idleness and said he had begun "to deem myself a coward and despise my own existence."

In the grip of that self-hating desolation, his heart oppressed and contracted, he even seemed to turn bitterly on Lee, angered at Lee's failure. He told Henry Clay Ford, treasurer of Ford's Theater, that when Lee had accepted his sword in 1861 from the Confederate Senate, Lee had sworn he would never surrender it, implying Lee was weak and dishonest. Ford retorted sharply that Lee was a brave general and Southern gentlemen and at Appomattox must have known what he was doing. Booth mumbled with a jeer that he was just as good and brave as Lee. There was an instant of disbelief between them, then Ford shot back, "Well, you have not got three stars yet to show it."

As the jubilant people of Washington, swept with a flood of ecstatic feeling of victory, were setting off fireworks to celebrate the surrender at Appomattox, and others were gawking in happy groups at the insanely bright streets with the big buildings newly ablaze with lights, fountains of fireworks in the sky, Booth's own flame flickered very low. The world seemed inane, tiresome, worthless, and empty. When a friend asked him if he wanted to go and get a drink, Booth quickly accepted, saying, "Anything to drive away the blues." One friend saw him drink a quart of brandy in two hours.[27]

As for the war, only Confederate General Joe Johnston was still in the field, facing Union General William Sherman. A victory by Johnston was the sole hope for Confederate military success and that hope was fading fast. Sometime in this period, Booth decided on murder. The telegram to O'Laughlen on March 27 is believed to be about the kidnapping attempt but supporting evidence is missing. But sometime in the next seventeen days, Booth decided on murder—had somehow found within himself the concentrated will to engage the Union in single combat and strike at its heart, killing not just Lincoln, but eliminating the whole upper echelon of the Union leadership, just as Harney had planned. Sometime between March 27 and April 14, Booth stopped to visit the Seward home on Lafayette Square and chatted with the household maid. We do not know what was said, but the visit would appear to have been a preliminary reconnaissance of a target.

No factual link has yet been found that ties the scheme of the New York crowd with the Harney mission, but it *is* certain that his belief that the South would continue to fight lay at the basis of Booth's act.

In the meantime, Lincoln was busy living the last week of his life. On the evening of April 11, it was raining, and Elizabeth Keckly, Lincoln's seamstress, looked out over the White House to a dense mass of darkened heads the likes of which she had never seen before. Close to the light, their faces could be seen clearly, but they stretched back into hundreds of dim shapes and profiles shrouded in dark. A great crowd had collected at the White House, and a great confused hum and babble rose over the sea of packed and pressed together forms. Lincoln's lank form at last appeared on a balcony to give what would prove to be his last speech. It wasn't a triumphal exuberance; there was no parading of Union superiority to please the crowd. Instead, Lincoln, his eye fixed on the future, launched into a sober, down-to-earth discourse, part of which touched on giving the vote to the newly freed colored man in Louisiana: "Concede that the new government of Louisiana is only to what it should be as the egg is to the fowl; we shall sooner have the fowl by hating the egg than by smashing it."

Mashed in the crowd, Booth stood, Powell at his side, both of their faces uplifted in the crowd and Booth completely incensed. He turned to Powell and hissed, "That means nigger citizenship. Now, by God, I'll put him through. That will be the last speech he will ever make."

LINCOLN WAS A tall, odd, and melancholy man. He radiated warmth and kindliness, yet his great reactor was cool at the core. Life approached him through his brain, his principles, and his calm, exact, and cold perceptions, not his feelings. Charles Francis Adams Jr. said Lincoln had "a mild, dreamy meditative eye which one would scarcely expect to see in a successful chief magistrate in these days of the republic." Lincoln was not a warmhearted man. He could be tender and considerate, yes, but he was not warmhearted—not according to his law partner Hearndon, who is certainly one of the most acute and admiring of his biographers. Hearndon said that if a warmhearted man was one who "goes out of himself and reaches for others spontaneously, seeking to correct some abuse to mankind because of a deep love of humanity, and he does what he does for love's sake, then Lincoln was a cold man." Lincoln acted consistently from his head, not his heart. He was gentle but hardly ever used terms of endearment, Hearndon noted.[28] Hearndon even remarks while Lincoln saw himself as the emancipator of the black man, "When he freed the slaves, there was no heart in his act." Hearndon added that while Lincoln could be tender and gentle, he acted chiefly from principled calculation: "In general terms, his life was cold—at least characterized by what many persons would deem a great indifference . . ." Hearndon adds, "He gave the keynote to his own character when he said, 'With malice towards none, with charity for all.' In proportion to his want of deep, intense love, he had no hate and bore no malice."[29]

That he was a man of comprehensive and unbending conscience, a heroic figure that had in him some inner strength that always beckoned him on, no matter how dark the hour, hardly needs to be stated.

Lincoln had about him something that was usually touching and poetic. Of all our presidents, Lincoln alone was visited by unique dreams and premonitions. After the election of 1860, lying exhausted on a sofa, he saw a double reflection of his face on a mirror on the wall. With one image so much paler and washed out than the other, his wife had taken it to mean he would be elected to a second term but would not live to complete it. Lincoln had agreed.

He once told a friend he believed he would come to "some terrible end," and after a visit to City Point on April 8, Lincoln had had a long conversation with his friends, reading from *Macbeth,* his absolutely favorite play, pausing over the passage,

Duncan is in his grave,
After life's fitful fever he sleeps well;
Treason has done its worst; nor steel nor poison,
Malice domestic, foreign levy, nothing
Can touch him further.

And then he stopped and read the passage over again, as if struck by its significance.

He later recounted to Ward Lamon, his burly bodyguard and close friend, a dream that apparently had occurred during this period. He told Lamon that some time around April 1, while he was at City Point waiting for the news of Grant's assault on Petersburg, which had ended the war, he had retired very late. "I had been up," said Lincoln, "waiting for important dispatches from the front. I could not have been long in bed when I fell into slumber, for I was weary. I soon began to dream." There seemed to be a deathlike stillness around him, but then he heard subdued sobs as if a number of people were weeping. He left his bed and wandered downstairs. There the silence was broken by the same pitiful sobbing, but the mourners were invisible. Lincoln went from room to room, but no living person was in sight, but the same mournful sounds of distress met him as he passed along. It was light in all the rooms, and every object was familiar to him. But why were all the people grieving as if their hearts would break? "I was puzzled and alarmed," Lincoln said. "What could be the meaning of this?" Determined to find the meaning, he kept on until he arrived at the East Room of the White House, which he entered.

"There I met with a sickening surprise," he said. "Before me sat a catafalque, on which rested a corpse wrapped in funeral vestments. Around it were stationed soldiers who were acting as guards; and there was a throng of people, some gazing mournfully upon the corpse whose face was covered, others weeping pitifully. 'Who is dead in the White House?' I demanded of one of the soldiers. 'The President,' was his answer: 'he was killed by an assassin.' Then came a loud burst of grief from the crowd, which woke me from my dream."

Lincoln slept no more that night.

On April 14, in a meeting with his Cabinet, he told of a dream he'd had the night before, a recurring dream that always preceded a great or important event of the war. Navy Secretary Gideon Welles asked what the dream had been about, and Lincoln described being "in some singular, indescribable vessel . . . moving rapidly towards an indefinite shore." He had had the dream just before the attack on Fort Sumter, and the Battles of Bull Run, Antietam, Gettysburg, Stones' River, Vicksburg, and Wilmington. "I have had this great dream last night, and we shall, judging from the past, have great news again very soon." The crusty Grant retorted that Stone's River was no victory and he knew of "no great results that followed it." But Lincoln concluded, "Something extraordinary is going to happen. And soon."

He had no idea that his time had come to die later that same day. What his wife and colleagues saw was a man that day carefree, frolicsome, and full of energetic joy, "like a boy out of school," someone said.

But dark and underhanded developments were already taking place that would join Lincoln's fate with Booth's. On the night of April 13, Booth had gone barhopping around the town, drinking heavily at his favorite watering holes. He then returned to his hotel and wrote a letter to his mother, then one for the newspaper, the *National Intelligencer,* for posterity. The next morning, he breakfasted with two young women. Booth then went to Ford's Theater where he picked up his mail. Then Booth stopped by a stable and rented a horse for his escape, and told the stable owner he would pick the horse up at four o'clock. Booth then visited Mary Surratt's boardinghouse. Mary Surratt rented a buggy to go to Surrattsville, thirteen miles away. Wiechmann, one of her boarders, who had rented the buggy, suddenly found Mary and Booth in conversation. Mary had a brown paper package tied with string that Booth had given her containing Booth's field glass. She also carried a message that would send her to the gallows. She was to tell Lloyd, the keeper of the tavern, "To have the shooting irons (two carbines) ready that night—there would be some parties call for them."

Clearly Booth knew that Mary was going to Surrattsville or perhaps he had visited her earlier that day and asked her to go. He would have no other means of knowing of her trip.

In the afternoon, Booth stopped at the Kirkwood Hotel on Twelfth and Pennsylvania Avenue. Atzerodt had registered there on Booth's instructions. His task would be to kill Vice President Andrew Johnson. Since Atzerodt registered at the hotel three hours before Booth had heard at Ford's Theater of Lincoln's attendance there that night, it would appear he had learned of Lincoln's attendance beforehand. There were only a few theaters to choose from in town. From his pocket Booth drew out a small card and scribbled on it, "Don't wish to disturb you. Are you at home?" The desk clerk left the card in the box of William A. Browning, the personal secretary of Johnson. It appears Booth was attempting to determine Johnson's schedule, using Browning as a "locator," but this has not been proved.[30]

At four o'clock, Booth ran into John Matthews, a fellow actor, on Pennsylvania Avenue. Suddenly, there passed by an open carriage containing General and Mrs. Grant, on their way to the train station. Matthews remarked the fact to Booth, who gripped his companion's hand, then hastily took to his horse, galloping furiously after the carriage.

An aide of Grant's, Horace Porter, would later say that a man strongly resembling Booth rode past the carriage staring fixedly at Grant. He was a pale, dark man, Porter said. For Mrs. Grant, it had already been a day of strange and menacing occurrences. While at lunch with General John A. Rawlings's wife, four men had come into the dining room and taken seats opposite their table. One of the men was dark and pale. Now that man had reappeared. As Porter said, "As Gen. Grant and I rode to the depot, this same dark, pale man rode past us at a sweeping gallop on a dark horse—black, I think. He rode twenty yards ahead of us, wheeled and returned, and as he passed us both going and returning, he thrust his face quite near the General's and glared in a disagreeable manner."[31] There is evidence that there may have been someone else, whose identity isn't known, who was assigned to kill Grant. When Grant was on the train, traveling between Baltimore and Philadelphia, someone tried to force his way into the locked car in which Grant and his family were traveling. The train crew seized him, but he escaped. He later wrote a letter to Grant, thanking God that his effort to kill the general had failed.

Where Booth went after that isn't known. He had supper at about 6 P.M., and by 7 P.M., was meeting with Powell, Atzerodt, and Herold to finalize their plans. According to Atzerodt, Powell was to go to Seward's house and kill him, Atzerodt was to kill Johnson at his room in the Kirkwood Hotel, while Herold would guide Powell to Seward's house then flee to a rendezvous point in Maryland. Booth would kill the president himself.

Booth made his way up a narrow alley at the back of Ford's Theater. It was a little after nine o'clock in the evening. At ten o'clock, tall, lanky Lincoln was seated up in the presidential box, engrossed in the play, a genial piece of popcorn called *Our American Cousin,* which was about half over. It was strange, Lincoln usually relished the performance of a play, but he hadn't wanted to go to the theater that night at all. In fact, thirteen people invited to attend had declined, including Grant, and Lincoln normally loved to see plays performed. But he had no taste for a play at Ford's that night. No matter. Mary's heart was set on going, anxious not to disappoint people's expectations, she said.

Booth entered a saloon next to the theater and ordered a whiskey. He drank it, then left by the front door. Booth mounted the curving stairs to the box. Inside, Major Henry Rathbone and his fiancée, Clara Harris, accompanied the presidential couple. During the second act, Lincoln suddenly felt cold and got up to put his coat around him. During the next act, Mary suddenly put her arms around her husband. "What will they think of me, draping myself on you like this?" Mary asked coaxingly. Lincoln replied, "They won't think anything."

They were his last words.

James Ferguson, who operated a restaurant next to the theater, had gotten a ticket in order to get a look at the famous Grant and was sitting opposite the presidential box when he saw Booth. There was a small anteroom that led to the president's box, and Ferguson saw Booth leaning casually against the wall by it. Suddenly he disappeared inside the box. Ferguson, his gaze turning to dread, saw the flash of a shot and the brief, evil gleam of a knife as Booth slashed at Lincoln's guest, Rathbone. From the stage, a startled actor, Harry Hawks, looked up to see a puff of blue smoke float out lazily on the air from the box.

5

★ ★ ★

THE CONFEDERATE GOVERNMENT had a responsibility for aiding the escape of its own conspirators, and Lieutenant Colonel John S. Mosby once again emerged to assume a major place. Had the Thomas Harney mission gone forward, Mosby was not only assigned to be responsible for infiltrating Harney into Washington, but for devising the means for getting him safely back out of the city and into the South. To do this, Mosby had a stay-behind group of perhaps twenty-five men, operating in the "Northern Neck" of Virginia between the Potomac and Rappahannock Rivers. For Harney (and Booth), there would have been a choice of three escape routes: across the Potomac River into Fairfax County, Virginia, or through southern Maryland (Prince Georges County or St. Mary's County), or north through Montgomery County. We know as established fact that Mosby's were the only units in action between the Potomac and James Rivers.

From here on, we just have bits and shreds of fact, but they allow us to infer what we cannot know. From the excellent researches of William Tidwell, a twenty-three-year operative of U.S. intelligence, we know that the Harney mission of April 1 was authorized as a high-priority mission by the highest levels of the Confederate government and that "a number of actions had been set in motion to support that operation" when the Confederate government evacuated Richmond the next day. As Tidwell says,

"Harney had been lost, but did that mean the end of the Harney operation." To find out what was happening, Mosby dispatched his friend Captain Robert S. Walker of Company B to determine the true state of affairs.

When the Confederates evacuated Richmond, many things were left up in the air. An agent Frank Stringfellow was trying to get back to Richmond, there were couriers from the secret line with information to deliver, and there was the Harney mission still unrecalled.

Mosby was put in a further quandary when on April 12, Union General Winfield Scott Hancock asked for his surrender. Mosby's reply was evasive, and he stalled for time. From April 22 to April 27, several hundred of Mosby's men were given paroles, but Mosby retained a group of rangers and was headed south with the explanation he was going to join General Joe Johnston in South Carolina fighting General William Sherman. Three different memoirs differ in their numbers. One said the number was three, another as many as thirty or forty.

We know that before April 15, Booth asked for directions to the homes of "Captain" Samuel Cox, a Confederate agent. We know he stayed at the home of Dr. Samuel Mudd. We also know that Booth was in the hands of Cox on April 16.

On April 21, Booth was moved from his secret camp on the Cox farm and put into a boat to cross the Potomac. An anchored Union gunboat aborted the attempt, but another try was made that proved successful. Greeting Booth in Virginia was none other than Thomas Harbin, an agent of the Confederate War Department, and another agent of the Confederate Secret Line, Joseph Baden.

In discussing future plans, Booth grew angry and affronted at what the two men told him, and he left in a huff. Booth and David Herold then went to the home of Dr. Richard Stuart, one of the prominent Confederate citizens of King George County. In a subsequent interrogation, Stuart said that Booth had told him he wanted to find his way to Mosby.[32] We know that after spending the night in the cabin of a black family, Booth hired the son of that family to take them in a wagon to Port Conway on the Rappahannock River. They arrived in early afternoon, and Booth and Herold then met three Mosby soldiers in the early afternoon of April 24, apparently by accident. One thing stands out, however. One of these soldiers was Mortimer B. Ruggles, second in command to Thomas Nelson Conrad of the earlier Lincoln kidnap plot (and very likely sent there to get Booth under Confederate control).[33]

On April 24, as Booth and Herold were approaching the Garrett farm, Mosby was only twenty miles away. When he was staying at Garrett's farm, an unnamed Mosby soldier rode in to tell Booth and Herold of approaching Union cavalry. It was Ruggles and his group who arranged for Booth to stay at the farm of Garrett, located near the Rappahannock, bringing Booth and Mosby to within twenty-five miles of each other.

On the afternoon or evening of April 25, a serving Confederate soldier, Allen Bowie, a twenty-seven-year-old sergeant in Captain Thornton's Company Lightfoot Battalion, Virginia Artillery, came calling. Tidwell concluded that the contacts by Confederate soldiers "imply the existence of some central direction in the (area) dedicated to the protection of John Wilkes Booth."[34]

We know it failed. Early in the morning on April 26, cavalry surrounded the tall, plank tobacco barn, and we know the rest, except for one final oddity. It took Booth two-and-a-half hours to die. The area in front of the barn was chaos itself during that time—doctors arriving, soldiers going to and fro, small crowds collecting, messages being sent and received. And in the middle of all the milling, noisy tumult, an unparoled private of the 9th Virginia Cavalry walked into the Garrett farm as though attracted by the commotion. Booth by that time had died. Tidwell said that the soldier was probably charged with determining for certain that Booth was dead, thereby ending Mosby's mission. Fortunately for the private, no one took much notice of the soldier, and he left without being questioned.

On that same day, Lieutenant Charles Cawood, the commander of the Secret Line station in King George County, would ask for parole, his war finally over.

Booth's ring was captured quickly, like fishnet being drawn close. Arrested were Herold, Mary Surratt, "Lewis Paine," George David Atzerodt, Samuel Arnold, Michael O'Laughlen. Only John Surratt would escape by joining the Vatican Guard.

Mosby's mission was ended. Mosby, the man who had stoutly opposed seccession at the outbreak of the war, had emerged from it a great Confederate hero. He wrote his memoirs, lectured, and became personal friends with Grant, who shielded him and who was not aware of the part Mosby had played in Lincoln's murder. And, indeed, Mosby never mentioned it for the rest of his life. Because of his unbridled and vicious guerilla activities, Mosby was the only Confederate soldier initially excluded from parole by order of Secretary of War Edwin Stanton, but Grant counter-

manded this. When Grant became president, Mosby was invited to the
White House and was able to procure government jobs for his sister and
some of his former followers. He refused one for himself, but was still accused by hard-line ex-Confederates as being a turncoat "seduced by self-
interest." He took to carrying a revolver, but someone in his hometown
took a shot at him, which spurred Grant to get his successor, Rutherford
B. Hayes, to bestow upon Mosby the U.S. consulship in Hong Kong. After that job was done, Mosby worked for a time for the Southern Pacific
Railroad until 1901, when he was laid off. What war couldn't do to him,
his having been fired was able to, which was destroy and embitter his
spirit. His temper grew savage, dictatorial, rude, and preemptory. Within
five years, he was dead, a harsh and disagreeable old man.

As for Lincoln's death, for his contemporaries it was for them what
John Kennedy's was for us. Everyone knew the exact time, the exact place,
and what he or she had been doing or talking to when the news of it was
received. The country as a whole plunged into unbearable sorrow. As never
before, the bulk of the country suffered as one a horrible ache of grieving
pain and loss. At the time, even the South recognized it had lost in Lincoln
its most dependable, fair-minded, and compassionate friend.

The ultimate tragedy of Booth's act was that it was utterly pointless. If
a belief is important only if it is true, then an act is valuable only to the degree it can make an improving impact on actual conditions. Like Benedict
Arnold, who lost his strategic sense after his treachery, Booth had no real
grasp of the Confederates' hopeless military situation. But after the surrender of Lee, there was no hope for further Confederate military success.
The surrender of Lee freed Grant's forces to move out of Richmond to join
with Sherman, forcing Johnston's surrender and the final end of the war.

Even today, to those of us who can inhabit that distant time only by
means of imagination, by the viewing of photographs, and by the reading
of documents and books, even we can feel a bit of the same sharp anguish
suffered by our forefathers. For his contemporaries, Lincoln's murder was
like having some towering, reassuring landmark, a compass point, ripped
suddenly and forever from a familiar and comforting skyline. People raised
their eyes to the spot only to reexperience the painful shock of dismay and
surprise to again realize that what once had stood there in all its glory had
vanished from them forever and left nothing of any worth to touch the
heart in its place.

The Traitor as Idealist:
CHAMBERS AND BENTLEY

*I find it heavy and dull those who think that good
must start with evil, that is with deaths.*

— MICHELANGELO

. . . man may be said to be a thinking being only in a very remote sense . . .

— SCHOPENHAUER

1

★ ★ ★

TODAY COMMUNISM APPEARS to us a collective hallucination, especially in the wake of its collapse in the Cold War. Its almost worldwide failure has discredited it to such a profound degree that it is hard to imagine the uncanny spell it was able to cast on thousands of sensible, solid American minds. Proposed as a system of human betterment, Communism's most sordid and disconcerting features included its idolization of force, its willingness to employ the vilest lies and treacheries to reach its ends. Deceit, fake identities, cover stories, theft of documents, even stony murder are things so seamy that they usually remain at the fringes of civilized life, but during Roosevelt's presidency they moved to the center. We don't expect to find Moscow-directed spies enjoying deep influence in the White House or hostile agents stealing secrets from key U.S. government departments, or American traitors infesting the country's intelligence services, and yet this happened.

When we read of the careers of Whittaker Chambers and Elizabeth Bentley, we are reminded of how hard it is to really know a thing in its true being. We wonder about how much Bentley and Chambers actually *knew* about Marxist-Leninism, even if as only a doctrine or a pseudo-religion. We wonder if they ever felt, as they went about their spying, the utter *foreignness* of the system they served. The ideology of communism was rooted in Russia, a country that had dominant feudal traditions, including an autocratic monarchy and an autocratic church, both stemming from an economic, political, and cultural history that differed remarkably and spectacularly from our own. In Russian politics, nothing was ever what it seemed to be. Russian culture in the nineteenth and early twentieth century was a culture of desperadoes with revolutionary movements often led or infested by czarist police agents. The nation was seething with treachery, betrayal, and outlandish conspiracies long before the coming of communism.

The heroism of Chambers and Bentley, both dedicated communist agents for a time, lay with their being able, from a mixture of resolve, anxiety, and intellectual integrity, to finally extract the moral meaning of their activities and summon up the moral courage to break free of their "dark night of the soul," as Chambers called it.

Their tragedy, shared by other American communists, seems to lay in the fact that by embracing their hatred for constituted society and by pursuing their hope for human progress no matter what the human cost, they somehow forsook the solid bone of life for a flimsy, romantic shadow. They gave a false reality to a fiction, and in so doing, impaired their own capacity for humanity.

It helps if we remember that by the 1930s capitalist democracy had pretty much discredited itself. The Great Depression had proved that capitalism was a system unable to properly feed and care for its own people. By 1932, the stock market had lost more than $74 billion, three times the entire cost of World War I. Prices paid for farm products had caved in, causing an avalanche of foreclosures on farmsteads. Five thousand American banks had failed. A third of a million children were out of school. Hundreds of men in cities slept on incinerator grates. Jobs were so scarce that men would leave home well dressed to go to another part of the city, change clothes, and beg or to sell cheap neckties, magazines, even vacuums door to door. In August 1932, someone asked the British economist John Maynard Keynes if history had ever seen anything like the Great Depression? He answered, yes. It was called the Dark Ages.

Such widespread and horrible economic failure made almost anything welcome as long as it was different. The collective all of a sudden seemed to promise more good than the unrestrained initiative of the individual. The appealing promise of the communist system was that its triumph would give an outlet to classes and segments of human nature not previously able to find sufficient expression. Under communism, the satisfied few would become the contented many, and the world of protest would finally merge with the world of privilege. For active strivers like Chambers and Bentley, there was in joining the movement the enjoyment of strength furnished by solidarity, the end of personal error and ignorance, and the sense of one's feet having at last been placed firmly on the right path—all very powerful and seductive intoxicants. The coming triumph of communism justified acts devoid of sympathy and humanity on the grounds that victory would result in an unmatched splendor of progress for humankind. The old melancholy lesson formulated by Jesuit-educated Sebastien Faure in the nineteenth century that stated "Every revolution ends in the reappearance of a new ruling class" was lost.[1]

CHAMBERS, THE MAN whom Kenneth Galbraith would call "one of the most avidly intellectual men of the century," was born Jay Vivian Chambers on April Fools' Day, 1901. Jay was named after his father, an illustrator who soon gave the belittling name of "Beadle" to his son because of the boy's watchful, grave way of looking at people and things. The boy was blond, with his mother's light blue eyes and a round, gentle face.

Laha was Chambers's mother. She hailed from Milwaukee, and was the daughter of Charles Whittaker, whose career proved disastrously uneven, full of sharp spikes and deep plunges, like the temperature chart of a fever patient. By the age of seven, Laha watched in dismay as business failures forced her father to sell their house in Milwaukee and move to Chicago, leaving her behind to attend the Home School, a private academy in Racine.

Once settled in Chicago, her father went into the business of making and selling brass castings, but this venture too was quick to collapse. The family lost everything, and Laha perhaps lost the most—her secret, treasured dream of one day attending an elite college on the East Coast.

Laha had a taste for theater and self-display and toured with stock companies in the midwest and west. She finally met her future husband at a cheap eating place in New York, which was owned by her father. Almost thirty, she was a waitress, living with her family in an unattractive, cramped set of rooms above the restaurant.

Following a two-year courtship with Laha and the inflexible opposition of his mother who thought Laha a bit of fluff, Jay and Laha married. The couple moved to Lynbrook, on Long Island's South Shore, a place Jay quickly despised. There was in him some contemptuous disdain for a provincial small town that took itself as the measure of all value. He viewed it as an oppressive, petty, and vulgar place where all zest, spontaneity, and free play of life had been smothered by the boredom of conformity.

Jay, plump, aloof, passive, was an illustrator with the *World* in New York. He promoted the impression of being the gifted artist whom others were born to pamper and support. But he was lazy around the house, letting it deteriorate, because his real interests centered on himself. He planted a large replica of the Venus de Milo in the middle of the living room floor, amassed oddities and antiques, and even mounted on the walls his collection of bookplates and the original and brilliantly touching Christmas cards that he created each holiday season for his friends.

Although the couple went through the motions of being in love and energetically meeting the responsibilities of parenthood, it was all a laborious sham. Jay cared little for family life. The minute dinner was finished, Jay went alone upstairs, donned an elegant robe, and played with his elaborate puppet theater, his collection of tiny matchbox houses he'd built, his bookplates, or his vast collection of penny toys, almost as if his adult life was a kind of falling back into childhood.

He was also a secretive bisexual, a man adept at living a life "divided into separate compartments," which was a talent his son would come to share.

Laha was more socially skilled and ambitious than Jay. She meant to succeed in the community for the sake of her sons, and she tried to have people like her. She was elected president of the local mother's club, and she belonged to an "exclusive" literary club made up of thirty-five members where she did dramatic monologues and readings. But she was showy, liked being noticed, and had florid, theatrical gestures and stagey mannerisms that put people off.

The marriage had soon frayed to ribbons. There were two children, Whittaker and Richard, his younger brother. They were witness to his father staying out late nights and the savage quarrels that occurred when the father at last arrived home, fortified by liquor. It wasn't long before Jay moved out, finding an apartment in Brooklyn.

Chambers's childhood was a lonely, bitter hell. Laha's overweening social pretensions prevented Chambers from even playing with the neighborhood children. His teeth were rotting because Laha never paid much attention to them. He was poorly dressed because his father was too selfish to buy him pants that fit. He was forced to wear his father's cast-off clothes "as a badge of shame," he wrote later. He became inert, didn't bathe, and let his hair grow until it straggled down over his collar. In high school he was the target of such endearments as "Girlie," "Stinky," and "Mr. Chamber Pot."

But like many who when young have no one to whom they can open their hearts, his inner life was full, rich, and incessantly active. By the age of eight or nine, he had begun to read Victor Hugo's *Les Misérables*. The novel's huge social canvas, its vast scope—what Chambers would call its "full-length picture of the modern world—a vast, complex scarcely human structure, built over a social abyss of which the sewers of Paris was (sic) only the symbol, and resting with crushing weight upon the wretched of the earth"—brought alive in him "the play of forces that carried me into the Communist Party, and (later) carried me out."

Three months past his eighteenth birthday, Chambers ran away with a friend, Anthony Muller. He worked at various odd jobs, but after four months on the road, unable to find work and out of money, Chambers returned to Penn Station to be met by Laha and brother Richard. He found out his father had returned home and was working as an art director at Frank Seaman, Inc., a midtown ad agency where Chambers was able to get work as a clerk.

Laha, a social snob, wanted Chambers to go to Williams College in Massachusetts. She disliked Jews, and she thought Williams College very elite and exclusive, in part because it kept Jews out. However, Chambers wanted to go to Columbia College in New York where there were Jews aplenty, and object as she might, Columbia was where Chambers went. Finding himself in the company of minds as wide-ranging and as full of a passionate craving for learning as his own, some new energy had been released in Chambers. Yet some damage from childhood remained. Even though he found a degree of relieving fellowship with classmates like Lionel Trilling and Clifton Fadiman, Chambers was still the defensive, lonely boy that a grade school teacher of his had described as "silent, observing, never taking part, imagining other worlds."

Chambers was soon seized by the conviction that "the most glorious career open to man was literature" and that to be a poet "is among the highest callings known to man." He shyly showed his first poems to teacher Mark Van Doren, who was himself a great scholar and fine writer. Van Doren was instantly moved to excited admiration. "We were convinced he would leap into fame," said Jacques Barzun, an awestruck undergraduate acquaintance.

But Chambers's displays of ability prompted him to become arrogantly slipshod in his habits. He missed classes, skipped tests, stole books, and exhibited a disconcerting ability to role-play, one day regaling a distinguished member of the English department with a totally fabricated escapade in a Harlem brothel, the account of which ended with Chambers flourishing a supposed syphilis test in front of the appalled professor's face.

In 1924, Chamber graduated quietly from Columbia, and soon after became a communist. Trifling with communism was a widespread fad among literary intellectuals at the time. Chambers had been taken by a friend to a meeting in a loft on the West Side of New York where some forty or fifty men and women drank glasses of hot tea and conversed in a babble of foreign tongues until the meeting was called to order, and then they abruptly switched to a laborious, heavily accented, hideous English containing those indigestible clots of Bolshevik jargon that were so to disfigure communist discourse and documents for many decades. Chambers was dismayed to see that the harbingers of a new social utopia "looked less like the praetorian guard of the world revolution than a rather undisciplined group of small delicatessen keepers."

For their part, they looked on him with suspicion because of his East Coast manners, cultivated demeanor, and elegant college diction. All the same, on February 17, 1925, he joined the party. He was quickly assigned to make newsstand collections for the party paper the *Daily Worker* in New York. He stoically took long train rides to Brooklyn or Queens to lug back heaps of unsold papers.

It is likely that Chambers's failed family played a large part in his choice of politics. The death of his brother, Richard, in 1926 was a crisis that would permanently sear its scar on the skin of Chambers's soul. Not long after Chambers had joined the party, Richard had dropped out of Colgate College and came back home. Laha's mother, who lived there, had gone quite mad in the meantime, jabbering about "old Jews" who had bored a hole in her ceiling and who were going to pump suffocating gas through it into the room to kill her. In addition, Richard had begun dressing oddly, wearing atrocious, ill-matching clothes and endlessly making the rounds of seedy speakeasies and bars in Lynbrook. The alcohol served by such places could be lethal, which would have suited Richard just fine—he had already begun to talk of suicide. One day, his face pinched and white, he approached Chambers and asked him to join him in a suicide pact. Chambers refused. "You're a coward, Bro," said Richard.

Alcohol drastically altered the dispositions and behavior of the brothers for the worse, causing them to quarrel, especially over the family, so Chambers began to skip his nights out with Richard. One night, Chambers came into the house to discover his father in a fit of merciless rage, pummeling Richard, so soddenly drunk that he was unable to dodge or defend himself. A blow by Chambers knocked the startled, astonished father to the floor, ending the fight. A short time after that, Chambers came home, but when he opened the door, choking gas smote his nose. He rushed into the kitchen to find Richard slumped over a chair, all the gas jets on the oven and stove wide open. After Chambers frantically revived him, Richard said to him, "You're a bastard, Bro. You stopped me this time, but I'll do it yet."

Chambers began to watch over his brother, sitting and waiting up late until Richard came back from the bars, befuddled, stumbling, and unsteady. Sometimes, Richard wouldn't appear at all, and instead there would materialize Laha's mad mother, mumbling paranoid inanities. In despair, Chambers would close his eyes, wishing fervently that "the house would burn down with all its horrors."

Chambers went on a brief trip west in the summer, and when he came back found that Richard had taken up with eighteen-year-old Dorothy Miller whom he sought to marry. Laha tried to break up the attachment, buying Richard a roadster, but Richard married Miller on May 29, 1926, and they moved to a little house in a nearby village. The family thought her a terrible specimen and snubbed the wedding. Laha refused to let the couple live at her house, so Richard got a job as a clerk in the Nassau County Surveyor's Office, and for a while Chambers simply went his own way.

The marriage was quick to collapse. Richard, lonely and distraught, continued to go on destructive alcoholic binges. He was living alone and grew increasingly lost. One night, he drove the roadster to the Lynbrook station with a friend, looking for his brother, but Chambers did not arrive on the train.

One morning, Chambers was awakened when the phone rang. A single, shrill terrible scream from Laha filled the house. The police had called. Chambers, his father, and Laha hastened in fear down to Richard's little apartment, crowded with police. Richard was lying with his head in the open oven. He was completely dressed, and his body was cold when they found him. A quart of whiskey stood empty on the floor.[2]

Richard was buried fifteen days before his twenty-third birthday. It was a warm early autumn day, with lakes sparkling in the distance, green, towering trees still in full leaf, and the mown grass very green. The cemetery was silent. The bright air was still and silent except for the peaceful droning and humming of insects. Richard was buried without a headstone. The coffin sank out of sight. Chambers was overwhelmed by a sudden unbearable, bitter spasm of angry grief and sorrow: "I felt that any society that could result in the death of a boy like my brother was wrong, and I was at war with it."

He had become "a thorough communist," moving from the party into the underground. With this new commitment, a flood of ecstatic power and strength washed over him. Suddenly, at a stroke, Chambers was no longer flawed, uncertain, inferior, no longer the product of a tragically dysfunctional family. Instead, he had been enlisted to serve a higher controlling agency, history and working for the betterment of the oppressed and poor. Where before he had been dejected, fragmentary, and unhappy, now he was unified, resolved, full of new command and purpose. There was no longer the selfish father, the feeble and failed brother, or the flighty, feather-headed mother. A higher purpose had taken him in hand. It was the beginning of what he would call his "fanaticism."

2

★ ★ ★

WHAT WOULD MAKE Americans want to work in secret, against their own country for the direct descendant of Vladimir Lenin's secret police? I can recall being startled in a class at Columbia College when my professor said that Karl Marx had been a liberal. Within my family, at my high school, and among my friends, he had never been presented to me in quite that light. But my professor was proved right. The truth is that communism developed as an antidote to the callous horrors and offhand atrocities of the Industrial Revolution, which are, to us, so vague and so distant that we have lost any power to clearly picture them.

Yet they were quite real, the exploitation of children being one of industrialization's most unfeeling abuses, especially in Britain, which had been industrialized longer than any other country. It was routine for small children to be forced by beatings to work terrible hours, sometimes sixteen hours a day, six days a week, for only pennies in daily pay. They were fed poorly and fought with pigs for slops in troughs, and working from 3 A.M. until 10 A.M., made them become so weary that they sometimes tumbled into machines and were mangled for life. They were constantly kicked, punched, and sexually abused, because only overseers with a driving force of terror could keep little children laboring under such painful strain for so long.[3]

Their parents were not much better off. The majority were living in slums where "hunger and dirt were king, where consumptives coughed, and the air was thick with the smell of latrines, boiling cabbages and stale beer, where roofs leaked and unmended windows let in the cold blasts of winter, where privacy was unimaginable, where men, women, grandparents and children lived together, eating, sleeping, fornicating, defecating, sickening and dying in one room, where a tea kettle served as a wash boiler between meals, (where) old boxes served as chairs, heaps of foul straw as beds, and boards propped across two crates as tables, where sometimes not all the children of the family could go out at one time because there were not enough clothes to go around, where decent families lived among drunkards, wife-beaters, thieves and prostitutes, where life was a see-saw of unemployment and endless toil, where a cigar-maker and his wife earning 13 cents an hour worked seventeen hours a day seven days a week to support themselves and their children, where death was the only exit and the only extravagance and scraped saving of a lifetime would be squandered on a funeral coach with flowers and a parade of mourners to ensure against the anonymity and ignominy of Potter's Field."[4]

Marx, the man whom historian Isaiah Berlin described as having the most "direct, deliberate and powerful an influence upon mankind in the nineteenth century," set out to change the system. Marx was a clumsy bruin of a man, full of titanic energy, exuding an incredible force of will, and armed with an acute and powerful intellect bristling with unshakeable convictions. In appearance, he displayed a thick mop of black hair on his head, and his eyes were deep-set and often flashed in excited, indignant rage. He had a black, bushy beard, and his skin was dark, prompting his children to call him, "The Moor." His voice was disagreeably harsh, and a colleague said, "He spoke of men and things in a tone of one who would tolerate no contradiction, and which seemed to express his own firm conviction in his mission to sway men's minds and dictate the laws of their being."[5]

As an intellectual, few men in history have proved more able or more industrious, and few have had more integrity or more sheer power to simply endure, inexhaustible and unshatterable. For years he poured out his soul, in all its vehement intensity, bottomless indignation, and blind, unwavering outrage, into books, pamphlets, and reviews. We can only point out a few features of his system, but a critical one was Marx's belief that economics was the rudimentary principle of human association. Human beings had to eat before they could think, he said, echoing Ludwig Feuer-bach, a German critic of religion. Another primary Marxian tenet was op-position to private property. To Marx, property was theft, and to own it was simply a way to ensure a lack of social justice. Social injustice to him was rooted in the fact that only a few owned property while the mass of the people owned nothing.

Another key tenet of Marx's faith was a belief in pitiless struggle as an agent of progressive development. For Marx, brute force, and destructive violence, was the engine that moved history forward on its path. History, for him, embodied a vast ruthlessness. The form that historical struggle as-sumed was an endless war between classes in society. Marx defined classes as a group of persons in that society whose lives were determined by the economic status that they shared or suffered in common. Marx believed that the war between the classes would automatically spew up an im-proved future.

History with a big "H" would be the means of this. Historical factors would ensure that the class war would result in the victory of the workers in the form of the "dictatorship of the proletariat." But this dictatorship was only a prelude to the abolition of all classes and the coming of a class-less and just society, fair to all, caring for all. All groups were corrupt except those who had redeemed themselves by unconditional faith in the violent proletarian revolution. For Marx, the ideal future would be brought to life only by the proletariat to whom everything was permitted in its name as a result.

As great as Marx was, he was a poor psychologist and never asked if there was some fundamental defect in human nature that had come to make the world what it was. All the great human systems, the great hu-man dreams, began with radiant prospects, yet all seemed, over time, to be dragged down and degraded by some element, some ineradicable flaw in human nature that ended with human beings exploiting their own and a system's weaknesses until its most current version bore hardly any resem-blance to the original. Writer George Bernard Shaw touched on the mat-ter when, in examining anarchism, he asked the question that if man were good and institutions were bad and man would be good again if institu-tions ceased to oppress him, "How did the corruption and oppression un-der which he groans ever arise?"[6]

Marx had no answer. Instead he offered a thrilling, sublime, splendid vision of a world in which there would be no bosses, coercion, authority, or ownership of property, just human beings living as they were meant to live, in harmony, by the dictates of reason, caring for each other and their needs.

It sounded too good to be true, and it was.

Perhaps the most sinister feature of Marx's system was its blind embrace of destructive force, its direct appeal to hatred, and its belief in unbridled terrorism as the chief instrument of achieving social justice. His follower, Lenin, would take the worst features of Marxism and make them the basis of his own system. It was on April 8, 1917, when Lenin and thirty other revolutionaries were put aboard a sealed train and sent by the Germans, Russia's wartime enemy, back into Russia, in Winston Churchill's words, "like a typhoid bacillus" to speed its collapse. When living in exile in Switzerland, Lenin had been stunned by the turn of events, bewildered by the fall of the czar, and staggered at the German invitation to help him return to his stricken, disorganized country.

Lenin was a fierce little man with a balding, bullet head and a neck like a bull, who, when it came to the revolution, was all business and hard energy. On November 6, 1917, his party, the Bolsheviks (Majority), struck and overturned the provisional government of Alexander Kerensky. Armed Bolshevik squads suddenly seized the railway stations, telephone exchanges, banks, bridges, and other public buildings. The next morning, riding in a Pierce Arrow car, Kerensky fled the Winter Palace, taking with him any hope of a liberal, democratic Russia.

Hardly a shot was fired. On the Nevsky Prospect, stores and cinemas were open, restaurants were crowded, and streetcars shuttled like glinting, metal beetles through the streets. Public lectures were packed with people. Performer Karsavina was at the Mariinsky, Chaliapin enraptured audiences in concert.

But a new personality had the city in its grip. As one historian observed, "He judged men not by their moral qualities but by their views, or rather the degree to which they accepted his." Revolutionary Russia was an agricultural country where the bourgeoisie was small and the proletariat even smaller. No matter. Theory would give way to ruthless practice. The Communist Party would not only *not* be broadly based, but instead it would be as secret as possible, moving with the utmost speed and determined ruthlessness. The apex of the party was to be Lenin himself. "The will of a class is sometimes fulfilled by a dictator," Lenin said, echoing philosopher Jean-Jacques Rousseau. Soon, a one-party dictatorship had been installed, and a secret police organ, the Cheka (the Extraordinary Commission for Combating Counter-revolution and Sabotage), had been set up as a state within a state, with its purpose to consolidate Lenin's grip by means of terror. The use of repressive state organizations and the application of terror were Lenin's specialties. Russia had to be cleansed of parasites, enemies, counterrevolutionaries, and conspiracies, and any secret opposition had to be utterly destroyed. "The preparation of terror is secret is necessary and urgent,"[7] he said. And Lenin and his minions began to enact this fiat without regard to justice, morals, or elementary human feelings or mercy.

Fortunately, there were some in Russia who still held fast to the old, heroic liberal dream of Marx's classless society. The final challenge to Lenin's new and suffocating regimentation came, of all places, from the Kronstadt mutiny of February 1921. It began aboard the Russian battleship *Petropavlovsk*. By that year, Bolshevism was rapidly sinking in popularity among the people. The hotheaded Russian sailors had always taken the lead in acting on revolutionary ideals, and they did so now. What they demanded shows to what extent Lenin had denied them old, revered Marxist ideals. They asked for an election of Soviet-governing groups by secret ballots instead of a show of hands at mass meetings (which could leave them open to retaliation or arrest). They asked that rival candidates be allowed to campaign freely. They charged that all existing governing bodies of Soviets were unrepresentative. They also called for the honoring of the old promises: freedom of speech and the press, free trade unions, the freeing of all political prisoners, the abolition of political parties in the armed forces, the setting up of a commission for review of all those put in prison or in concentration camps, the formation of peasants' unions, and the right of peasants "to do as they please with all the land."

The sailors' revolt spread only slowly through the country, and allowed Lenin to finally muster the force to drown it in a sea of blood. German socialist leader Rosa Luxemburg commented sadly that the new system reproduced the worst features of the czardom that it was designed to replace.

3

THE YEARS FROM the 1920s to the 1930s was called by U.S. spy-hunters "the era of the great illegals."[8] Some Soviet spies worked as diplomats, using an embassy position, such as "Second Political Officer," for cover, and enjoying diplomatic immunity and other privileges much as the American and Russian diplomats do today. However, there were others who, while remaining Soviet citizens, hid their real identities and their purpose by assuming "legends" or fake biographies that were established by means of forged documents. The technique had been launched in the Berlin *residentirua* in 1925. These illegal agents worked for the most secret part of the Communist International (Comintern), called the OMS, whose mission was to assist the so-called autonomous communist parties outside of the Soviet Union. These agents were the dominant players for they were harder for the enemy to identify and recognize and more difficult for an open society to catch. The OMS had its own expert staff to recruit and handle operatives, and, at great risk, they traveled throughout the world recruiting and running agents. Joszef Peters was one of Moscow's most outstanding operators in building these networks.

Known as "Pete," Peters was short and dapper, sported a Groucho Marx mustache, and possessed a charming smile on a face that had alert, intelligent, assessing eyes under thick brows. His mental abilities were great. Peters had a mind that had the talent of extracting the meaning of a situation like a man coring an apple. He was also fertile in hatching clever plans and stratagems. As a handler, Peters knew that agents were vain, insecure, and sometimes very brave, but always in need of fresh proof of their usefulness and importance. They also had to have a liking for living in the world of feigning and deceit. But to Peters, the best agent was an idealist, one driven by beliefs of such passion and purity that money or other worldly contaminations simply could not corrupt them. The handler's job was to turn new recruits into devout trustees of Moscow's aims, programs, and ideals without telling them what they really served. American communists were to be left the illusion that they were good, progressive American patriots, when in fact they were Russian ones.

One longtime recruiter for the Soviets was Hede Tune Massing. Tall and strikingly beautiful, she had married Comintern agent Gerhard Eisler at the age of seventeen in 1920, and she herself would become highly placed in the Comintern. In 1981, having broken long before with the Communist Party, she explained why communism was so seductive to the American elite. What rendered gullible "the privileged of America," she said, was "an idealistic approach. . . . It would be almost impossible to recruit the working class . . . but easy to win recruits among the intellectual and middle class." Why? She explained, "Communism appeals to the elite. What does it offer? Great ideas. The freedom of all time. Marxism. A different economic system. Thoughts. New medical experiments. The world . . . the world . . ."[9]

Elizabeth Bentley, who would defect to the FBI in 1945 and end by crippling more key Soviet spy networks in the United States than any other one person, related how her seduction by the Russians was accomplished.

Bentley had a superior personality with a great power to charm. She was assertive, lively, articulate, and perceptive, with a manner that turned people's hearts in her favor. She was extremely attractive to men. She was ample-breasted, stood five foot seven, and weighed 142 pounds. After studying at Vassar, she traveled abroad, making three trips to Italy. She then pursued a master's degree at Columbia, and in 1932, spent a summer at Middlebury College in Vermont studying Italian. By 1934, having completed her master's in Italian at Columbia, she made contact with a communist front called the American League Against War and Fascism (ALAW&F). Many of America's literary intellectuals like Sherwood Anderson and Theodore Dreiser were part of it, and from the first, Bentley found herself impressed by her new colleagues. They "had an inner sure-ness that I lacked," she said. She soon found a circle of friends who wel-comed her warmly, casually, totally, acting as if they had known her all their lives. Especially impressive was a woman in the group, Lee Fuhr. Fuhr's life had not been easy. As a teenager, she had worked long, grueling hours for little pay in the cotton mills of New Jersey. Her husband had died soon after she'd gotten her nursing degree and was pregnant with her first child. Undismayed, she simply dug down and applied herself, finding that she was not only able to support herself and her child by being a nurse, but had enough strength of effort left to put herself through a year at Teacher's College. With a college degree, she would be able to attain her supreme goal—to work in public health.

Talking with Lee made Bentley feel "a new breath of hope." Her list-lessness vanished in the face of Lee's energy and vision. Fuhr talked of a unique new society being built in the Soviet Union. "The means of pro-duction are in the hands of the people not owned by private interests," Fuhr said.

In 1934, most of the country was out of work, and Bentley knew there was no going back to the small town ways in which she had been brought up. Small town America had clearly been replaced by a "vast impersonal industrial civilization," and if life was to have any meaning, it had to be reconciled "with the basic Christian ideals my parents had taught me," she said.

Lengthy conversations continued, and one day, Bentley and Fuhr were talking of groups that could actually build a new society. Fuhr said that the league was too cumbersome for the role. What progress required was a small, disciplined group of people to provide cohesiveness and drive.

Bentley asked where such people could be found.

"You don't have to find them. They already exist," said Fuhr.

They were the Communists. They would rally the progressive forces to fight fascism and war, Fuhr said.

Bentley became a Communist in 1935.

BY 1934, CHAMBERS was a member of one of the fastest rising Russian spy rings in Washington, the Ware Group. Harold Ware, in his forties, was a vigorous character, trim, muscular, with a frank, open face, always ready to tell colorful stories. After getting a degree in agriculture, he had hoboed from farm to farm, following the grain harvests in the Great Plains and the

Dakotas, and then had traveled to Russia where he remained for nine years helping the peasants solve their farming problems.

Once a consultant to the Department of Agriculture, Ware had set up a small think tank, Facts for Farm Research Inc., which published a monthly journal *Facts for Farmers*. Using this publication as a cover, Ware began to spot and recruit Soviet agents. By 1934, Ware headed a clandestine network of seven cells—small groups of secret operatives, working under the direction of a Russian handler.

Chambers, introduced by Peters, met Ware at a Manhattan automat, and the two men struck up one of those friendships that is based on instantaneous affinity. "We had the same romantic interest in conspiracy, the same apprehension of the difficulties of organizing intellectuals, and a common interest in farm problems," Chambers said later.

It was Peters's plan to use the Ware Group to get inside America's chief government agencies to gather information and subtly veer U.S. policy in the service of Russian aims. Peters's sense of strategy was superb. He had mastered enough information to have a particularly brilliant grasp of those American industries whose technological progress might one day prove useful to Moscow. The Ware Group were not the rough-cut foreigners who spoke heavily accented English while sipping glasses of tea that Chambers had known early on. At least five members of the Ware Group had degrees from Harvard and one was a Phi Beta Kappa from the University of Chicago. They were clearly not workers and few exhibited any traces of Marx's proletarian worldview. Some gave the promise of rising to the very top of their profession where their access to U.S. secrets would be unbounded.

In addition to the Ware Group, Chambers was also working in New York with Itzhak Akhmerov, codenamed "Bill," another Soviet handler who was a leading NKVD (the Russian secret police, later evolving into the KGB) "illegal" intelligence operative. Since a birth certificate was proof of U.S. citizenship and had to be submitted to any government agency for employment, "Bill," a tall Estonian with a tired, almost lipless face, kept a team of researchers that included Chambers to busily ransacking back issues of the nation's daily newspapers on the lookout for birth dates that would be roughly equivalent to the ages of spies about to be brought to the United States. When an appropriate date was found, a Soviet agent would write to the hospital claiming he had lost his birth certificate and required a new copy. When he got one, a new spy's career was born.

In 1935, after Ware was killed in a car accident, Chambers began a full-time life as a courier of stolen U.S. government documents. He lived in Maryland, and his routine was simple. He first arranged a rendezvous with a fellow spy at a neutral site in Washington, like a park, playground, or coffee shop. Chambers then met with a ring member and was handed documents stolen from a government agency, which he quickly slid into a briefcase. Chambers then drove back to Baltimore to an apartment owned by the Soviet underground. Photographic equipment stood ready in the kitchen, direct light supplied by a peering gooseneck lamp. Chambers put on gloves to avoid leaving any traceable fingerprints and set to work photographing the documents. When at last the hanging strips of film were dry, he drove back to Washington to return the originals to members of the ring who would replace them in the government files. Chambers would then take the film up to New York, delivering it to his handler.

Soon, "Bill" disappeared, replaced by a feminine, red-headed, paranoid, panicky, unpleasant man named Boris Bykov. Bykov was from Odessa and was an agent of the GRU, an organization that had originated with the Registry Section of the Cheka. Under Lenin, Cheka officers had controlled the press, shot and imprisoned counterrevolutionaries, protected the party elite, suppressed religion and churches, regulated prisons, and run the special forces of border guards to keep foreigners out and Russians in. The Registry Section, whose job was to provide cover for Soviet spies, was transferred in 1920 to the 4th Bureau of the Red Army and renamed the Military Intelligence Directorate or GRU. The GRU faced a formidable rival in the NKVD, which was determined to replace the GRU as the lead agency in Soviet foreign intelligence operations. (It should be remembered, however, that the GRU's greatest achievement would be stealing the secrets of the American atomic bomb.)

With the arrival of Bykov, Chambers's career as a spy now took a dramatic new turn. Bykov and Chambers bristled at each other from the first, warily circling each other like two street dogs. When Peters left the two alone after introducing them, Bykov completely panicked, endlessly walking the New York streets, performing countersurveillance, convinced he was being tracked by American "secret police."

But if he was full of flutters, they were misleading. Bykov was a tireless driver when it came to work. Before Bykov's arrival, Chambers had only received pilfered U.S. government documents a total of three times! With the arrival of Bykov, the output of the Ware cell really took off. For

Chambers, dealing with Bykov was a rocky road. Bykov was a man given to violent mood swings, and he was capricious, arbitrary, and insolent to his agents. He often sharply quizzed Chambers on his political views, spied on his mail, and had him followed. Often Bykov even tried to put Chambers's nerves on edge by telling him he had to go to Moscow or declaring other ultimatums meant to test his courier, hoping Chambers proved as big a coward as himself.

What most horrified and offended Chambers were not his boss's tormenting ploys, but his handler's startling moral vulgarities. When explaining how to recruit new agents, Bykov told Chambers they must first be put "in a productive frame of mind," which meant softening the moral fiber by means of money. Chambers recoiled in shock. Americans were "Communists on principle"—they worked for ideals, not money or material gain, he said. Bykov scoffed, "Who pays is the boss, and he who accepts money must do something in return." In other words, get some clear means of coercion using some material leverage over your people at all costs.

If cash gifts were out of the question, Chambers must resort to plying his contacts with expensive gifts. Christmas was coming, and Bykov gave Chambers $600, instructing him to buy some Bokhara rugs, made in the Soviet Central Asian republics. Turning to an art dealer friend, Meyer Shapiro, Chambers had him buy four colorful carpets at the shop of an Armenian wholesale dealer who worked for the communist Amtog Trading Corporation. Two rugs were to prove fateful to their recipients: one went to a friend of Chambers named Alger Hiss and another to a man who, within a decade, would be a big star in the Roosevelt administration, a Treasury Department official named Harry Dexter White.[10]

If White was merely a cell contact from whom he received documents, Hiss was a man who saw, felt, and thought about life as Chambers did. Hiss was "as close a friend as a man makes in life," Chambers said later. When they met in 1934, they couldn't have been more different in background. Hiss came from a prominent Baltimore family that was shattered when the father, Charles, a member of a Baltimore import firm, killed himself by cutting his throat with a razor, then calmly lying down and bleeding to death. This occurred when Hiss was two-and-a-half years old. Hiss would not find out how his father died until he was ten when, by chance, Hiss overheard a neighbor say of him and his sister, "Those are the children of the suicide." In May 1929, his older sister Ann, unhappily mar-

ried, died in atrocious agony after swallowing the contents of a bottle of
caustic household cleaner. His older brother Bosley, a promising reporter
with the *Baltimore Sun* and with whom Hiss was very close, would die of
a kidney ailment at the age of twenty-five. Bosley had been born the same
year as Chambers and clearly touched some tender point in Hiss's heart.

As a boy, Hiss had proved hardworking, pulling a wagon from his
neighborhood of Bolton Hill to Druid Hill Park—at that time way beyond
the "civilized" center of the city—to fill up glass bottles with spring water.
Footsore and tired, he then carted the full bottles back and sold them
to customers. Even as a young man, Hiss appeared the picture of well-
mannered courtesy and candor. At Johns Hopkins University and Harvard
Law School, he had proved an outstanding student with an incredible
memory and an agile mind that was the more admirable for the tireless
drive to improve that lay behind it. He was impressive enough to become
a protégé of Professor (and Supreme Court Justice) Felix Frankfurter.
Hiss's gift for friendship and his social and intellectual talents enabled him
to obtain a much-coveted clerkship with the Supreme Court's aging but intellectually brilliant Judge Oliver Wendell Homes.

By this time, Hiss had married Priscilla Fansler, a New York writer and
art historian, who became a Communist and aided Hiss in his espionage
work by retyping stolen State Department documents on a Woodstock
typewriter. In 1933, after several years of work at a New York law firm,
Hiss went to Washington and took a position with the Agricultural Ad-
justment Administration (AAA), which Roosevelt had set up to boost
America's slumping farm production. Once in Washington, Hiss's rise was
like that of a rocket: spectacular and rapid. All his career moves were first
approved by Peters. From the AAA, he went to the Nye Committee, where
he had access to voluminous secret War, State, and Navy Department documents on information on munitions. He then moved to a 1935 to 1936
stint at the Justice Department. Because of their social polish, their wide
culture, and their expansive geniality, the Hisses mingled easily and as
equals with influential New Dealers young and old.

From the time they met, Hiss and Chambers felt they could open their
hearts to each other. As ideas flew back and forth, admiration mounted in
both, along with excitement and warm sympathy. To Chambers, Hiss was
a man of "great simplicity, with a great gentleness and sweetness of character." Hiss exhibited the humility of a man who knew the importance of
his mission, and the prestige he earned by serving it. Except there was a bit

of the desperado in Hiss, Chambers saw. He noted that Hiss accepted his role as traitor with an almost heroic indifference to its morality. Hiss made it clear he was not the kind of man to nurse his conscience as though it were a sick friend and knew that "the revolutionary cannot change the course of history without taking upon himself the crimes of history."[11]

The Hisses had first lived in a fourth-floor walk-up on Twenty-eighth Street N.W. Then came two places in Georgetown. Then they moved to a nice house with a kennel for the family dog on Wisconsin Avenue N.W. in fashionable Georgetown. Chambers was often the houseguest of the Hisses. In fact, he would say later that the Hiss home had become a kind of "informal headquarters" for him.

Being a modest man himself, Chambers was impressed by the spare modesty of their life. The Hisses cared nothing for fancy food, and their houses were just "pulled together," furnished with nothing lavish or assertively showy. Hiss drove a dilapidated Ford roadster whose windshield wipers didn't work. Chambers discovered this when he drove the car one day in the rain and had to reach out and work the wipers by hand.

When Hiss bought a new Plymouth, against the rules of communist discipline, Hiss, generous as always, insisted the car be turned over to the party so that it could be of use to some poor party organizer out West somewhere. Peters and Chambers had tried to talk Hiss out of this, but he became stony and stubborn. Chambers gave up. He knew a used-car lot run by a communist and had the car taken there. But the incident was typical of the kind of gentle, giving soul Hiss had and of the fraternal solicitude he felt for his fellow members.

4

YEARS PASSED.

By 1937, Whittaker Chambers's group operated efficiently like an old-fashioned spinning mill. The Soviet handlers went about to inspect the machinery, noting that here a spindle had stopped, that there was one that made too much noise, that another was not quite functioning properly, making adjustments until all was humming smoothly in unison.

Chambers had by then rented an apartment in Baltimore, across the street from Druid Hill Park and its conservatory. Chambers told Boris Bykov that his dual duties of courier and document photographer was not only inefficient, but it put the ring at risk. Bykov agreed, and Felix Inslerman took over the job of photographing the documents. Now Chambers would turn the documents over to Inslerman at a prearranged meeting place near Union Station in Washington. Later that night, the two spies would meet again, and Inslerman would return the originals. A few days later, Inslerman would hand Chambers the developed microfilm who would then drive it to New York to give to Bykov. Later they would use the precaution of leaving the film undeveloped so that if Chambers were ever stopped, the film would be exposed the instant the canister was opened.

As the operation grew, its targets became increasingly ambitious. Successes included the theft of a formula from U.S. Steel, intelligence on the staff at the Aberdeen Proving Ground, data on the firing tables of a new U.S. sixteen-inch gun, and a summary of the top secret Norden bombsite that would help to destroy German and Japanese cities in World War II. There was an incessant demand from Bykov for any information about the anti-Comintern Pact signed by Germany, Italy, and Japan in 1926. Alger Hiss, in fact, provided vital information from America's neutral diplomatic outposts about the intentions and capabilities of Germany and Japan, Moscow's two main potential enemies. The chief objective of Bykov—infiltrating the U.S. government at levels where undercover Communist agents could help steer the government toward policies useful to Moscow—was succeeding beyond his dreams, at one point causing Bykov to exult, "We have agents at the very center of government, influencing policy!"

Yet as the months passed, a vast cloud of doubt was beginning to crawl its lengthening shadow across Chambers's mind. The great purges were sweeping Moscow, and Chambers could no longer avert his mind from what was happening. As mobile as he was in his job, Chambers was able to pick up news about Russia and the Communist Party, and what he heard about Moscow made him wonder if the whole bent of his character was fit for the life he had chosen. The purges had begun in December 1934, with the single, sudden murder of Sergei Kirov, a senior Soviet leader. As Chambers would come to learn, a crisis had developed that autumn within the top leadership of the Soviet Union, based in part on the resistance of old party members who opposed Joseph Stalin's promiscuous use of terror to suppress contending opinions within the party. Kirov's killing unleashed what U.S. diplomat George Kennan called "a . . . sinister, unidentifiable terror," which was to continue, in one degree or another, until Stalin's death in 1953. No one even in the U.S. government at the time was close to realizing that the total of those executed would reach between nine and ten million people.[12]

As the purges gained ominous speed, the blood of suspects began to swamp the country in a great flood, or so it seemed to some. Immediately after the death of Lev B. Kamenev and G. Y. Zinoviev, two old and loyal Bolsheviks, Stalin ordered the shooting of 5,000 party members already under arrest. As Charles Bohlen, a U.S. Ambassador to Moscow, noted, one of the inexplicable features of the purge was the pitiless onslaught against Soviet military leaders—perhaps 10,000 of the rank of colonel or higher were either shot or sent to concentration camps. No U.S. diplomat could quite make sense of it, and only much later would it be known that their crime was that they had resisted Stalin's efforts to try and place himself in partnership with Adolph Hitler at the very time Hitler was emerging as a truly lethal threat to the Soviet Union and as Stalin was portraying himself to the world as the dauntless enemy of fascism.

Soon Chambers's ardor for the communist cause had burnt out. He knew too much. By 1937, the whole framework of his earlier faith had reached a turning point. It had become clear to him that anyone found suspect by Stalin was being arrested and killed, and Chambers at last was face to face with facts about the ghastly, inhuman character of the system he had chosen to serve. A deep, lightless gulf began to yawn open between him and his handlers. It became unbridgeable in the late winter or spring of 1937, when, on one of his frequent trips to New York, Chambers paid a call on a communist colleague only to find a third man was there.

It was John Sherman.

A communist agent, Sherman had just returned from Moscow in a state of frenzied and inflamed agitation. He grabbed Chambers and demanded they go outside, where he talked inexhaustibly of the purges and also told of being mistreated and snubbed in Moscow. Sherman said he had been granted a new post in London, but Sherman had no intention of going there. Sherman burst out with passionate intensity, "I will not work one week longer for those murderers!" and he then told Chambers he was going to break with spy work.

When Bykov heard of Sherman's and Chambers's exchange, he asked that Sherman "meet" with representatives of the NKVD. Sherman fled. Bykov was startled, convinced Sherman had phoned the American "secret police." Bykov insisted that Chambers phone Sherman's hotel, but Sherman was long gone. Bykov sulked, disgruntled and unforgiving.

Then another nasty shock occurred.

The exceptionally brilliant liberal philosopher John Dewey was holding a Commission of Inquiry to expose the dishonesty of the spectacular show trials which Stalin was using to rid himself of his challengers by accusing them all of being German spies. Meyer Shapiro showed Chambers a transcript that made clear the blatant rigging of the trials. Chambers was shaken to the core. Chambers spitefully passed the transcript on to Bykov who recoiled, only able to say, "The boss is cooking us a strong mush."

But gripped by his own inner fear, Bykov quickly lashed out in accusation at his agent. Chambers was to cut all ties with Shapiro, he said.

But cutting all ties did not mean stifling all thought. There was a necessity in Chambers's soul driving him to look below the surface and to question what others took for granted. That fixed, habitual look that the world wears for most men did not exist for him, because he was forever unmaking his world and then rebuilding it in thought, dissolving what to others were solid facts and discovering what to others were old truths. Nor was he alone. Lawrence Duggan, a fellow Soviet spy in the State Department, was also struggling over the show trials, wrestling with what he was being told by others and what his own common sense told him was the truth. Duggan could not swallow the treachery of the old Bolsheviks, which Stalin kept claiming. Had the founders of the revolution all really been spies and saboteurs in the pay of Germany from the first? It was too improbable, too brutal an upending of idols that Duggan had been taught to revere and respect.

"(Duggan) cannot understand events in the U.S.S.R," wrote his Soviet handler. "The disclosure of Trotskyite-fascist spies in all branches of industry and the state institutions embarrass him enormously. People he has learned to respect turn out to be traitors to the motherland the socialist cause . . . he repeats again and again: he cannot understand it, he is embarrassed, he cannot sleep."[13]

Neither could Chambers. Chambers was still floating adrift in a sea of indecisions, and floundering in that tormenting, unsettled state of self-questioning and moral disgust when there came the war in Spain. The civil war there would provide the sharp, jarring blow that would forever shatter Chambers's faith in the plaster colossus of the cause. The crisis was acute because an authentic workers' revolution, a real Marxist revolt, had actually occurred in Spain, the first instance in history of what Karl Marx and Friedrich Engels had dreamed of. In contrast to Lenin's revolution, the revolution in Spain wasn't set in motion by a small cadre of trained, professional revolutionaries, but had resulted from the widespread ferment among the Spanish Left that consisted of homegrown anarchists, a new Marxist Partido Obrero de Unificacion Marxista or POUM party, and the Syndicos Libres. It was a group that included miners, anarchists, union men, socialists, communists—all of whom combined in a Popular Front that attacked the right-wing church, army officers, the Carlists, the monarachists, the small and grand bourgeoisie, and the wealthy land-owners.

Stalin, of course, had been quick to declare the expected communist pieties of support for the uprising. "The Spanish struggle is not the private affair of Spaniards. It is the common cause of all advanced and progressive mankind," he said. To Chambers and Elizabeth Bentley and the other hoodwinked American Communists, the war in Spain seemed a noble international crusade to rescue democracy and preserve authentic socialism from the menace of tyrannical fascism. Lee Fuhr even went off to work as a nurse in Spain, as she was so convinced of the worth of what had happened. But in secret, Stalin made his grim decision to throw the whole weight of the Soviet power against the revolution, his purpose being to totally crush it out in blood. A man obsessed by an appetite for supreme domination was not about to support a real working-class revolution that was not subject to his full and strict control. Stalin supplied arms but only to factions that he felt would fall under his will.

By September 1936, a new Stalinist terror was racing like fire through Madrid, Barcelona, and Valencia. The OPGU had its own special prisons and torture chambers, and its own units for executions and kidnappings. It operated entirely outside the Spanish government's Ministry of Justice, becoming an empire within an empire, just as it was at home. During the remainder of 1937 and the rest of 1938, Stalin murdered Leftists and anarchists and anyone hostile to his plans. When that work was done, as was his habit, he then ferociously turned on his own. Throughout 1937 to 1938 all over the world, Stalin began killing those very agents who had helped him terrorize the Left in Spain. General Jan Atonovich Berzin was recalled and executed, the head of the NKVD office in Paris was cornered and forced to take cyanide, and the headless corpse of Rudolph Clement, who had organized rebel arms smuggling, was found floating in the Seine. Walter Krivitsky, the head of NKVD intelligence for Western Europe saw a dear friend and colleague, Ignatz Reiss, a dedicated communist disillusioned by the show trials, finally defect only to be machine gunned to death by a Lausanne, Switzerland, roadside. Reiss's murder would in turn prompt Krivitsky to defect, and Stalin's goons would chase Krivitsky for three years. He would finally be found murdered, shot in the head, in a Washington hotel next to Union Station only the day before he was to testify before the U.S. Congress.

5

★ ★ ★

To Whittaker Chambers, no amount of explanation could excuse Joseph Stalin's actions in Spain. With the avalanche of Spanish atrocities piling up, Chambers found himself living in terrifying fear and uncertainty, always looking over his shoulder. His duties now were done numbly and mechanically. Gone was that feeling that the measure of his worth as a person depended on how useful and effective he could prove to the cause.

By 1937, a plan for defection was taking shape in his head, but defection wasn't simple. The father of British philosopher Karl Popper once remarked about being a Jew that it wasn't a club from which you could simply resign. Neither was communism. Plus Chambers was no imperturbable rocklike embodiment of unshakeable will. He was a timid, nervous, lonely man, afraid for his own skin, and with good reason. Defection was no smooth road, but a sharp right-angle turn, and no one knew what the road ahead led to. Since he had concentrated on the functions of being a courier and contact for top spies, Chambers knew he posed a palpable danger to his handlers. As a defector, he would be a loose thread, and a loose thread, if pulled, could unravel the entire intricate tapestry of the networks that the Soviets had woven carefully in Washington.

They would certainly try to kill him. Like water closing over a stone, his earlier handler, "Bill," had completely disappeared, and Chambers knew that the Russians would only be deterred from violence by the threat of exposure. Even if Chambers escaped assassination, he had, after all, been a Russian spy, and he feared U.S. federal prosecution, dreaded the degradation of being held up before the public as a traitor, and feared what his exposure might do to his wife, Esther, a young artist he had met in 1926 and married five years later. But he had to do something. Within the underground, suspicion had grown so great, floated so completely free of the ballast of sensible skepticism, that no one trusted anyone anymore. This came clear at a lunch with Peters and Chambers in New York at a restaurant called Zimmerman's Budapest. At a neighboring table sat Arnold Ikal, a friend and an expert Soviet forger who worked for the 4th Department, who was known to U.S. officials as "Mr. Reubens." The usually expansive Ikal looked worried and gray as he sat at the table until Chambers asked Peters, "What's wrong with him?" "You," Peters replied. Ikal suspected that Chambers had been assigned to spy on him by Moscow.

For several months, Chambers had been strengthening his hand against Boris Bykov, secretly pocketing documents from the State Department that had been given to him by Alger Hiss. They consisted of sixty-five, densely printed, retyped cables, three rolls of microfilm, and four handwritten notes. From another source, he squirreled away two more rolls of microfilmed documents from the Navy Bureau of Aeronautics. These were what he called "life preservers." Even though he loved Hiss dearly and affectionately as a friend, Chambers had not given him or anyone else in his circle the slightest inkling of his pending course of action.

Still he hesitated. Was it because he was a man slow to bring himself to the point of action? Was he cowardly, or, by mean of his intelligence training, did he have the intelligence agent's skeptical caution about performing the irrevocable act? According to former British spymaster J. C. Masterman, one of the rules in running agents is "never to commit an irrevocable act."[14] Lord Melbourne, the British prime minister under Queen Victoria, once said the same thing slightly differently: "When I hear people say something must be done. I know they contemplate on doing something damn silly." So perhaps Chambers had that rare strength of will that refrains from the obvious action. One thing was sure: survival was his aim. Without it, there could be no salvation.

On April 1938, without a word to any associates, he and his wife left Baltimore and drove to Daytona Beach, Florida. Reaction by the Russians was immediate. Bykov began to visit friends and members of family, asking for Chambers's whereabouts. Bykov paid a visit in person to Chambers's literary agent Maxim Leiber, urging him to go and find his client. Otto Katz, a well-known Moscow thug and assassin, was put on his trail. Moscow hardened to stone. Unforgiving Kremlin superiors demoted Peters, and Bykov was recalled to Moscow, where he lived in frantic terror of execution. In Moscow, NKVD superiors were already telling each other that Chambers had been a German spy from the first, long before his defection.

Chambers, in hiding, knew his commitment to communism was as dead as a severed power line. He had taken his pilfered documents in the fall of that year and sent them to his wife's nephew in Brooklyn for safekeeping. He instructed the nephew that if he were killed, the package was to be given to the U.S. government. All he wanted was to leave the underground behind him—to wake up and have it be gone. Yet he still harbored sensitive scruples and held a deep horror about damaging those Communist friends or associates who had retained their mistaken faith, like Hiss.

Because of his special liking and affection for the Hisses, he visited them at their Georgetown home at Christmas. Their smug satisfaction would cause the iron to enter Chambers, ending any reluctance about public disclosure of the ring. When he arrived at their house, Alger wasn't home, but Priscilla was. She greeted Chambers distantly, they talked, and Chambers excused himself to use the toilet. Near the bathroom was the bedroom door and on it a telephone. As Chambers closed the bathroom door, he stopped to listen, the doorway half open, and heard Priscilla talking in a low voice on the phone. When he reappeared, she hastily hung up.

When Alger came in, the three sat and had dinner and a weak, cramped note of warmth entered the mood. But when Chambers unburdened himself about how disturbed he had been about Stalin's actions in Spain and vented his other misgivings, he was met with no answering sympathy from either of the couple. Instead he was startled when Priscilla burst out, "What you have been saying is just mental masturbation." It was a brusque, almost brutal dismissal of his concerns from Priscilla, who turned icy and unfriendly.

Chambers saw that to a closed mind like hers, coming to doubt communism was more than an intellectual error; it was evidence of a wicked perversity of will. Alger himself appeared to have lost his grip on the real. A little later in the evening, he imparted the incomprehensible news that the world was in fact "tottering on the verge of proletarian revolution."[15] Chambers was incredulous. He saw that nothing he could say could prompt any fresh questionings or qualms of conscience about the path Alger had chosen to take. Still, Alger was a friend, and Chambers felt he owed it to his treasuring of his friend's talents to try to get Alger to break with the underground. Chambers reasoned and pleaded, he protested and expostulated, and argued facts, but Alger turned a stone ear. Alger was emotionally moved by the passion of his friend's entreaties, but he was a convinced communist and that fact ruled out any possible reexamination of his premises. The two men stood at a juncture that would compel they part. It was an emotional moment. Both men had tears in their eyes as they said goodbye. When they met again, it would be as enemies in a contest that brooked no quarter.

But new, tender roots of life were stirring in the dead, stony ground of Chambers's heart. In April 1939, he applied for and obtained a job at *Time* magazine. A friend had described to a *Time* editor the ordeal of Chambers's defection, now two years past, and the editor, very much moved, had offered Chambers a job. Finally, Chambers was back in the daylight world of ordinary America, where the best-selling pop hit record was Hildegarde's "Deep Purple," where a singer named Frank Sinatra was making $25 a week doing one-night stands at a hotel in Englewood, New Jersey, where Lou Gehrig's farewell to baseball had saddened fans, where the Lone Ranger was being heard three times a week by twenty million people over 140 radio stations, where Joe Louis inflicted a twenty-three-stitch gash on Two-Ton Tony Galento; where the top three box office stars were Mickey Rooney, Spencer Tracy, and Tyrone Power, and where Hollywood was riding the crest of what one historian called its "supercollossal glory."[16]

Slowly, very slowly, that knot of distrust that had stayed like a clenched fist far down in him began to loosen its grip. Chambers had become friends with Isaac Dan Levine who had a virulent animosity toward revolution in all its forms. This same dislike was becoming a permanent characteristic in Chambers's own mental outlook. To Levine, big words merely made people unhappy, and communism was above all a repository for big words. But Chambers was still reluctant to face any dangers to himself. He would expose his former cell members only if he could first obtain immunity from prosecution from his treason. If he were given help, he would offer to give help, but not before. Levine had grown close to Soviet defector

Walter Krivitsky and wanted Chambers and the Russian defector to meet. Chambers was reluctant. After his experience with Bykov, he had developed an unreasoning dislike of Russians, but Levine persisted. Levine had helped Krivitsky do a series of articles exposing communism for the *Saturday Evening Post,* and he assured Chambers that Krivitsky was a truly different type. And he was. Krivitsky was an earnest man with deep-set, dark, intelligent eyes, showing a face with a high forehead, big ears, and thin lips. Krivitsky was living in the United States under an alias with his wife and son, his murder only two years away. At the meeting with Levine and Chambers, Krivitsky came into the room, small, slight, his hair brushed back from his forehead, and sat down and fixed his eyes on his feet. Then he asked Chambers in German, "Is the Soviet government a fascist government?" Chambers had answered, "Yes, the Soviet government was a fascist government." Then looking at Chambers for the first time, Krivitsky said in German, ". . . and Kronstadt was the turning point."[17] How many people in the world knew of the tragedy of the Kronstadt mutiny, Chambers thought. And it was as though a dam had burst. Alert, excited, bound fast by fascination, both men began talking at once.

Chambers knew Krivitsky had worked for the GRU in Berlin where he'd watched Stalin court Adolph Hitler and murder Russian generals who had opposed collaboration with Germany's ruthless new dictator. Krivitsky had also been witness to the killings in Spain and Stalin's determined undermining of the worker's revolution. Krivitsky told Chambers that communism's fatal moment had been in 1921 when Lenin had suppressed the sailors at Kronstadt. The pile of cigarette butts rapidly rose in the living room ashtray. Each knew things the other needed to know. Krivitsky filled in details about Bykov, and Chambers told him about Arnold Ikal, the forger. They began to finish each other's sentences as their excitement mounted. "It was like fitting a jigsaw puzzle together," Levine said later. "It was astonishing." When Levine woke up in the morning, the light was still on in the room, and both men were still there, jabbering intensely like monkeys in a tree. But Krivitsky sounded a sinister note. Stalin's shadow lay across the Roosevelt administration. It was "honeycombed" with Moscow's agents. Anything told to any U.S. official got back to Moscow within twenty-four hours, he said. The safest course was to testify in a public forum. The two men talked for hours and left as friends, but the impact of Krivitsky on Chambers was profound. Chambers's exasperated revulsion with communism was complete. Egged on by Levine,

Chambers finally agreed to meet with U.S. government officials. He had wanted to meet with Roosevelt himself, but settled for Assistant Secretary of State Adolph Berle. This short, stout, square-faced, trim, forty-four-year-old man had been a child prodigy who, his friends said, had continued to be a child long after he had ceased to be a prodigy. The youngest man ever to graduate from Harvard Law School, he was a brilliant professor at Columbia Law School when Roosevelt had found him. He became an administration standout. He was one of the New Dealers, a known anti-communist, and the founder of the New York Liberal Party. His keen mental abilities extended to management of U.S. intelligence operations, especially at the State Department where he was in charge of counterespionage. The Chambers-Krivitsky meeting occurred on September 1, 1939. That day, at dawn in Europe, German armies had knifed into Poland, and in Washington, there was a sense of catastrophe, of lights going out all over the world, and of a foreboding that lay like a smothering weight on the city. Chambers and Levine took a taxi up to Woodley Oaks, the beautiful French mansion high on a huge hill near the present-day Washington Cathedral that Berle, Roosevelt's assistant secretary of state, was renting from Henry Stimson, soon to be the secretary of war.

Dinner was quiet and decorous, and when it was finished, the men went out in back. Night had fallen and a breeze blew, moving the trees and cooling the air. A servant brought them drinks on a tray. A deep gloom had settled on Berle's spirit. He noted that the United States would be at war within forty-eight hours. Chambers felt a certain inner shrinking at first, but his will gained strength and force from the drinks, and he began to speak of the Washington ring. Out came the names. Alger Hiss, Donald Hiss, his brother, Lawrence Duggan—all men who had irreproachable reputations and well-known and respected names in the Washington power establishment. There was Noel Field, whom Hiss had tried to recruit, now with the League of Nations in Geneva, and Lauchlin Currie, a special assistant to FDR himself. Chambers mentioned Harry Dexter White in the Treasury Department, and he talked of secrets stolen, including the plans for the two U.S. battleships obtained by the Russians and the sketches of the Norden bombsite. It must have stunned Berle. When Chambers at last fell silent, Berle took Chambers and Levine into his study and wrote up Chambers's disclosures titled "Underground Espionage Agent." The notes ended with an ominous observation. Ikal, the forger, and his wife had been unmasked as Soviet illegals by the State Department and forced to return to Russia where both had disappeared. Berle ended with a chilling coda: "Note—When Loy Hendersen (a State Department official) interviewed Mrs. Reubens (Ikal) his report immediately went back to Moscow. Who sent it? Such came from Washington."

So there was profound penetration of the Roosevelt government. Krivitsky knew it, Berle knew it, and most of all, Chambers knew it. Berle sympathized. He told Chambers that he must tell no one of his interview, and that the matter had to handled with the "utmost delicacy." Any leaks could spoil all by resulting in a delay of the investigation. It was after midnight when the two men left Berle's house.

Alone, Berle was pensive and troubled, and in part unconvinced. He, like most counterintelligence officers, liked a story when it matched other factual accounts already on hand. But Chambers was not a suspect, and Berle was somewhat skeptical of Chambers's reliability. He knew ex-communists and, although estranged from the movement, they had still seemed impressed by "the all-powerful quality" of having been a conspirator. They also shared an unfortunate tendency of "exaggerating their own experience" in retelling it. Still, Berle would make discreet inquiries.

In fact, he never would. As a matter of routine procedure, he should have immediately alerted the FBI or filed a record of the interview with a military or counterintelligence agency, or even notified the State Department's personnel and security office. Had he done so, severe and lasting damage to U.S. interests would have been forestalled, but Berle did none of these things. In March 1941, *only* after Krivitsky was murdered would Berle finally ask the FBI if it were investigating Chambers, and the agency said it was not. When Berle finally gave Chambers's notes to President Franklin Roosevelt, Roosevelt laughed. When Berle tried to press the issue, Roosevelt responded to Berle that he should "go jump in a lake."[18]

Berle's spasmodic, ineffective efforts ceased altogether. Nothing of substance would be done because Roosevelt "never took seriously the possibility that his administration might be penetrated."[19] The telling details of widespread treason and betrayal within the Roosevelt government just lay there mute in Chambers's notes, like a coiled poisonous snake in the bottom of a closed wicker basket.

6

★ ★ ★

WORLD WAR II would see the Soviet spying reach dangerous heights of unprecedented success. The antecedent of much of this triumph can be traced to a mysterious denseness of thought on the part of American political leaders that dated back to the 1920s. Many U.S. politicians had replaced a detached, unemotional observation of America and the world with a self-flattering illusion. America, they seemed to say, was the place of the Great Promise, the land where people had only to make honest exertions at betterment in order for a fuller, richer, freer life to be had by all. In foreign policy, there seemed to prevail a deeply rooted and idealistic belief that if America were honest, generous, and aboveboard in her dealings with foreign countries, those countries would be inspired to match her in trustworthiness and goodwill. At the end of World War II, even as the Soviets were busy undermining U.S. policies, General Dwight Eisenhower said to alarmed U.S. diplomats, "You have to give trust to get trust."

Certainly the counterintelligence capabilities of the United States in the 1920s and 1930s can best be described as hopelessly feeble. In 1929, when Henry Stimson, President Herbert Hoover's secretary of state, was shown decrypted cables produced by the famous Black Chamber decoding group, he recoiled in outraged shock, declaring it "unethical" for America to be reading the "messages coming to our ambassadorial guests from other countries . . ." Stimson quickly disbanded the Black Chamber.

But just because America was blind to its own weaknesses didn't mean that others weren't already at work to exploit them. In fact, Soviet efforts to subvert the American government knew no rest. For year upon year, little bands of Russian spies, bound fast by the fiery and inflexible servitudes of ideology, labored without pause with relentless perseverance to obtain crucial secrets. And opposing them was . . . what?

After Roosevelt became president, he exhibited an astonishing ignorance of the aims, methods, and character of the Soviet system or else he arrogantly chose to ignore them. Roosevelt in 1936, was a broad-shouldered man of fifty-four whose polio-paralyzed legs were partly offset by his long arms and huge, hairy hands. The popular image of him, exuding intense vitality, his leonine head thrown back, his cigarette holder canted up at the sky, embodied the nonchalance of elegance and his bottomless confidence in himself.

He had acted with extraordinary vigor to save the country from the Great Depression, yet his views on foreign policy were often callow, quirky, and frivolous. For example, in 1935, he sent a New York attorney to see Italian dictator Benito Mussolini in the hope that better ties with Italy would block the expansion of Adolph Hitler's Germany.[20] Russia, unfortunately, was a particular blind spot. Roosevelt, who had recognized the Soviet Union in 1933, regarded himself as a "progressive" and saw in Joseph Stalin another "progressive" like himself. Just as Roosevelt had talked of "Developing Capitalism in One Country," Stalin was developing "Socialism in One Country." The historian Paul Johnson notes that Roosevelt, in the grip of a vanity that craved to be thought forward-looking, rated Soviet Russia as more reliable and promising for obtaining world peace than Britain, blithely ignoring the fact that Russia was a "totalitarian predator."[21] Roosevelt knew that American communists took their orders from Moscow, but he had a personal dislike of Germans and seemed more interested in thwarting any subversion by Hitler. As a British historian of intelligence observed, Roosevelt saw Soviet spies more as crude labor agitators, rather than as smart, suave, personable, well-informed American bureaucrats with business or law degrees. From the mid-1930s on, Roosevelt ". . . never took seriously the possibility that his own administration might be penetrated," the historian said.[22]

The warning bell alerting the world to Roosevelt's gullibility rang out sharply in Washington in 1936. Few noticed. If the United States had any department able to act as a counterintelligence force against Russian spies, it was to be found in the State Department's Division of Eastern European Affairs, an organization that had existed since 1924. It was headed by Robert F. Kelly, a Russian expert whom diplomat George Kennan called a "discreet bachelor." A graduate of Harvard and the Sorbonne, Kelly was a tall, taciturn man whose mind missed nothing. Kelly had been active in the 1933 U.S. talks that recognized the Soviet Union. Those talks had relied on voluminous files of material that Kennan said had been "collected from every possible source on every aspect of Russian life," including newspapers, periodicals, and other literature. The vision of Kelly's department was not only steady and objective, but it was intellectually conscientious. His department's staff had taken pains to verify every fact in the files with collateral evidence. Kelly's group had also amassed meticulous files on Soviet subversion in the United States.

Counterintelligence is simply a huge research project based on consulting massive archives, and Kelly's files were unmatched. Where the FBI saw Soviet agents as equivalent to anarchists or labor radicals, Kelly's understanding was lucid, subtle, and comprehensive. Kelly had instantly understood that the recognition of the Soviets had provided them with new launchpads for spying on U.S. soil and, like the young State Department experts on Russia such as George Kennan and Chip Bohlen—sharp, learned, hard-minded experts who had an encyclopedic knowledge of Stalin's system and its aims and methods—Kelly believed that the Soviet system was a grave threat to American freedom and that the ultimate national interests of both countries were locked in profound conflict.

But there was in the White House a growing conviction that improved relations with Stalin was a prize to be had at any price. The president, First Lady Eleanor Roosevelt,[23] and some of the president's key aides all came to feel that Kelly's carefulness in examining and questioning Soviet declarations was somehow unfriendly and would jeopardize the betterment of ties. The growing menace of Hitler darkening the horizon only added weight to this group's views.

It wasn't long before Kelly realized a terrible force was at work against him. Kelly was keenly aware that diplomatic recognition of the Soviets had acted to give them new bases of operation on U.S. soil. His division's files would be at the core of any attempts to unmask Soviet spying. Epithets began to be muttered against Kelly and his group who were called "ungentlemanly" and "anti-Soviet." Joseph E. Davies, the new U.S. ambassador to Moscow and a big contributor to Roosevelt's campaign, declared, "It is bad Christianity, bad sportsmanship, and bad sense to challenge the integrity of the Soviet government."[24]

One day Kelly was suddenly asked to report to the undersecretary of state's office, where he was told his division was to be liquidated and its functions transferred to another department. Kelly's priceless, indispensable files were to be turned over and destroyed, which would leave a fumbling FBI having to start its Russian spy-hunting from scratch. Kennan later blamed this "curious purge" on indications of "strongly pro-Soviet" influence in the upper reaches of the government, manly, in this instance, from First Lady Eleanor Roosevelt.

He would be right, and that influence would swell and worsen with the coming of World War II.

In June 1941, already having conquered most of Europe, Germany had invaded Russia, scoring some of the biggest victories in the history of warfare. On July 10, 1941, in the Battle of Minsk, the Germans captured 323,898 Russian prisoners and destroyed 3,332 tanks and 1,909 guns.[25] In the first year of the war, the Russians estimated they lost 4.5 million men, 9,000 planes, and 15,000 tanks.[26]

The war put America in an awkward position. In 1939, after a decade of neglect, the armed forces of the United States ranked nineteenth in the world, after Portugal's.[27] Roosevelt had to decide which theater of war was the most important. Thanks to key advice from a graduate of the German War College, Albert C. Wedemeyer, Roosevelt made the critical decision to wage the primary war against Germany with a second front against Japan. Always sensitive to the public, in the back of Roosevelt's mind was the clear realization that American casualties had to be kept to an absolute minimum. As a result, the Russians would have to bear the brunt of the war.

They did. From June 1941 to June 1944, the Soviet armies confronted 250 Nazi and satellite divisions along the thousand-mile-long Eastern Front. Even after D-Day, Britain, the United States, and their allies confronted only ninety divisions in Italy and France. For the better part of the war, the two formidable heavyweights, Germany and Russia, were to be the ones to slug it out.

Roosevelt's unrealistic political attitudes toward Russia would soon become a screen that acted to block out what was real. In the summer of 1943, former U.S. ambassador to Russia William Bullitt submitted a memo to Roosevelt, an old friend, in which he pointed out that while Hitler's victory in Europe would be an intolerable menace, domination of Europe "by Stalin's communist dictatorship would be as great a threat."

Roosevelt airily replied, "I have a hunch Stalin is not that kind of man. . . . I think that if I give him everything that I possibly can and ask nothing from him in return, noblesse oblige, he won't annex anything and will work with me for a world of democracy and peace."[28] At the time, Stalin, in secret, was considering the possibility of making a separate peace with the Nazis.[29]

Roosevelt had taken a similar buoyant and breezy line a year earlier with Winston Churchill: "I know you will not mind my being brutally frank when I tell you that I think I can handle Stalin better than either your Foreign Office or my State Department. Stalin hates the guts of your top people. He thinks he likes me better, and I hope he will continue to do so."

This personal conceit, this unsound belief of Roosevelt in the power of his charm and his special certainty of touch with Stalin and his ability to influence, divert, or even soften the hard calculations of Soviet national interest was to prove wildly wrong and result in tragedy. At war's end, Stalin would possess and hold 500,000 square miles of former European territory.

Experts like Bohlen and Kennan saw clearly the jagged rocks toward which Roosevelt's foggy course was steaming at full speed. A wartime alliance of necessity did not mean the United States had to abandon its reservations about Stalin. Where Roosevelt spoke airily of noblesse oblige, Kennan understood that Stalin had none. Of capital importance, Kennan saw clearly that what the West did or did not do would have little effect on Soviet foreign policy, which came from "basic (Russian) inner necessities," the chief of these Moscow rendering its illegitimate government as legitimate by picturing the West as "evil, hostile, and menacing," using the bogyman of capitalist encirclement to impose political unanimity at home.[30]

It didn't matter. More and more Roosevelt saw Stalin and Russia through the vague, roseate haze of his own wishful thinking, and as the war ground on, the callow superficiality of American ideas about the Soviet system only deepened and increased. In March 1943, *Life* mounted to new heights of gullible fatuousness when it praised Lenin as "perhaps the greatest man of modern times," and declared that the Russians "were one hell of a people: (who) to a remarkable degree . . . look like Americans, dress like Americans, think like Americans." The NKVD was in the eyes of *Life* only "a national police force similar to the FBI."[31]

To criticize Russia acted only to aid the Nazis went the line, and when William L. White wrote an article about Russia after a visit in 1944 that criticized the low Russian standard of living, the oppressiveness of the secret police, and the inefficiency of its industrial techniques, a pack of wild dogs raced in to rip and tear at him. Typical was the *New York Times* reviewer who said, "Mr. White fires no guns for Fascism, but he rolls ammunition for it."

More and more people were being asked to believe that Stalin had no designs for imposing communism on the world. In 1943, when Russia abolished the Comintern, its overseas agency for subversion, many Americans fell for it. Joseph Davies, who was in Moscow when the announcement was made, said in an article that Stalin intended "to cooperate with, not stir up trouble for, (Russia's) neighbors." In a book *Mission to Moscow,* Davies said that the "Russia of Lenin and Trotsky—the Russia of the Bolshevik Revolution—no longer exists." And as for Stalin, he was far from being a bloody tyrant. Instead, "A child would like to sit in his lap and a dog sidle up to him."[32]

The great majority in America heaved a sigh of relief, but not everyone. Former Russian correspondent Louis Fisher sounded the skepticism of a knowing few when he said that in abolishing the Comintern, "Stalin has only torn up a label. He loses nothing. He must be laughing at us for being so naïve as to celebrate the death of a name."

Fischer was right, and the bulk of the country, including Roosevelt, was dead wrong. By the mid-1940s, just when Roosevelt saw Russia as perhaps its most essential partner in achieving postwar peace, Moscow Center had penetrated every major branch of Roosevelt's administration, and the chief U.S. intelligence agency, the Office of Strategic Services (OSS), had not a single agent reporting from Moscow on Russian activities.[33] The Communist Party in the United States, never much liked in America even during the war, had suddenly dissolved itself to become the nonpartisan Communist Political Association, supporting Roosevelt for president. This was fine, but it wasn't real and didn't matter.

Chambers had been part of this debate, violently opposed to the notion that any criticism of Russia was an insult to the joint war effort. He was working for *Time* in the "Books" section, but hungered to be in "Foreign News." But even in "Books," he displayed that impatient intolerance of a man who is certain he possesses the deciding facts and who is forced in frustration to deal with the dense who still clung to a shabby, discredited falsehood and mistook it for truth. Critic Malcolm Cowley said of Chambers, "He believes that conspiracies, traitors, and spies surround us on every side and is determined to wipe them out." Chambers's tryout in "Foreign News" was a disaster. He attacked the pro-communist line with such savagery that he was quickly recalled to "Books."

And meanwhile, all during the 1940s Russian espionage continued to seep through the government like water spreading through the crevices of a sponge.

peint par Wilckenson a Boston

GENERAL ARNOLD
*Qui avec le Général Gates aidoit à environer le General Lieu=
tenant Bourgoyne, que toute l'Armée se rendit Prisoniere,
et l'obligea de mettre bas les Armes.*
So vend a Londres chez Thom Hart.

The most infamous traitor in American history, Benedict Arnold held the rank of
general in the Continental Army until 1780, when he betrayed his compatriots at
West Point. Although the plot was discovered, Arnold escaped to later
lead two vicious campaigns under the British flag in Virginia and Connecticut.

*(Emmet Collection, Miriam and Ira D. Wallach Division of Art, Prints and Photographs,
The New York Public Library, Astor, Lenox and Tilden Foundations)*

MAJOR JOHN ANDRE.

Major Andre

(From a Miniature by himself)

Major John André, a British spy serving in the American army, negotiated the betrayal of
West Point with Benedict Arnold. Known for his charm and mourned
by some as a romantically tragic character, André was captured, tried, and then hanged at
Washington's headquarters for his part in the plot.

(Emmet Collection, Miriam and Ira D. Wallach Division of Art, Prints and Photographs,
The New York Public Library, Astor, Lenox and Tilden Foundations)

A zealous Confederate from a family of Unionists, John Wilkes Booth secreted himself into the presidential box at Ford's Theatre on the night of April 14, 1865 and shot Lincoln at close range. Jumping to the stage, he shouted, "The South is avenged!"

After nearly two weeks of a desperate manhunt, John Wilkes Booth was found hiding in a barn in Bowling Green, Virginia. Following a brief standoff, he was fatally shot on April 26, 1865.

$30,000 REWARD

DESCRIPTION

OF

JOHN WILKES BOOTH!

Who Assassinated the PRESIDENT on the Evening of April 14th, 1865.

Height 5 feet 8 inches; weight 160 pounds; compact built; hair jet black, inclined to curl, medium length, parted behind; eyes black, and heavy dark eye-brows; wears a large seal ring on little finger; when talking inclines his head forward; looks down.

Description of the Person who Attempted to Assassinate Hon. W. H. Seward, Secretary of State.

Height 6 feet 1 inch; hair black, thick, full and straight; no beard, nor appearance of beard; cheeks red on the jaws; face moderately full; 22 or 23 years of age; eyes, color not known—large eyes, not prominent; brows not heavy, but dark; face not large, but rather round; complexion healthy; nose straight and well formed, medium size; mouth small; lips thin; upper lip protruded when he talked; chin pointed and prominent; head medium size; neck short, and of medium length; hands soft and small; fingers tapering; shows no signs of hard labor; broad shoulders; taper waist; straight figure; strong-looking man; manner not gentlemanly, but vulgar; Overcoat double-breasted, color mixed of pink and grey spots, small—was a sack overcoat, pockets in side and one on the breast, with lappells or flaps; pants black, common stuff; new heavy boots; voice small and thin, inclined to tenor.

The Common Council of Washington, D. C., have offered a reward of $20,000 for the arrest and conviction of these Assassins, in addition to which I will pay $10,000.

L. C. BAKER,
Colonel and Agent War Department

Whittaker Chambers exits New York's Federal Courthouse, December 6, 1940, where he testified before a grand jury. Although secret State Department documents were discovered on his Maryland farm, the *Time* magazine senior editor refused to reveal the nature of his testimony.

(AP Photo/jl)

Former State Department official Alger Hiss enters the Federal Courthouse in New York, December 7, 1948, to answer accusations made by Whittaker Chambers. Chambers implicated Hiss, the president of the Carnegie Endowment for International Peace, with involvement in communist activities prior to Wold War II.

(AP Photo)

Flanked by her police guards, Elizabeth T. Bentley listens to the testimony
of government employee Victor Perlo at an Un-American Activities
Committee hearing in Washington, August 9, 1948. Bentley, the hearing's star witness,
accused Perlo of disclosing confidential information.

(AP Photo/Stf)

A U.S. Federal Marshal escorts John A. Walker Jr., left,
from the Montgomery County Detention Center in Rockville, MD,
to his federal court appointment in Baltimore, October 28, 1985.
Walker pleaded guilty to the charge that he and his son, Michael,
organized a network of spies who sold naval codes to the Soviets,
allowing them to decipher one million classified cables.

(AP Photo/Bob Daugherty)

FBI agent Robert Phillip Hanssen was arrested on February 18, 2001 and charged with espionage. Hanssen was accused of acting as a Soviet and Russian spy for more than fifteen years.

(AP Photo/FBI)

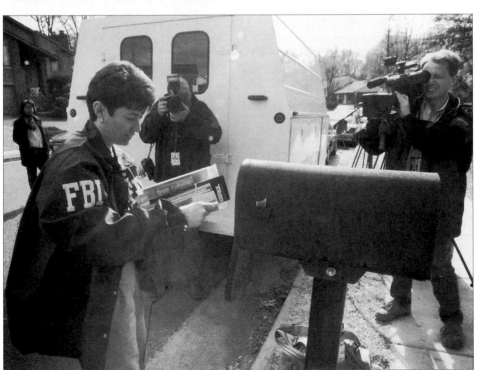

An FBI agent removes mail from Robert Phillip Hanssen's Virginia home. A veteran FBI agent, Hanssen was charged with providing the KGB with the names of three Russian agents working with the United States in exchange for cash and diamonds.

(AP Photo/Doug Mills)

7

By 1943, Elizabeth Bentley stood at the very crux of Soviet espionage operations in the United States. The bespectacled, bookish-looking Vassar graduate had become a major agent. She had fallen deeply in love with a small, stocky man in his mid-forties who at first had seemed to her to be a bit colorless and shabby. He wore a battered brown hat, a nondescript suit, and unpolished brown shoes. When they went to their first dinner together, it was supposed to be routine, yet two hours later both were bent head to head, and Bentley found herself pouring out experiences she had not told to other people. The man's eyes were blue, his hair a bright red, and he had very broad shoulders and strong, square hands. But his mind displayed piercing intelligence, and was quick, keen, and incisive.

It should have been. He was Jacob Golos, one of the most senior NKVD agents in the United States. Long married and with a son in Russia, he had spent his life in the underground. By 1940, he had had twenty new Soviet agents under recruitment, and would get more, some of them supreme performers. Golos not only ran key networks in the United States, but in Canada as well. In later KGB records, his accomplishments would be labeled "colossal."

To Bentley, Golos remained a mystery until one night, when burning documents at his apartment, she found a card that said Golos worked for the OGPU, the secret police forerunner of the NKVD, and the GRU's main rival in the United States. She was not put off. Golos somehow reminded Bentley "of my New England parents. There was the same, simple plain way of life, the same capacity for hard work, the same unswerving loyalty to an ideal, the same shy kindness and generosity . . ." She looked upon him as "the ideal Communist." There was a strong feeling of being comrades, of sharing a worthy cause in common, and of the excitement of finding mutual meaning in ideas plus "an inexplicable comfort and warmth in our nearness," she would say.

Golos was a maverick, with a fierce, fully fashioned, independent will, who, in spite of the party hierarchy, refused to value the judgments of others above his own. He was the person on the spot, and his assessment of matters would prevail because his mind had an alert appreciation of evidence and could draw the correct inferences to which the evidence pointed. His view of his superiors was colored by a dark grudge Golos bore them. Back in 1939, a Justice Department had accused World Tourists, a front company Golos ran that supplied fake passports for Soviet agents, of committing espionage on behalf of Moscow. To quell the attention-focusing commotion, Golos's superiors had picked their star spymaster to plead guilty in court. He never forgave them. Pacing up and down his room, utterly weary, he said to Bentley in ferocity and despair, "I never thought I would live to see the day I would have to plead guilty in a bourgeois court."

He threw himself on a bed and turned his face to the wall.

Golos in time would punish them for their choosing to sacrifice him. Golos ran Moscow's two key, top-producing spy rings in Washington, the Perlo and Silvermaster groups. The latter was the most indispensable. Nathan Gregory Silvermaster, Chambers's old contact, had begun to work for Golos in 1941. According to one U.S. historian, the Silvermaster group generated the NKVD's most valuable information in America and it increased in pace and volume like a swollen torrent rushing through a lock. The stolen secrets came from the navy, the army, the Department of Justice, the Treasury Department, and the Office of Strategic Services. One Silvermaster spy in the OSS had even given Moscow a heads-up over U.S. efforts in 1944 to persuade Hungary to surrender in order to splinter the Nazi position in the Balkans—which was why, for a time, Silvermaster would be the only American in the KFB Hall of Fame.[34] More secrets were culled from rising NKVD stars like mild, short, bespectacled, Harry Dexter

White in the Treasury Department and Lauchlan Currie, a personal assistant to Roosevelt.[35]

In the beginning, the take of the day could be processed on three or four rolls of microfilm with thirty-five to forty exposures per roll. But made more ravenous by their success, the Russian handlers boosted their demands, and the group soon found itself working to the fullest extent of its capacity, almost worn dead from lack of sleep. Soon, Bentley was carrying as many as eighty rolls of film up to New York every two weeks. By the spring of 1943, as an added security measure, the rolls were being forwarded undeveloped to the Soviet Embassy's NKVD lab, accompanied by an itemized list.

But an extraordinary crisis soon arose that was to wreck the smooth-running machine of Soviet operations. Golos, never a well man, had suddenly died of a heart attack. Bentley was dazed, stricken, devastated. The sweet intimacy of their love was made manifest in one particular incident that occurred around Thanksgiving, 1943. Golos and Bentley for some time had been jointly running his networks. Since many of their agents paid communist party dues, did not receive salaries, and were only supplied money for traveling expenses, she and Golos made it a point each Christmas to buy them a present in appreciation of their work: a steamer basket of fruit and jams, jars of Russian caviar, a bottle or two of Scotch—just some token to tell them their loyalty had been noticed.

Loaded down with packages, Bentley tottered into World Tourists to find Golos in his office. She eagerly began to open packages to show him what she'd purchased. But when she took out some toys she'd bought, he simply looked at them. He sat very quietly for a moment with tears in his eyes, then Golos pulled her to his lap and placed his cheek against hers. "You know," he said wistfully, "one of the things I regret most is the fact we never had any children."

A few days later he was dead. Bentley's heart was dead too, and the NKVD began to take Golos's networks away from her. The Russian "legal" NKVD agent in Washington told Bentley to cut all ties with the Perlo group, and this she grudgingly did. The Silvermaster group was next on the NKVD list. The Russians knew that to control the Silvermaster group meant pushing Bentley out of the way, but so did she, and this time she rebelled. Bentley had a certain redoubtable pride in her own competence, her own initiative, her own sense of responsibility, instilled in her by Golos. What she had learned to do could not be undone, and she set her teeth in resolve to continue her lover's work as talent spotter, group controller, and recruiter. Golos had run his spy rings as one-man business, and she felt exactly the same. She refused to be sidelined and set herself to resist with every means in her power.

Itzhak "Bill" Akhmerov, who headed one of the four NKVD *rezidenturas* in the United States, made the first move. He and Bentley met in New York.

Things went well at first, but when "Bill" asked Bentley to introduce him to the Silvermaster group, she turned stony and remote. She said they were afraid to deal directly with Russians. Akhmerov was brought up short. He would say later that Bentley carried out his instructions "gladly," but at any mention of his having direct contact with the Silvermaster group, she became "an absolutely different person," contrary and stubborn.

Since she had seen through his game, he quickly changed tactics. First "Bill" offered to raise her salary. Bentley replied primly that her income was equal to her needs. "Bill" offered her more money. Bentley blazed at him in fury. "What kind of racket is this where they pay you for doing your duty?" she asked.

"Bill" then offered her a gift, a Persian lamb coat.

She refused.

How about an air-conditioning unit for her flat? Bentley didn't budge a hair.

But the pressure of her handlers continued to tighten like a vise.

By the end of 1944, a defeated Bentley returned to the Silvermaster group to collect stolen secrets for the last time. Back in New York, she handed the package of papers to "Bill." He smiled at her with pity in his eyes. "Goodbye and good luck," he said softly, reminding her she would meet her new contact in two weeks. Akhmerov had won, but in winning, the Russians had committed a grave miscalculation. Bentley came away believing that Russians were out only for Russians and tolerated Americans only when the latter were their subservient and submissive tools, and she would not be one. In the flush of his self-satisfaction, Akhmerov would have no inkling that what he had done would prove to be the beginning of the end for the heyday of Moscow's critical American spy rings.

Bentley's next Russian contact meeting was a flat failure, and Anatol Gorsky, the Washington NKVD station chief, now stepped upon the scene. It was he who had first ordered Bentley to sever all ties with the Perlo group, and as Bentley waited outside a drugstore, carrying a copy of *Life* magazine, suddenly there he was. In his thirties, with blond hair brushed straight back, he was a picture of "well-fed flabbiness," according to Bentley.

They ate at Naylor's, and as Gorsky lit a cigarette with a gold lighter, he remarked, "I hope the food is good. Americans are such stupid people that even when it comes to a simple matter like cooking a meal, they do it very badly."

Her dislike was total and instantaneous. The international communist movement was in the hands of the wrong people, she thought. But there are many roads to persuasion and Gorsky was taking a gentler, higher one than had "Bill." Perhaps warm praise and high expectations would work where blunt appeals to self-interest had failed. Gorsky spoke glowingly. He told Bentley that she had a great future before her, and suddenly announced she was being awarded the Order of the Red Star, one of the highest Soviet decorations.

Gorsky hastily pulled a facsimile of the decoration from his pocket, but Bentley, while producing amiable smiles and exclamations of pleasure, remained inwardly stony and disgusted, seeing in the award only a more vulgar version of the Persian lamb coat. Pledging to Gorsky that she would work even harder to justify such an honor, she inwardly lodged another sour grudge.

Her disenchantment mounted by the day. She could no longer hope. She could no longer believe. Pleasure is the true face of despair, and she succumbed. She already had a male lover, but took another, Peter Heller, a man Gorsky suspected of being a U.S. agent. Gorsky ordered Bentley to dump Heller and take a vacation, and, to stem Bentley's mounting instability, Gorsky planned "to load her up so much (with work) that she has no time to think too much (and) no time to practice romance." Plus she was to stay away from any contact with old agents.

Relations only grew worse.

Bentley showed up surly, peevish, and drunk at the next meeting, asking Gorsky for fresh monies and threatening to testify before the House Un-American Activities Committee. She also charged that Akhmerov had tried to rape her and threatened to kill another Russian male who apparently tried to take advantage of her.

Gorksy ended the conversation and quickly scuttled off. Oddly enough, Akhmerov continued to be fascinated by this woman who had refused to yield to his will, saying in one cable, "She is a rather attractive person," and in another, "I think she is undoubtedly one hundred percent woman."

But as time passed, he too began to doubt, and Gorksy finally knew he was up against a woman who was part lion and part fox and knew it was the fox that he feared. He introduced a more sinister, proven plan to rid himself of the difficulty. In a cable to Moscow, he said that Bentley "is alien and hostile to us personally." If she decided to turn on them, the damage to Moscow could be severe. He said there was but one remedy left and "the most drastic one—to get rid of her."[36]

The Kremlin, however, stayed calm. It ordered no hit, but instead counseled caution, discounting the idea that Bentley would ever become a double agent. But whatever loyalty and goodwill Bentley had felt had soured in her for good.

On August 23, 1945, aged thirty-seven, Bentley entered the field office of the FBI in New Haven, Connecticut.

8

★ ★ ★

IT WAS 1946. America's fashion makers had revived the bare midriff and the strapless wired bra. The first DuMont TV sets had begun to appear in American homes at the rate of a quarter million per month. Dr. Spock was popular. There were celebrity weddings—pop bandleader Artie Shaw to movie siren Ava Gardner, Judy Garland to Vincent Minnelli, Gloria Vanderbilt, twenty-one, to conductor Leopold Stokowski, fifty-eight. There were less sanguine developments: the number of American supermarkets was tripling and would soon total more than 20,000. In California, the first eight-lane highways known as "freeways" were in the planning stage and on paper.

At the close of 1945, the great wartime American military machine was being wrecked and dismantled. The army was sending home almost a million men a month by December 1945, the navy another quarter million.

The war was over and the Nazis were broken, but the whole of Eastern Europe was suffering a nightmare of ghastly suffocation, like a man whose head is thrust suddenly into a tightening plastic bag. In Hungary, parts of Germany, Rumania, Bulgaria, the Baltic states, and eventually Poland and Czechoslovakia, the Red Army held power. It quickly suppressed opposition groups and eliminated personal freedoms, and people once again began disappearing without a trace into prisons. The Soviet puppet governments, so-called "people's republics," were a hideous eclipse of what should have been the bright, ecstatic deliverance of victory.

President Franklin Delano Roosevelt's part in this gigantic failure is not to be underplayed. As a wartime leader, Roosevelt not only had to direct where the war was going to *go*, but also to tell Americans what the war was going to *mean*, and he had sold the war to the American public as a struggle for self-determination for small countries. In August 1941, in a secret meeting at Placentia Bay, New Foundland, with Winston Churchill, the two leaders issued "The Atlantic Charter," in which they said they respected the rights "of all peoples to choose the form of government under which they will live" and that they desired to see "no territorial changes that do not accord with the freely expressed wishes of the people concerned," among other provisions.[37]

They were wonderful, stirring idealistic words, and that's exactly what they remained—lofty rhetoric directed at the upper echelons of American public opinion. Churchill at that meeting exempted the British colonial possessions from the charter they drew up, and at the same meeting, Roosevelt himself approved the joint Russian-Anglo invasion of Iran, a neutral country, on trumped-up charges of harboring Nazis, but really in order to better supply Stalin with Iran's north-south railroad.

But Eastern Europe was a stark tragedy. It was partly the result of the fact that Roosevelt had conducted the war through his joint chiefs of staff and sidelined the State Department, and chiefly because the department had experts like George Kennan and Bohlen and Averill Harriman, the U.S. ambassador to Moscow, who would have told him things he did not want to hear. As Kennan watched the Red Armies overrun Eastern Europe, he thought that the United States should have forced a showdown. Russia should be made to collaborate in founding truly independent countries in Eastern Europe or forfeit U.S. aid for the remainder of the war, he said.[38]

Harriman said that in the summer before the war ended, he had tried four or five times to talk to Roosevelt about Eastern Europe, but could get nowhere.[39] Roosevelt's optimism about Joseph Stalin proved an enormously stupid misjudgment. In all the Soviet-occupied countries, there was no right of assembly or political association unless it first got approval of the Soviet Army. There were no radio shows, no stage plays, no cinemas, no books or pamphlets, or no news except those approved by the Soviet Army.

Yet, up until a few months before his death in 1945, Roosevelt had still been bedazzled by Stalin, had still been fearful of provoking him, and was still wanting to compromise with Moscow for the sake of building a world of peace and democracy. In February 1945, Roosevelt postured pompously at Yalta about "free and unfettered elections . . . on the basis of universal suffrage and the secret ballot," when he knew there was absolutely no such possibility. The purpose of such words was to seduce Polish voters at home.

Roosevelt's Yalta statements truck Kennan as "the shabbiest kind of equivocation," a sham and a fake meant to conceal from American ethnic voters the dark reality of what the necessity of wartime collaboration had brought to pass.

But then Stalin had always known what he wanted out of the war: solid real estate. "This war is not as in the past," he told fellow communists. "Whoever occupies a territory also imposes on it his own social system" as far "as his army can reach."[40]

But despite years of unbroken espionage success, with secret spy rings working with antlike industry, the Soviets were about to endure a brutal shock.

It began in the fall of 1945. The Soviet embassy in Ottawa was housed in a three-story building on Charlotte Street, in a shabby middle-class neighborhood. On the second floor of the building, the secret cipher branch was housed in a room behind a big thick steel door shielded by a velvet curtain. Behind that massive door was another, even more massive, manned by the NKVD, which, when opened, let the visitor into a corridor full of more steel doors, these a lot smaller. It was the most secure area of the embassy, the home of the GRU in Canada, the site of secret radio communications with Moscow, of the storage place of top secret files.

Igor Sergeivitch Gouzenko, the man who would set in motion the disruption and curtailment of key Soviet espionage efforts in North America, worked as a modest cipher clerk for the GRU, Whittaker Chambers's old outfit. Gouzenko had come to Canada in 1943, and he had wanted to defect from the first.[41] He knew that he had valuable gifts to give. While working at the GRU center in Moscow with forty other clerks, he had inadvertently strayed across evidence of a mole highly placed in British counterintelligence, and later discovered a cable that disclosed a Soviet agent named "ALEK" who had given to Moscow information on the U.S. atomic bomb and other extremely sensitive information.

Gouzenko disliked his comrades. He was an idealist who had recoiled at the petty, sordid avarice he saw in the corner-cutting embassy diplomats who purchased luxury goods and covertly shipped them home, concealing the costs in department budgets. But he hesitated until the summer of 1945, when he made a clumsy mistake at work. His angry boss, Colonel Nicolai Zabotin, gave him a withering reprimand, and the GRU in Moscow demanded the clerk be recalled. When Gouzenko got home and told his pregnant wife the news, she sank to the floor, sobbing. But he was ready. For some time, Gouzenko had secretly made lists of Zabotin's agents and contracts. He had copied correspondence and cables, and on September 5, 1945, Gouzenko made his break. He stuffed his documents and some pages from his superior's diary and made his way from the embassy.

Now his real troubles began. What Gouzenko was trying to reveal was a plot startling in its meaning and dread-making in its extent. But he had expected if not a warm welcome, then at least an expression of interest. He got neither. Talks with the editors of Ottawa's newspapers left them suspicious, and visits to Canadian officials left them cold. Incredible as it seems, even after Roosevelt died in April 1945, the spell cast by Stalin over U.S. foreign policy remained in full force. A British intelligence analyst said that Stalin's reputation for being a tough customer had had the effect, "making almost any concession to Stalin's demands seem necessary. . . . The furtherance of good relations with the Soviets has become all consuming."[42] As an editor told Gouzenko, "Nobody wants to say anything but nice things about Stalin these days."

But not everyone's instincts had been dulled by the platitudes of politics. Keener minds in the intelligence establishment saw the depth of Western penetration, and it filled them with deepest alarm. Gouzenko's documents showed that the upper reaches of the British, American, and Canadian governments were riddled with shadowy Soviet agents of influence. What the analysts were staring at was a widespread, brilliant, subtly contrived threat whose genius lay in its patient capacity for camouflage, its ability to hide itself in the institutions it had set out to destroy.

The Canadian government was convulsed, its mood ranging rapidly from helpless confusion to vows of heroic revenge to ideas of timid apology. The Canadian Prime Minister Mackenzie King sat numb and in shock

at the news of the defection. What if the Russians broke off relations because Canada had sheltered Gouzenko? With all the backbone of a choco-
late éclair, King dithered and fluttered and did nothing. But on September
30, as President Harry Truman crossed Lafayette Park in Washington to
take his 120-paces-a-minute fitness walk, documents arrived at the State
Department on Virginia Avenue. The package was from Lester B. Pearson,
the Canadian ambassador to the United States and its papers clearly summarized Gouzenko's allegations.

A grim, new hour had dawned.

ANOTHER AMERICAN WAS working that weekend. Sitting in his office at
the State Department, the senior official who read Pearson's memo was
riding perhaps the most satisfying crest of his career.[43] After a patient period of preliminary flickering, there had burst out in Washington the dazzling light of a new star. Alger Hiss, as new director of the president's
Office of Special Political Affairs, had just recently moved into a nicer,
roomier office. After his jobs with the AAA and the Nye Committee, and
after a short time in the office of solicitor general, he had gone to the State
Department in 1936. Throughout the war, Hiss's career had been one of
irresistible ascent and accomplishment. Unlike some others, he had not
been transferred to the NKVD but had remained with Soviet military intelligence (GRU). Hiss had enjoyed the honor of attending the Yalta Conference, and afterward had flown on to Moscow in the State Department
plane as special assistant to Secretary of State Edward Stettintius. Hiss
then became secretary general at the U.S. conference in San Francisco and
had since become the chief advisor of the U.S. delegation to the UN General Assembly. He had worked as a deputy in the State Department's Office of Special Affairs, had plenty of access to valuable secret military
information, and had finally become the office's director. But one of Hiss's
greatest personal satisfactions lay in knowing that he commanded from almost everyone the admiration and applause due his outstanding ability
and remained able to weave his own spells over the town's elite.

As Hiss read the Canadian documents, his eyes fell on a line where
Gouzenko spoke of an assistant secretary in the State Department who
was "a Soviet plant." Instantly Hiss felt as if someone had removed the
solid floor from under his feet. He slowly reread the statement. Gouzenko
wasn't exactly accurate. The position he named was wrong, but it was
close enough for Hiss to be unable to breathe for a moment. For years,

Hiss had been secretly and continuously worn by the intolerable burden of his double life, and now there was this. But as Hiss sat and pondered, there was a sudden sense of hope. After all, Gouzenko's startling shot had been fired blind and had only grazed Hiss, not hit him. It showed only that Gouzenko was groping, full of hearsay and guesswork. For now, Hiss felt certain he was going to be safe.

But the vague guesswork of Gouzenko was not to last for very long.

The House Un-American Activities Committee (HUAC) had been everyone's joke for the past ten years—a purveyor of the bigoted, the out of date, the customary, the habitual, and the unthinking. Headed by Martin Dies, a Texan who hated Roosevelt, and John Rankin of Mississippi, who hated Jews, it had, for a decade, tried to sabotage, baffle, smear, or frustrate Roosevelt's reforms by casting the silhouette of huge communist conspiracy against the public wall. Yet few had been frightened, and the committee's efforts had seemed superbly futile—like a man who heaps up and tears down piles of sand.

But since the end of the war, there had been a lot of vigorous activity behind the scenes, and if most Americans did not yet know who the scene-shifters were, they saw that when the curtain went up, it revealed an entirely different tableau. By Christmas of 1945, in a "winding line from the Adriatic to the Baltic," vast regions of Europe lay under Stalin's power. By Christmas 1945 all countries each of the line except for Greece had communist governments or coalition governments in which communists shared power with others.[44] In 1948, America's great wartime ally, Russia, had taken over Czechoslovakia, blockaded Berlin, and tried to drive out U.S. forces stationed there. The temperature of the Cold War plunged to freezing point, and resentful doubt and wrathful suspicion had replaced the American public's ignorant credulity regarding Russia's good faith.

Elizabeth Bentley had already testified in secret before a grand jury in New York. Her testimony lasted thirteen months, and in it she named eighty-seven alleged Soviet spies, among them Hiss. Eleven of the spies she named would be allowed to resign. Some were never called to testify. Some were. But her exposure of the Perlo and Silvermaster rings, agents in the White House, the State Department, the War Department, the Treasury Department, and the Office of Strategic Services (OSS) would prove catastrophic to KGB networks in North America.[45]

The onward rush of bitter national disillusion swept on and would reach its ugly climax in the Hiss-Chambers case.

Chambers testified before HUAC three days after Bentley, naming thirty-seven spies. Gentle, troubled Lawrence Duggan, only forty-three, was one. The State Department employee who had been made so distraught by Moscow's show trials could not envisage the disgrace of his own. Duggan jumped to his death from a sixteenth-floor Manhattan window after two witnesses identified him as a communist. Twelve others named by Chambers either kept still or swore that the allegations against them were false.

The Hiss case was not long to come, and in the beginning, Hiss seemed unassailable. By 1948, he was listed in *Who's Who in America,* and in the Washington, D.C. , *Social Register,* and his friends filled the top ranks of the Washington elite. Plus many found Hiss very impressive as a person. There was a smooth trace of Harvard and Massachusetts in his well-modulated voice, and he played at Gibson Island tennis tournaments and escorted his wife, Priscilla, to Baltimore cotillions. He had the winning talent of entering into productive, rewarding social relations with everyone.

Except all of a sudden, planted squarely like a lion in his path, was the rumpled, fat figure of Chambers. He was still at *Time,* as a senior editor. A stumpy, unattractive man, with a pale, unhealthy complexion, roundish face, and heavy-lidded eyes, to many he was simply a loser, a former traitor, a sometime homosexual, a man who could point to no influential connections beyond his employer, Henry Luce of *Time.*

True to habit, Chambers's own conduct was equivocal. It was full of shifts, evasions, and feints, presenting a confusing mixture of reformer, traitor, crusader and a man not quite able to muster the courage to come completely clean. It was hard to determine which had the supreme claim on his behavior, his hatred of communism or a certain protectiveness about his past as a communist spy and a scrupulous reluctance to inflict damage on people like Hiss who had been part of it. When a grand jury had asked him about the Ware Group and if its primary purpose was espionage, Chambers had calmly and fluently lied his head off, saying that its mission was mainly to infiltrate the government.

But on August 4, Chambers identified Hiss as a communist before the committee, and the very next day Hiss appeared. He looked erect, tan, confident, and fearless. Ready to vouch for his loyalty were some of the most illustrious names in America, beginning with the Secretary of State Dean Acheson. Hiss was not going to duck behind a constitutional amendment, but face the communist charge square on. He would adopt the tactics Bentley had urged on Greg Silvermaster in 1942, when questions had been raised about Silvermaster's loyalty. The spy had been dejected and full of despair, saying, "It's no use fighting this thing," but Bentley, made of far tougher stuff had flared, "Stand your ground, put on an air of injured innocence: you are not a communist, just a 'progressive,' whose record proves you have always fought for the rights of labor. Rally all your 'liberal' friends around."

Silvermaster followed her advice, and now, so did Hiss. He answered every committee question boldly, decisively, finally, full of the strength of righteous certainty. His performance was so impressive that John Rankin, a senior member of the committee, came down afterward to shake Hiss's hand and Senator Karl Mundt thanked him for his "very cooperative attitude." Everybody was pleased and happy except one person, one of the committee's best interrogators, a young man named Richard Nixon. He had never taken his eyes from Hiss's face the whole time.

Hiss had resigned abruptly from the State Department to become head of the Carnegie Endowment for International Peace, but rumors had silently fumed and floated in Washington that Hiss had been forced out of office, that he had once been a communist. Nixon knew of FBI interrogations of Hiss, but they had resulted in nothing. But Nixon felt that Hiss was fundamentally dishonest.

The question was how to prove it to the world.

For days Nixon fretted, fumed, frowned, and then he had his idea: Chambers was recalled.

On August 7, the plump, dowdy man made his way to the thirty-two-story Federal Courthouse on Foley Square to the dark paneled first floor courtroom. The whole story, an almost encyclopedic knowledge of the Hiss family, again reeled out of Chambers's incredible memory. Out came the addresses of the Hisses' homes (and the leases), the grades of Priscilla Hiss's son from a previous marriage, descriptions of the Hisses' Volta place house that had had their gilt Hitchcock chairs, the intimate, endearing nicknames Alger and Priscilla had for each other, an account of the mirror with a gold eagle on top, and a description of how the walls of the Hisses' Volta place house were papered halfway with a mulberry pattern. There were details about books, children, servants, furniture, the kennel for the dog on Wisconsin Avenue.

And then came the hobbies.

Both Alger and Priscilla were fanatical bird-watchers, and Chambers told about how ecstatic Hiss had been when one morning he'd spotted a prothonotary warbler on the Potomac. Chambers had unwittingly laid a trap. After the committee had recalled Hiss, an amateur ornithologist on the committee named John Howell would ask Hiss if he'd ever seen a prothonotary warbler. Hiss instantly came to life. "I have," he said, with a gush of animation. "Right here on the Potomac? Do you know that place?" And he bubbled on about the "gorgeous bird."

His answer sank in deeper than he knew.

But that was to come.

At first, Hiss stoutly maintained he didn't know Chambers, but the committee wanted to know how a stranger had acquired such an incredibly detailed knowledge of the Hisses. Suddenly Hiss recalled he *had* known a down-and-out freelance writer named George Crosley. Hiss had met him in the 1930s and had let him sublet an apartment in a Hiss home. In fact, the Hisses had put up Crosley two or three nights in a row at their own home because the subletters' furniture van had been late to arrive, a lie Priscilla would later be caught in.

"How tall was this man, approximately?" asked Nixon, suspicious.

"Shortish," said Hiss.

An investigator asked what kind of car Crosley drove.

"No kind of automobile," Hiss replied. "I sold him an automobile. I had an old Ford that I threw in with the apartment and had been trying to trade it in and get rid of it. . . . It wasn't very fancy . . ."

"You gave the car to Crosley?"

"Threw it in with the apartment and charged the rent and threw in the car at the same time."

"Did the Ford have windshield wipers?"

Hiss said airily, yes, hand-operated, adding, "You had to work them yourself."

Questions came now like rain. What were the Hisses' nicknames? Did they have pets? Where did they board them? Had Hiss ever had a boyhood occupation?

With each answer, Hiss kept violating what one U.S. congressman would call "the first law of Pits"—when you're in one, stop digging.

Nixon was totally disbelieving of Hiss. Nixon was not an honest man and he knew that weakness when he saw it in another. He and other committee members could also see Hiss was beginning to buckle under the fearsome pressure.

Then Nixon hit upon an idea that would flush Hiss from his cover like a panicked quail. One day as Chambers was entering the House office building in Washington, committee staffers told him he must take a five-hour train ride to New York. On that same day, committee staff had approached Hiss at his uptown New York office near Columbia University. Could Hiss come to the Commodore Hotel and meet with Congressman John McDowell and Nixon?

When Hiss arrived there, he found quite a crowd, including a stenographer at her machine. He was administered the oath and told to smoke and be comfortable.

Nixon told Hiss that he had felt it would be in everyone's interest if the committee could determine, once and for all, if Crosley and Chambers were the same man.

Chambers was duly brought in and took a seat on the sofa.

Hiss was choked with panic. He stood six feet tall, six inches taller than his accuser. Nixon had Chambers speak. Hiss looked at his teeth. He stalled as long as he possibly could.

At last Hiss asked Chambers, "Are you George Crosley?"

"Not to my knowledge. You are Alger Hiss, I believe."

"I certainly am."

"That was my recollection," said Chambers with the calm of one who is conscious of ample reserves.

A few minutes later, in a panic, Hiss positively identified Chambers as George Crosley. McDowell turned to Chambers. Was this the Alger Hiss he had known?

Chambers was utterly calm. Positive identification, he said.

Hiss stalked over to him, fists clenched. He was about to do the most stupid thing in his life, and he wasted no time in doing it. "I would like to invite Whittaker Chambers to make those same statements out of the presence of this committee without their being privileged for suit for libel. I challenge you to do it, and I hope you do it damned quickly," he seethed.

He towered over Chambers who remained seated on the couch.

"Sit down, Mr. Hiss," said HUAC investigator Louis Russell.

"I will sit down when the chairman asks me to sit down," Hiss shrilled.

"Please sit down, Mr. Hills," urged Russell.

"I will sit down when the chairman asks me to sit down," Hiss snapped.

"I want no disturbances," Russell said.

McDowell said with heavy authority, "Sit down please."

"You know who started this," spat Hiss.[46]

9

★ ★ ★

ALGER HISS WAS now hung out over a precipice. By taunting Whittaker
Chambers, Hiss had lied himself into trouble he would not easily find a
way out of. His challenge of a trial would force his old friend to produce
evidence in a court of law that would decide who was telling the truth. It
was no longer the word of a glamorous, distinguished, and successful
member of the Eastern elite against a dumpy deadbeat who lived on a
farm in Maryland.

On August 27, 1948, as a guest on the Sunday morning talk show
Meet the Press, Chambers said that Hiss had been a communist "and
could be one now."

And suddenly there it was.

Advocates of both sides froze and fell still, waiting for the avenging
lightning to flash from the clouds of Hiss's wrath, but instead, an absolutely dumfounding thing happened: nothing. Weeks went by. Still there
was to be heard nothing but silence from Hiss. Then on September 27,
Hiss finally sued for defamation, and Chambers, brought to bay, would
stun the country by proving that this highly respected American diplomat
and former friend was a Russian spy. According to Chambers, from May
or June of 1937, for more than a year, until Chambers defected, Hiss had
placed in Chambers's hands "every classified document, cable, report, and

dispatch that he could get his hand on."[47] Some had been summarized in Hiss's own handwriting; Priscilla had copied others at the family Woodstock typewriter. Hiss was not only a spy, Chambers claimed, but he'd been a recruiter, a top Soviet talent spotter, working to subvert Noel Field and Lawrence Duggan in the State Department.

Hiss's attorneys had been visibly stunned at the advent of the documents, but Hiss, made desperate, proved a nimble and adroit liar. He acknowledged that the contents of the documents were of the type he had handled, but said he had no idea how they'd gotten into Chambers's possession. He put on a great act of sanctimony, saying the documents should be forwarded to the Justice Department without delay.

Hiss appeared to have escaped the snare, except Chambers, as usual, had kept something up his sleeve. For years, Chambers had secretly kept back three strips of microfilm, moving the film from one location to another in his house afraid that communist agents or the Hiss defense team might break in and burgle them. On his farm, Chambers took committee investigators to a strawberry patch overgrown by a pumpkin vine. He broke off a pumpkin, took it into the kitchen, and cut a circle, taking off the top, as if to make a Halloween jack-o'-lantern. Inside the pumpkin shone three metal cylinders and two developed strips of film, wrapped in wax paper.

As he had promised, he was going to undo communism by "those arts, which Communism taught me."

Hiss was indicted on two counts of perjury on December 15. On May 31, 1949, his first trial began, ending in a hung jury on July 8, chiefly because of a biased judge. The second trial opened November 17, and Chambers was more self-assured, intent, and hard-driving than ever. The national mood had grown even more depressed and somber. In July, the United States entered the NATO alliance, and the Truman administration had asked for $1.5 billion in aid for the Western European democracies threatened by the huge Soviet Army in the middle of Europe and by internal Soviet subversion. Worse, China had fallen to the communists, and in September, a B-29's sensors in the Pacific picked up radioactive residue that meant the Soviets had exploded its first atomic bomb, an exact copy of a model developed in 1945 by the United States. When he'd defected, Igor Sergeivitch Gouzenko had warned of how the Soviets had stolen from America the information used to make the Soviet atomic bomb, and now the nation was angry and on edge.

As the new Hiss trial began, there was a new witness this time, Hede Massing, the Soviet talent spotter, who told of warning Hiss off attempts to recruit Field from a group already controlled by her. This, of course, supported Chambers's earlier allegation that Hiss had been a tireless spotter of talent, always on the lookout for new operatives.

There was the damning documentary evidence as well. When Hiss once again claimed that the documents produced by Chambers could have been stolen from his State Department wastebaskets, the prosecutor asked sharply that if that were so, why was it none were crumpled or creased or folded?

Hiss replied lamely that it was a mystery.

But the most convincing piece of evidence dealt with the car and a $400 loan. Hiss had initially testified that he had given the car to Chambers, thrown it in with the rent, but when a title transfer showed otherwise, Hiss said he had given Chambers the "use of the car."

But in 1937, Chambers had been in need of a new car in order to flee with his family to Florida. After trading in the old one, he found himself $400 short of being able to buy a replacement. The FBI recovered records showing that on November 17, 1937, Priscilla Hiss had withdrawn $400 from a savings account. Four days later, Chambers bought his new auto. How had Chambers known about the $400, the prosecutor asked. Was he psychic? The prosecutor jeered. But Priscilla told the court she had taken the money out in cash to buy furnishings for their new Volta home. She had no receipts and the withdrawal had almost wiped out their savings, she said, but the money was spent on furnishings. But the lease showed that the Hiss family had not occupied the new home at Volta until January 1, 1938. Once again, the prosecutor brutally pounced on the weak story. He produced a dozen check stubs of Priscilla's written for the same period recording payments of $10 and $15. "Do you tell this court that you cashed all those small checks between the dates I have described when you had this (four hundred dollars) in your purse?" he asked Priscilla. In the jury, there were derisive smiles. Hiss was found guilty of perjury on both counts. At the verdict, his face turned a sick gray. There was a convulsing tightening in Priscilla's throat. He was sentenced to five years in Lewisburg federal prison.

CHAMBERS HAD TRIUMPHED, or had he? Many could not conceal their loathing for the whole school of human experience of which Chambers was representative. First of all, he contradicted beliefs that many of the socially progressive elite of America had accepted to be true without any rigorous examination of them. One of these was an admiration of the Soviet Union. The historian J. M. Powers talked of critics of the Soviet Union and Adolph Hitler, and wondered, why they "did not have more effect, and why these appalling regimes should have been so widely admired." But in every country, there are people of standing, stringent decency, and definite account who think they represent the most developed segment of public opinion, and that they are more concerned with progress, human fairness, and expanding social obligation to larger and larger fields of humanity than others are. To these people, Chambers was a defiler, a Bohemian, a homosexual degenerate, a self-confessed traitor, and a liar, and therefore a man from whom no truth could be expected to come.

His assault on Hiss had seemed an act of mindless malice and perhaps his chief effrontery was to have placed himself on an equal plane with themselves, the most enlightened and progressive portion of America. They felt justified in discounting whatever he had to say.

As we've noted, Hiss made an outstanding public impression, and Chambers did not. But as Nixon said, "Like most men of quality, (Chambers) made a deeper impression personally than he did in public." Nixon added that Chambers "seemed a man of extraordinary intelligence, speaking from a greater depth of understanding; a sensitive, shy man."

But unfortunately, few saw that.

As Chambers wrote later, "It was, not invariably, but in general, the 'best people' who were for Alger Hiss and who were prepared to go any length for him. It was the enlightened and the powerful, the clamorous proponents of the open mind and the common man, who snapped their minds shut in pro-Hiss psychosis, of a kind which, in an individual patient, means the simple failure of the ability to distinguish between reality and unreality, and, in a nation, is a warning of the end."

As Chambers's biographer Sam Tanenhaus observes, Hiss's adherents had sealed their eyes blind to history. The advent of NATO, the subjugation of Czechoslovakia, the Berlin airlift, the Marshall Plan— ". . . Hiss's sympathizers failed to grasp what had been occurring before their eyes," Tanenhaus said.[48]

Literary critic Leslie Fielder said the failure stemmed from ". . . the implicit dogma of American liberalism," which rigidly made the assumption that in a political conflict "the liberal per se is the hero."[49]

But Chambers, the victor, had actually lost more than he won. After the sharp and punishing battle with Hiss, he was out of his job at *Time,* and when he tried to return to a career as a journalist, could find no footing. To survive financially, he had sold off property from his farm, but he had also gotten a literary agent, and suddenly there came the vivid stimulant of something promising in prospect. A conservative editor at Random House, David McDowell, had read two chapters of an autobiography Chambers had begun and McDowell thought them splendid. McDowell wanted Random House's publisher, Bennett Cerf, to read them as well, but as McDowell took the gutsy step of inviting Chambers to the Random House offices, Cerf had blurted angrily, "Get him out of here."

But McDowell reproached Cerf with Cerf's own beliefs—if he were a true liberal, how could Cerf choose to deny a writer a fair hearing because Cerf simply disliked him? So Chambers was admitted, and both former graduates of Columbia soon discovered they had more in common than they thought. Both were soon chatting away about friends they shared. Cerf took some chapters home, but although not impressed, agreed to publish the book, offering Chambers an advance of $15,000, half of which was to be paid on signing.

But Chambers's agent had approached major magazines to talk about serialization. It was an innovative idea to serialize a book in those days— no one had ever done it. Henry Luce at *Time* was interested, but delayed too long. The manuscript went to the *Saturday Evening Post,* a major competitor. *Time* chafed at its rival's activities and made a bid of $30,000 for the book. But *Time* offered too little too late. The *Saturday Evening Post* bid $75,000, and Chambers closed the deal.

Now new, taxing exertions began for the ex-spy.

Chambers stayed on his farm with his wife and two children, working on his book, sometimes writing for twelve-hour-long stretches, beginning at eight and stopping only for lunch or to do work on his barn. The book was scheduled for release in book form in June 1952, but its first serialized portion appeared in the *Saturday Evening Post* in February titled "I Was the Witness." Later, the title of the book was simply *Witness.* In one passage, he began, in a letter to his children, to explain the word's meaning: "I was a witness. . . . A witness in the sense that I am using the word, is a man whose life and faith are so completely one, that when the challenge comes to step out and justify his faith, he does so, disregarding all risks, accepting all consequences."[50]

This, of course, was a task that for years Chambers had been unable to face, always lacking the will to amass the courage to overcome his own timid fears for his own safety. But he quickly acknowledged this with touching modesty, saying, ". . . a man may be an involuntary witness. I do not know any way to explain why God's grace touches a man who is unworthy of it. But neither do I know of any other way to explain how a man like myself—tarnished by life, unprepossessing, not brave—could prevail so far against the powers of the world arrayed so solidly against him."[51]

He was, he said, a witness to God's grace and the fortifying power of faith.

Witness is a work of the first distinction. In its transparent candor, its power of depiction, its self-insight, its relentless brilliance of reasoning, the book is a masterpiece. Chambers's writing instantly has about it that personal accent that represents a special way of looking at life, and he shows on every page the born writer's relish for words. One can perhaps wince when he says, "I see in Communism the focus of the concentrated evil of our times," because we can think of so many things just as evil and just as self-deceived. But Chambers is an unswerving, honest man, and is unerring—sometimes painful—of where the true moral center of gravity lies in a given situation, which makes his book a still unsuperseded classic.

The public saw this. The book was a smash hit, but it wasn't long before the swift-moving torrent of residuals had shrunk and dwindled to a trickle. Chambers owned plenty of land and he began to sell off parcels to keep afloat. He finally got a job at the *National Journal,* published by friend William Buckley, much his junior but a close friend, and at the age of fifty-eight, Chambers also became a full-time student. He enrolled at a local college, Western Maryland, earned a B.A., then worked on a master's of arts degree in romance languages.

When the dean asked what he planned to do with his M.A., Chambers said he had no idea. He said that he only expected that "I shall be different than I am at this moment."

He was a brilliant student, bragging to writer Arthur Koestler that he was getting straight As. In June 1961, his son John got married, and a month after the wedding, Chambers felt sharp chest pains. His heart trouble had begun in 1952, but he had paid it no attention, eating as he wished, getting what exercise he could from his farm work. Now, for the next few weeks, Chambers would feel suddenly drained and experience a feeling of constriction in his chest or a sharp pain in his shoulder, never truly well. The final blow fell on July 8. Chambers felt severe chest pains and knew instantly that his case was grave. He phoned his doctor at midnight, but she was elderly, like himself, and he felt pity for her and told her to wait until morning to come and see him. His wife stayed awake to watch over him, but worn out and made groggy by anxiety, she finally dozed off in the early morning. She awoke in a scare at seven to find Chambers lying motionless on the floor. The doctor arrived and pronounced him dead.

On July 11, the news was made public to the world. Some scoffed, some smiled with grim satisfaction, but others were pierced to the heart. Koestler wrote that Chambers was one of the most "misunderstood men of the time." He then added simply, "The witness is gone. The testimony will remain."

ELIZABETH BENTLEY WOULD outlast him by only two years. An alcoholic, she spent the waning part of her life anything but content, fulfilled, or tranquil. In 1952, she had been arrested in Connecticut for a hit-and-run and spent a night in jail for leaving the scene of the accident. The very next day she had another accident when a truck ran into her. Her conduct remained uneven. FBI files noted she had been in fights, gone on several drinking sprees and was "increasingly difficult to handle." She was cracking up, the agency said.

By 1956, she had dropped from the news and almost out of sight of the FBI. She did some lectures on communism and taught at a school in Hartford that left her very dissatisfied. She was reluctant to talk to the FBI, but turned to them in 1959 with a request they help her establish her bona fides as a teacher. FBI Director Herbert Hoover responded with a tribute he had given her before the Senate. In November of that year, she wrote she had found a position with the Long Lane School for Girls, a Connecticut state correctional institution in Middletown. She died a lonely spinster in 1963. She was fifty-five years old.

Her alumni magazine at Vassar noted at her passing that she was "an admitted communist spy during World War II who renounced communism and helped expose Red espionage in this country."

The Traitor as Petty Thief and National Catastrophe:
JOHN WALKER JR.

*Every counterintelligence man's dream is to be able
to secretly read the enemy's communications.*

—ROBERT LAMPHERE

We had an ally, the enemy. We knew all the enemy's plans.

—COLONEL HOFFMAN ON GERMAN RADIO INTERCEPTS
AND GERMANY'S VICTORY AT THE BATTLE OF TANNENBERG

1

★ ★ ★

THE FBI MEN were growing impatient. It was four o'clock, a Saturday afternoon, which meant they were working a weekend. Nothing had happened for hours, and the chance of making a dramatic collar was evaporating fast. The whole day had been a bummer. Even though the agents knew that the suspect always slept late on Saturday, the FBI had begun surveillance at 7 A.M. The stakeout teams had been stationed at major intersections through which the suspect would have to pass if he left home. For safekeeping, a bureau aircraft loitered overhead at 3,000 feet, flying lazy eights. Hours had passed, and the suspect hadn't gone out, except that one time.

Just after noon had struck, the suspect had emerged from his two-story brick and clapboard house. At the sight of him, everyone had stiffened, and their gaze had grown keen. The man had proceeded at a leisurely pace as he had come down the walk of his house at 8424 Old Ocean View Road in Norfolk and got into his brand-new blue and silver Chevy Astro van. His name was John A. Walker Jr., or "Jaws" to the agents, a retired Navy petty officer. He was a short man, bearded, wearing gold, wire-rimmed glasses and a dark toupee. The agents watching him knew little more than that about him—except that he was probably a traitor.

As the van had pulled away, the stakeout crew had followed him, letting an agent named Hodges have the eyeball, except the suspect had gone only a disappointingly short distance, parking at a waterfront lot and going to a houseboat he owned named *Jaws*. For the next few hours, Walker had worked at putting a fresh coat of paint on her hull before he had returned to his house. Bored and restless, the field agents' minds kept straying to the chores left undone at home, the lawns that needed to be mown, cars that had to be washed, priceless time that could be better spent with wives and kids rather than watching some round-faced man painting an expensive toy. The chores were immediate, the arrest an abstract possibility. Besides, the bureau had never in its history ever captured an American spy passing documents to his Russian handler, and it didn't seem likely it was going to do so that day. By 4:30 P.M., the disgruntled group met in a nearby parking lot. Robert Hunter, the tall, blond, good-looking FBI agent in charge, agreed to call it a day, but he wanted the team ready to go tomorrow, Sunday, May 19th, 1985.

To Hunter, there was something big in the air, and tomorrow was very likely to crest in a momentous climax. The FBI had been tapping the suspect's home and business phones and had heard him say he had an errand to do the next day. To each of his callers, Walker gave a different account, named a different destination or event. But to Hunter and the FBI professionals, there was no doubt something was up: KGB professionals had a penchant for weekend drops.

The tired team finally dispersed.

CI-3 was the central weapon of the FBI's war on Soviet and Eastern Bloc spies. In the Cold War days, there were 4,250 Soviet and Eastern diplomats in the United States, confronted by about 300 FBI counterintelligence professionals. There were twenty FBI squads, each with its own specialty. For example, CI-2 watched the KGB KR counterintelligence section that wiretapped and tailed other KGB agents to ensure their loyalty. CI-3 watched Soviet military spies and worked with CI-6. CI-6 focused on the Soviet military officers not assigned to the Soviet military office or SMO, while CI-3 watched the ones that were. CI-3 was the primary squad handling the Walker case. The Norfolk office was the office of origin (OO), while Washington was the auxiliary office (AO).[1]

Saturday night proved unnerving for the agents, and several slept poorly. But on Sunday, all were in place, when, at about ten after twelve, Walker came out of his house. He was wearing the same gold-rimmed glasses, a black nylon windbreaker, blue jeans, and a deep blue pullover shirt. He locked the house door, then got into his van and pulled away from the curb. Although a retired navy communications man, Walker currently earned his bread as a private detective, and his job required knowledge of surveillance and how to counter it. Soon, without warning, Walker began turning into driveways and going down dead ends, each affording him a vantage point from which to detect a tail. One time, he pulled over to the side of the road and just sat. "He just sat in his van and looked around," Hunter said. "He was looking to see if anyone was following him—looking for surveillance."

It was smart but dumb. The FBI had earlier nailed a Soviet agent working for the Pentagon because the man practiced elaborate countersurveillance as he went home from work every day. Had the man simply gone home every evening, the FBI would have dropped him and begun "spot" surveillance of some other Defense Department employee. But the unusual precautions had put the bureau on the alert.

It was the same case here. Even before that day, the conviction had grown upon Hunter that he was dealing with a man so crooked that Walker could easily hide behind a corkscrew. Walker's counterspy antics made Hunter even more certain than ever that Walker was a Soviet spy.

He would be right.

Walker drove endlessly in the hot, bright May afternoon until at last he turned and headed north toward Washington.

He wasn't alone. Twenty FBI cars made up the squad in pursuit, while overhead the single-engine FBI plane radioed back reports to a command car carrying Hunter. A variety of cars tailed Walker, sometimes passing him only to turn back and creep up on him again, a pattern repeated by them all. By 4 P.M., Walker crossed over the Potomac River on 495 into the Maryland suburbs of the city. The FBI cars quickly converged on a mall and hastily switched their license plates from Virginia to Maryland as other cars kept Walker in sight. He was soon going down River Road, slowing down at certain utility poles. Potomac, Maryland, is a showcase of million dollar homes with swimming pools and tennis courts with area roads climbing and plunging over steep hills. It was the dead, deserted calm of Sunday. No cars were on the road, making it easy for Walker to spot any suspicious vehicle.

The grim hunt was on.

★ ★ ★

BY CONSENT OF most U.S. counterintelligence experts, Walker is the most catastrophic spy the United States has ever had. In war or peace, security of a country's secret communications is everything. As a U.S. intelligence official once said, to have the enemy be able to read your communications is like playing poker with someone who already knows what you have in your hand. In the Battle of Tannenberg, fought on August 30, 1914, the first collision between the Russian and German Empires in World War I, the Russians suffered 30,000 killed and 92,000 prisoners. It was described by General Ironside as "the greatest defeat suffered by any of the combatants during the war," and the Russian catastrophe began to slowly turn the wheels of revolution and began the fatal erosion that caused the collapse of the Romanov monarchy. As a result of its victory, Germany, fighting a two-front war, was able to free forty-two divisions that were sent to the West to fight the French and British in a four-year-long stalemate.

How was such a victory won? There were errors on the part of the Russian command—an attempt to fight a war of maneuver that the Russian troops were incapable of performing—but the chief ally of the Germans was their ability to read messages the Russian leadership was sending to huge groups of soldiers in the field—for example, "On 25 August, the 2nd Army proceeds to the Allenstein-Osterode line; the main strength of the army corps occupies XIII corps . . . XV corps . . . XXIII corps . . . the I corps to remain in District 5, to protect the army's left flank . . ."

This was, in fact, nothing less than a complete picture of the combat as the Russian generals perceived it. It was priceless inside knowledge, a giveaway of "unprecedented in the whole of military history," wrote code expert David Kahn.[2] Although there has been a lot of pointless noise made about renegade CIA agent Aldrich Ames being the super traitor of our time, Ames betrayed Soviet agents and U.S. intelligence operations against Russia. He caused death and terrible damage. But the man who arrested Walker, Hunter, said very clearly, "Ames is no Walker." Hunter added that Walker "was the Soviets' trump card in the event we went to war. Ames identified Russians who were betraying their country, which caused the deaths of several of those traitors. Walker put our entire Navy at risk and is believed to have caused the death of unknown numbers of our men in Vietnam. Which was more devastating? You decide."

The jury is still out on Robert Hanssen, but not on Walker. In 1985,

an FBI agent showed up at my office where I was a national security reporter for an aerospace publication. Wiry, small, but bursting with energy,
the agent was someone I had known for some time. We went across wide
Fifteenth Street to get hot coffee at the Madison Hotel. The agent always
carried a .38 in his black briefcase, and he could look around the room of
the restaurant and tell you which waiters were "locals" working for the
KGB. He was in a fit of incensed and vindictive outrage as he leaned forward over coffee and told me of a spy, a U.S. Navy officer named Jerry
Whitworth, who worked with Walker, and how Whitworth was the "most
deadly spy in U.S. history" who someone should take and shoot in an ally.
The FBI agent was a nice man, a man with a family. It wasn't like him to
talk like this. I broke the story of Whitworth, and the perils posed to the
U.S. Navy by his treachery, but the full story of Walker I never knew until
now.

WALKER'S GRANDMOTHER ANGELINA had come from the coal fields of
Pennsylvania, just as her husband had. In 1907, her husband-to-be, a sixteen year old from Italy, Arthur Scaramuzzo, had stepped down from a
train, all his belongings crammed into one bag. He went to work in the
coal quarries at Scranton, site of the largest bed of anthracite to have ever
been discovered in America. He believed in the American dream and his
values were an immigrant's values: hard work, thrift, piety, and devotion
to family. He was five foot seven inches tall, with broad shoulders, and at
night he studied to learn English. In 1908, he married Angelina, a Catholic
like himself. Years passed and he prospered. He lived in a two-story frame
house, and soon was head of a large family of four girls and four boys.

Angelina was a generous soul, always busy doing things for people—
collecting baskets for the needy at Christmas, mending clothes, baking
bread for a bed-bound neighbor. One of the daughters, Peggy, born in
1913, was a beauty, and she felt entitled to more of society's fine things
than her parents had enjoyed. Peggy had auburn hair and fair skin, and
her beauty made her arrogant. She had singing talents that seemed to add
to that sense of being a better, special person for whom exceptions must be
made. Once when her mother asked her to go to the corner market on
some errand, Peggy snapped, "No. There are some things a young lady
just doesn't do," and the humiliated mother was forced to make the trip
herself.

Peggy had large claims on life, and in 1932, she met a man who felt the same as she did. He was John Walker Sr., lean, handsome, clean cut, with considerate manners, and a shared passion for music. Johnny Walker Sr. had grown up in West Scranton, the son of an engineer, he said. Peggy was smitten instantly: "Johnny was so handsome, and I was so much in love with him. We were so full of life. Nothing was going to stop us, man. Nothing!" She said this to a reporter at the age of seventy-four.

But something would. Peggy may have exulted about being full of life, but she was, alas, a bit more full of life than she thought. She was eight months pregnant when she married, and soon gave birth to a son, Arthur James.

It was a desolate time in America. The country lay numb and disoriented under the Great Depression, with millions of unemployed wandering about like so many ants. Johnny Sr. luckily got a government job, but the money he made was meager, and Peggy was forced to work. For a person who thought themselves born to a higher plane, being forced to become a housewife who fixed meals and changed diapers was a stinging setback, and Peggy instantly filled with unforgiving resentment. But there was a bright spot in the dark of her discontent. In July 1937, she gave birth to a son, Johnny Jr., a boy she took a shine to from the first.

Johnny Sr.'s job as a government clerk soon staled on him. He got another with a coal company, but dropped it after a powerful relative obtained a position for him raising money for the Franklin D. Roosevelt Library. For a time, the couple's cup seemed filled with contentment to the top. Arthur, the old immigrant father, was puffed out with pride at his son-in-law—the American dream was real!

Even when Johnny Sr.'s job ended in 1941, the powerful cousin came up with another that required that sales representative Johnny Sr. represent Warner Brothers in a tristate area, but Peggy's complaints began to fall like cold, continuous rain on her husband—his work took him away too much, he had an eye for other women, and he didn't love her anymore.

Tragedy struck in September 1944 when Johnny Sr. was almost killed in a car accident. By the time he had recovered from his terrible mangling, he had lost his Warner Brothers job, and he faced the humiliation of climbing down the ladder of life from the high and fulfilling place he had earlier reached on it. He glumly went from door to door selling pots and pans, he worked as a department store clerk, he even drove a cab. The haughty Peggy was compelled to take two jobs.

Her corrosive temper only grew worse, and Johnny Sr. began the suicide of his reason by taking to the dangerous restorative of drink. Drinking unfortunately made him thin-skinned, suspicious, and irritable and increased his wife's dislike. The Walker home became a hell of horrors, a place of shrill arguments, shrieks, blows, slammed doors, a place inhabited by two hateful adults and terrified, cowering children.

The darkest day came on November 12, 1948, when a real estate company foreclosed on the family house. Johnny Sr. had failed to make the mortgage payments, and now the movers had appeared. Out went their cherished property, including the boys' Maplewood bed set, Johnny Jr.'s piano, and his mother's plush studio couch. Johnny Sr., the man once thought by the neighborhood to be a celebrity, was broke and in disgrace. Once a larger-than-life figure to his boys, he had shriveled to something pitiable, contemptible, and small.

Once again, Johnny Sr.'s powerful cousin came through with a job, but it wasn't much of one—manager of the Roosevelt Theater in Scranton. But the family was again forced to work.

And in his son, Johnny Jr., there now smoldered an unquenchable hatred of his father. A favorite saying of his was that he would not end up like his father. He repeated it all the time. And he was right. He wouldn't be like his father—he would do and be much worse.

2

From the beginning, John Walker Jr. was a malign spirit to whom skill of pretense came naturally. He had the sinister gift of being able to become whatever the person with him wanted to see him as being, like the lizard that takes the color of the place you put it on. To some, he seemed ambitious, sure of himself, energetic, determined to get ahead in life, frugal, and independent, vowing not to be a failure like his father. Yet like a moon, he had a dark, forbidding side that only a privileged few ever saw. "Jack is cunning, intelligent, personable, and intrinsically evil," said Charles Bennett, a childhood friend who knew him best. With Bennett, Walker stole tires and rolled them down hills at people, threw rocks through the windows of St. Paul's Catholic Church, stole money from unattended coats at school functions, and stole coins from church sanctuaries where donations for the poor were left by worshippers.

Once the two even stole a tin of hosts from the church.

Another one of Walker's obvious gifts was an ability to bend others to his will and, to govern people through their vanity. By instinct, Walker thought himself smarter and more talented than others, and spoke to them as one having been empowered by some unchallengeable authority. "It was almost hypnotic," Bennett said. "I can't explain it, but he became my

Svengali. There was just something about him that drew me to him. He had a certain manipulative power."

His father, Johnny Sr., thinking that regimented coercion could help create a conscience seemingly absent in his boys, sent them to a strict Catholic school, St. Patrick's. There were no grays at St. Patrick's, only blacks and whites. Arthur excelled there, becoming an excellent athlete in several sports, and was even named the most popular student in the school. Johnny Jr. felt the place was a cheerless prison and resisted. His duties were all disagreeable drudgery, done under compulsion, affording no sense of satisfaction or growth of self.

At home, however, times had improved. His father had made a spectacular comeback. He'd left his job at the Roosevelt Theater to work for a radio station, WARM. Because he was a newcomer assigned to the graveyard shift, Johnny Sr. developed a charming and imaginative show called the Night Walker, where he whispered into the microphone love poems against a background of soft music. The show was a huge and instant hit, and Johnny Sr. was soon earning $4 per hour, which most people were getting for a full day's work. But once again, Johnny Sr. fell behind in his bills, he was seen with other women, and quarrels ensued that were so loud, ugly, and harsh that neighbors summoned the police.

In 1954, Johnny Jr. always found a way of escape by buying things. Taking a hefty $590, he bought a 1949 blue Ford to speed around in. By then, he had assumed a persona of scoffing, arrogant superiority. He felt superior not only to people, but to people's rules and laws as well. What Walker could not afford, he stole. When he needed money for tires for his car, a friend named Smiley suggested that they could break into a gas station and steal either the tires or the money. The two boys hit one station but came up empty. They then targeted a men's clothing store; Cuozz and Gavigan's. A foot patrolman discovered them at the rear of the store, and Walker fled in his car. The policeman flagged down a passing car and gave chase. Walker had relaxed, thinking he'd lost the cop, when suddenly at a stoplight, the policeman jumped out, gun in hand. "Stop! Police!" he yelled, but Walker squashed the gas pedal to the floor. The policeman dropped to one knee and fired, but Walker escaped.

A few days later, a tip from his mother turned him in. From jail, Walker called his father, begging him to post his bail. His father was instantly transformed into a person of Olympian detachment. "No," he replied, "he might learn something if you keep him in jail a few nights." His son would say later he was almost raped in jail. "I hated my father so much that night," he said.

In May 1954, Walker committed four burglaries and was guilty of six more that he had secretly confessed to Scranton police. There was even another, far more serious offense. Three months before his arrest, a Scranton Transit Company bus had been held up by an armed teenage bandit and $38 stolen. Walker later bragged about the robbery to his other brother, Jimmy, displaying a moneychanger he'd taken from the frightened driver.

Walker was caught and sentenced to the Camp Hill state correctional institution, receiving a suspended sentence. It was then Arthur suddenly appeared, home on leave from the U.S. Navy. He was quick to get his brother to approach a U.S. Navy recruiter. Because of Walker's record, Arthur went to the courthouse to talk to the sentencing judge. "Your Honor, my brother wants to join the Navy, and I think it would really help him out," he said.

It seemed straightforward, manly, and forthright, and it worked. Arthur returned to submarine duty, and Walker was on his way to boot camp. It was October 1955.

He was assigned to duty on a destroyer when he met Barbara Crowley, the daughter of George and Ann Crowley, at a roller skating rink at Revere Beach in Boston. Born November 1937, Barbara came from a large family of seven children that was in her words, "as poor as it could get." Her father was a welder who worked for Bethlehem Steel at the huge, sprawling Boston shipyards. Her family home was located in Chelsea, a down-at-the-heels working-class suburb. At the age of five, when an accident disabled her father, her mother was compelled to work as a waitress. Barbara's sister baby-sat, and the brothers sold newspapers. At the age of eight, her father died. Her mother soon remarried, and the family moved to Maine. However the stepfather's working pay was paltry, and when he fell ill with a brain tumor that left him partially paralyzed, the family suffered the pressing, wretched helplessness of real want.

Barbara felt to the full the unexpended frustration having been denied any solid opportunity to advance in life. Her inflexible circumstances were made even more painful by the fact that she had always loathed her stepfather. Disliking a parent is akin to hating a shoe that doesn't fit—there is no possible way to escape the torment. Barbara was in ninth grade when her stepfather told her she could not return to school, and instead she was sent to a factory where she spent the day cutting up frozen fish in a mood of sullen rebelliousness. It was a setback that inflicted immense and intimate suffering on her idea of herself. Thanks to her hatred of her stepfather, Barbara bolted from home the minute she legally could—on her eighteenth birthday. She had moved in with the family of a girlfriend in Boston, taking a job as a keypuncher at the Federal Reserve Bank. She caught every admiring eye, her sister said. Although only one hundred pounds, she had a "Jayne Mansfield figure" and long, black hair that fell sexily to her shoulders. "She was a strong-willed person," the older sister said. She was not "snotty" but intelligent and "carried herself with a certain pride."

One night Barbara and the friend had gone to go to a roller skating rink to relax. Barbara had been reluctant to go, but her friend had wanted her to, and Barbara had agreed simply to be agreeable. Like many people who are inwardly aggressive and ambitious, she was outwardly shy, and her haughty aspect captured Walker at once. "Barbara could turn up her nose at anybody," he said later. "She had that Boston-better-than-thou attitude."

Walker was drawn instantly to her looks, but further conversation with her revealed not only a character he liked but also someone with a work ethic he admired. Barbara had that staunch determination that wants to live with strenuous energy even if that energy brought fatigue to her or even pain. No obstacles were going to stand between her and her goals. She was on an 8:05 subway every morning going to work, she was rising in the world.

Walker was conquered instantly.

It wasn't mutual. In spite of Walker's capacity to be endlessly agreeable, she didn't want to see him again. When Walker drove Barbara and a girlfriend and her date home, Barbara got out a block ahead of where she really lived, still defensive and secretive about her background. But they started dating, and by the summer of 1957, the initial mistrust and misgivings had worn away, and the two were deeply in love.

But there soon arose an unlooked for and inescapable dilemma: Barbara was pregnant. For a woman of drive and ambition, it seems incredible that she had neglected to take precautions, especially since she hadn't wanted to have a child. Yet, from some underlying mental laziness or fatalism, she hadn't bothered, letting herself drift along on the dangerously inert hope that somehow the pregnancy wouldn't happen.

When Walker heard of the pregnancy, his passionate attachment fell apart as though it had been put together by pins. Walker's sense of convenience was his law of right or wrong, and this was inconvenient. He bitterly blamed Barbara for not having been more careful. His next instinct was to save himself and jump clear, ditching Barbara flat—simply blotting her out of his mind and leaving her behind to contend with her own plight. But then he felt softened and sentimental when he thought of her family. "I thought, 'Hey, this could be really good. I would have one of those great Italian families like my grandpa Scaramuzzo, where I would come home from work and Barbara and the kids would be waiting for me, and I would tell them stories like Grandpa did. Only I was going to do it right, not like my mother and father had done.' "

But Barbara had not been entirely open with Walker. The sweet days of courtship during which two strangers are trying to find a way into each other's lives also bristle with irrational but vivid fears of offending and thereby losing a new love. Barbara had wanted nothing to lessen her desirability. She was ashamed of her parents and their poverty, and she had hidden their existence from Walker. Her mother and stepfather had returned to live in Boston, and, marshaling her nerve, Barbara took Walker to the cramped apartment in a sad, run-down section of Chelsea and told him then that they were her real family, not the nice jolly Italian family of her friend's where she lived.

But Barbara saved the day by saying, "I've not always been proud of my family, but I wanted you to meet them and know that I want something different from this for myself." Accomplishment, to exert yourself to the full and rise in life—those were Walker's aims as well.

The couple went to elope in New Hampshire only to find the legal age for a marriage license was twenty-one. But then Barbara discovered they could get married in North Carolina as long as the woman was nineteen years old, and they drove to Durham where they became a legal couple on June 4, 1957.

When Walker called his parents, his father seemed quickened by the news, but his mother only feigned her joy. "If you're happy, then I'm happy, Johnny-boy," she said.

Then came disturbing news. Barbara had developed toxemia, and the doctor warned that the baby might be born dead. Behaving with a steadfast bravery and considerate gallantry quite unusual for that day, Walker asked to be with Barbara in the delivery room. He brought her flowers and behaved with affectionate support. He was with her when a normal baby was born, named Margaret Ann, after their respective mothers.

"We named her after you, Mom!" a jubilant Walker told Peggy.

But Peggy tasted a bitter flavor from the past at hearing the news. She would later tell a reporter she was mentally comparing her own marriage to her son's. She had met her husband on a blind date, like Barbara and Johnny Jr. She and her husband had wanted a life rich with success and life's better things. She and Johnny Sr. had also married in haste because of a baby. Peggy was pessimistically wistful: a couple needed time to be just two, time to discover the real self of the other that they loved, time to form closer ties of affection and not be bothered by a baby.

Peggy went and clasped her rosary and, lips whispering, prayed.

WALKER SOON RECEIVED a transfer to the aircraft carrier *Forrestal*, but it meant Barbara had no choice but to go stay with his parents, Johnny Sr. and Peggy. Like dynamite and fire, Barbara and Peggy met and exploded. Peggy was a narrow, imprisoned spirit, with pouncing, tireless eyes alive only to Barbara's faults. Peggy seemed to detect in Barbara some of her own old imperiousness, which only deepened her bitterness. "She was lazy," she said of Barbara. "She expected to be waited upon."

Barbara had her own tale to tell. She talked about how she had done the cooking and how she and Johnny Sr. also did all the housework while Peggy, she said, " . . . didn't do anything but go to work and come home and bitch, bitch, bitch."

When he returned and heard what happened, Johnny Jr. told his brother Arthur he was quitting the navy. He couldn't stand aircraft carriers and navy life was hard on Barbara. They also had hardly any money. Arthur told Johnny Jr. to try and get himself assigned to submarines, and shortly Arthur obtained an assignment for Johnny Jr. on a sub tender. Johnny Jr. was elated. In the meantime, Barbara had another baby, Cynthia, and would be pregnant again two months later.

As a husband, Walker was always on his rights, and as chief breadwinner, he declared he was exempt from helping around the house. It is, of course, the beginning of the death of love when one party in a marriage reserve rights or standings to themselves while not allowing their partner the same privilege—it destroys any pretense of equality. Walker didn't care. He worked sixty hours a week, he said, and she didn't work, and she was the wife, and that was that, period. The whole idea of mutual assistance in the service of the aims held in common clearly meant nothing to him.

3

★ ★ ★

IN JUNE 1960, John Walker Jr. was approved for submarine duty. For training, he went to submarine school in New London, Connecticut, and his wife went back to Scranton. Once again, Peggy Walker and Barbara Walker were like hostile cats sewn up in the same sack.

John Walker Sr., utterly sick to death of the quarreling, angrily bolted out of the house to move back to his mother's place in Scranton. With vindictive relish, Barbara lost no time in telling John that the malice and uncontrollable temper of his mother had driven his own father from the home. When he heard this John Jr. flared into anger, forever affronting Peggy by saying, "If you were half the wife Barbara is, he wouldn't have left you," referring to his father. Peggy smarted profoundly, but she attributed her son's comments to "that witch Barbara."

Other moves and assignments for the Walkers quickly followed: first to San Diego, then to San Francisco, then to Vallejo, California, to serve on the USS *Andrew Jackson*, a nuclear-powered submarine. The relocations of the Walkers would total fifteen in five years, trying for any family. But Johnny Jr. was beginning to detect in his wife abiding, persistent defects of character that threw a shadow of disappointment and uncertainty over the future. For one, she was incredibly lazy around the house. When he came back from a brief cruise, Johnny Jr. found that dirty clothes had been left on the floor, soiled dishes and silverware jammed the sink, and chaos was to be seen strewn everywhere. Plus Barbara, in a mood of spiritless stupor, had begun to watch television for hours and hours every day.

To Johnny Jr.'s disgust, Barbara was fast becoming something hardly useful and decidedly inferior. He explained, "When Barbara and I first met I viewed Barbara as someone who was poor as hell but who had lots of ambition. She had pulled herself out of a sewer and I figured she would claw her way to the top. We were similar in that way. We were going to make something of ourselves." Now this. In his view, he was a thoroughbred who had found itself hitched to a horse cab.

When she went into labor again on November 1, 1962, Johnny Jr. expressed his aggrieved displeasure by an act of petty spite. He dropped Barbara at the hospital to have the baby, then went to play a game of baseball with some sailor friends. Barbara, stung to the quick, named the boy Michael Lance Walker instead of after her husband as they had planned. When Johnny Jr. found out, he was blazingly furious, but she felt a delicious, gratifying moment of revenge.

Things would go rapidly downhill from there.

FOR A TIME Walker seemed to try to absorb the spirit and meaning of the navy. There would be a whole succession of favorable fitness reports, and Walker appeared to effortlessly rise aboard a veritable escalator of advancement, earning seven promotions in nine years. On December 29, 1964, after a background investigation, he was cleared to work with top secret and cryptographic materials, and by August 1965, he became a radioman aboard the nuclear-powered submarine the USS *Simon Bolivar*. Walker was ecstatic. "I was beginning to peak. I was at the top of my profession," he exclaimed.

He was, for once, speaking the truth.

The navy's entire, sprawling, wide-flung worldwide system of top secret communications depended upon the radiomen who operated it. The Classified Materials System (CMS), developed by the National Security Agency (NSA), was run by a chain of code handlers, and the first people in the chain were couriers who ferried code-keying materials for code machines in tamperproof packages under armed guard from the huge, tightly guarded NSA printing plant at Fort Meade, Maryland, to the Navy Accounting Center in Washington, D.C. From there, the Armed Forces Courier Services men delivered the materials to trained personnel at navy shore stations or to Registered Publications Systems (RPS) custodians on ships throughout the world.

The RPS custodian (also called CMS custodian) was in charge of the message center vault in the crypto room, and he not only kept a record of anyone who had seen any NSA codes, but the reason why they had seen them. When it sailed to sea, a U.S. submarine usually carried a five-month supply of codes, called keylists, for its coding machines. Walker soon found that his job was to give code-keying materials to other radiomen whose job was to load the key into a code machine. Every day, the materials, each of which had a number for its use, were kept careful track of, logged in, logged out, and then destroyed under the supervising custodian, in this case Walker. The destruction of the materials was always witnessed by two people who then signed the accountability log.[3]

Walker, like other custodians, was drilled to be extremely security conscious. The military's security rating system begins with "confidential," then moves to "secret," which means information vital to national security, and is followed by "top secret," which means data absolutely crucial to the nation's welfare. A breach in "secret" material can cause major damage to a country, but a hemorrhage of "top secret" materials can be the cause of catastrophe. Not only did custodians like Walker require top secret (TS) clearance, but they also required a clearance for special intelligence (SI), which is highly compartmentalized. As a radioman moved up the ranks, he or she attracted more counterintelligence and security scrutiny. Any radioman eligible to become a CMS custodian was investigated, not only by the National Security Agency, but also by the FBI in separate probes. The commander almost always selected the custodian, and the CMS custodian was almost invariably the chief or senior radioman of the station.

By April 1967, Walker was made a watch officer or CMS custodian of a message room whose task was to communicate with every submarine operating in Atlantic waters. His promotion came at an ominous time. The late 1960s was a period of intensifying competition between the U.S. and Soviet Navies. The Cuban Missile Crisis had brought both sides to the nuclear brink in 1962, and to many military thinkers on both sides, the world was not going to end with a whimper, but with a horrible, blinding, annihilating bang.

In any all-out war with the Soviet Union, the United States was going to rely on its "strategic triad"—a force made up of land-based Intercontinental Ballistic Missiles (ICBMs), B-52 land-based bombers—airplanes as long as sixteen-story buildings that carried nuclear weapons—and a formidable flotilla of Strategic Ballistic Missile Submarines or SSBNs. Each part of the U.S. triad posed a different engineering problem for the Russians. Solving each problem meant forcing on Moscow to make greater increases in Soviet defense expenditures, and each solution reached would absorb more of Moscow's economic resources into defense research and development. To take one example, in order to retaliate against a first strike by U.S. ICBMs, Russia, a country of eleven time zones, would have to have in place a strategic surveillance network able to give early warning of an imminent U.S. attack, a system costing billions of dollars. Soviet satellites would have to be positioned to be able to observe any unusual activity around known U.S. missile fields, while ground-based Russian spies within the United States would try and track the whereabouts of senior U.S. military leaders involved in any launch of ICBMs. In Russia itself there would have to be in place vast, secure communications networks linking Soviet leaders in underground bunkers in Moscow to subordinate centers of command and control at Russian Missile fields sprawled across the huge country. This system too cost billions. And there are even more complexities involved.

Dealing with U.S. missiles whose whereabouts were known or could be tracked were bad enough, but a sharp needle of fear pierced the hearts of Soviet war planners when it came to the U.S. fleet of SSBNs. The Soviets knew that even if a first Soviet strike destroyed all U.S. land-based missiles, the U.S. submarine force at sea would survive and be able to savagely lash back and hurl a torrent of unimaginable horror upon Russia's military targets, ports, nuclear facilities, cities, towns and people.

In the early 1960s, the U.S. Navy won the race against the Soviets to be the first nation to position missile-carrying subs off the enemy's shore. The boats were "Polaris" subs, which were 382 feet long, sixty feet longer than any attack sub, and armed with sixteen nuclear missiles that could strike targets 1,100 miles away. By the late 1970s, the Polaris subs were replaced by U.S. "Trident submarines," which were truly fearsome things. Snub-nosed, five hundred fifty feet long and forty-three feet tall, the Trident was equipped with twenty-four nuclear missiles, each with a range of six thousand miles. They were stored in green-painted silos wryly called "Sherwood Forest" in neat compact rows behind the submarines' "sail."

The firing sequence was complicated, beginning with an Emergency

Action Message, but within six minutes, all twenty-four missiles would be screaming across the sky, carrying 336 warheads, each equal to 50,000 tons of TNT (the Hiroshima warhead was equal to 20,000). The warheads would reach an apogee, then plummet at many times the speed of sound.[4]

A single U.S. sub was capable of inflicting fifty million casualties.

This U.S. sub force was especially terrifying to Russian planners because it cruised the ocean deeps so quietly and in such secrecy, that the Soviets never were sure of where it was. The quietness of U.S. subs denied the Soviets any knowledge of how, where, when, and from what direction an annihilating U.S. undersea missile strike might come. The Soviets lacked the technology to track the boats and knew only that the boats were lurking somewhere out of sight in the world's oceans, biding their time. To have this deterrent in place was absolutely critical to the U.S. balance of power in the Cold War.

But if American U.S. subs enjoyed a superiority in stealth over those owned by the Russians, the U.S. Navy was not risking any relaxation of effort. They didn't want to be caught napping, while its deadly rival made any naval improvements. By the late 1950s, the U.S. Navy began to create an underwater detection net made up of sonic buoys called the Sound Surveillance System (SOSUS) to detect Soviet ships and subs. The buoys were laid chiefly at shallow water choke points and on the ocean bottom ridges and highlands. The buoys not only picked up and tracked the vessels, but recorded their specific sound signatures for future references, recording the data on scrolls of paper that were played over by pens and scrawled slowly out of continuously rotating drums.

In the beginning, Soviet subs posed no real threat to U.S. forces because, in building their subs, the Russians had gone for speed, using two sets of propellers and sometimes two reactors. All submarines use propellers, but the Soviet two-prop design left their boats speedy but very noisy. The noise was called "cavitation" and occurred when a propeller rotated in the water at high speed, creating an area of low pressure behind the edge of the blade. The lower pressure worked to vaporize the water, which turned to little bubbles. Because of water pressure, the boiling clouds of bubbles collapsed, and the water came rushing forward to buffet the blades, making a clearly trackable noise, plus causing the craft to vibrate and the propellers to wear out.

For years, the U.S. Navy had pretty much solved the problem of noise while the Russians lagged far behind, a fact that would prompt Admiral James D. Watkins, chief of Naval Operations, to state that as long as U.S. codes stayed unbroken, "we remain convinced that our SSBN is still one hundred percent survivable" after a Soviet first strike.

It was for this reason that the codes became the chief Soviet target of its intelligence collection efforts. U.S. Navy secrets sat at the very pinnacle of importance for U.S. security. Not even the secrets of U.S. nuclear weapons performance were as closely guarded as day-to-day tactical navy communications, and Walker's job sat right at the center of that covert world. Because of the nature of his job, only he would be allowed to be in the watch room alone so that he now enjoyed unfettered access to this extremely sensitive information. As part of his new job, Walker was required to read every top secret message sent or received by every U.S. sub in the Atlantic, which meant that into his office flowed messages from spy satellites, warships, submarines, and shore stations. If a Russian sub had been spotted off the coast of France, the information was sent instantly to Walker's office. If the Pentagon had dispatched a submarine to the Mediterranean, Walker was the man who relayed the sub's orders that directed it to the Strait of Gibraltar.

The job was a real step up, and Walker enjoyed the sense of increased personal power that accompanies an enlarged and improved ability. He had a position of official, recognized prestige, and the praise and respect of superiors.

Walker had indeed reached a new peak of performance and accomplishment. Except professional success wasn't matched by personal moral growth. Walker was fundamentally dishonest, and at work he remained a sneaky conniver, always trying to manipulate his environment and the people in it. In whatever Walker undertook, there lurked an unseen, self-seeking, ulterior purpose. For example, he joined the ultra anti-communist John Birch Society, and Barbara dutifully hosted coffees for recruits and members. Walker had also enrolled in a "great books of the western world" club and read the selection each month, and in the beginning Barbara also tried to read the books, but could not apply her mind and quickly lost interest. Yet as Walker later admitted, the joining of the Birchers and the great books club "was all show." He portrayed attitudes of open-mindedness, breadth of interest, and intellectual drive only to soften up the attitude of peers and superiors. He was not interested in really *being* a consistent and perpetual learner, but only in being *seen* as one. He always read a selected book in a place that ensured his boss and his fellow crew members couldn't miss seeing what he was reading.

Meanwhile, his marriage had begun to crumble. The great historian Sir Herbert Butterfield once noted that the collapse of civilizations usually comes not from great catastrophes, but from little complicities and petty breaches of faith on the part of very nice people. In a good, sound marriage, there is an adapting to each other's faults, a dissolving of the walls between the partners. Not here. Walker's hard work to raise himself in the navy's ranks and social scale had filled him with such an exalted sense of his merits that he began to act as though the last person able to appreciate his talents with the thunderous applause he deserved would be his wife. By the late 1960s, he had become incessantly unfaithful. This became obvious to Barbara in the spring of 1966 when she got a phone call from a close buddy of Walker's. "I think my wife is in love with your husband," he said. The phone call was numbing, shattering, yet only a few minutes later, there was a knock on Barbara's door.

There stood the wife, all of twenty-two. She said she was leaving her husband for Walker, and one can only imagine the rush of anxious, torturing unrest that flooded through Barbara, but she kept her head and asked the woman in. How had she gotten there? She had driven her husband's car, the young wife replied.

Well, if the women got divorced, she would lose the car, Barbara said smoothly. Animated by the cold alert energy of profound dislike, Barbara displayed in her conversation with her rival an amazing adroitness of mind. The woman, eager to give all for love, had thought only of its delights, not of any of its disagreeable penalties and consequences. Barbara explained to the woman that her husband would no longer support her after a divorce, and she would be forced to go to work, something the woman hadn't thought of. And for the next hour, with great energy and cunning, Barbara worked at undermining and destroying the woman's illusions and chilling the attractions of the affair.

Afterward, left alone, Barbara had her own sense of hurtful insult that smothered her heart in poison. Clearly her husband had slept with another woman. It stung like a stab wound. Yet she knew it wasn't the woman's fault. She knew Walker and the way he worked. Walker had "set her up for the kill," she said later.

She was surprisingly ignorant of the fact that Walker had been and was being constantly unfaithful to her in various liberty ports around the world. She also realized that the reasons that had put off the young woman getting a divorce also applied to her, and in reliving mentally the conversation with the young wife, she found it sobering for her own prospects. In the event of a divorce from Walker, the amount any navy judge would require him to pay would be so paltry that she and the children would not be able to continue living as they had. Up until that time, she and Walker had manifested an amazing fiscal discipline in their marriage. Every time he'd gotten a raise and more pay, they'd immediately put the new money into a savings account on the theory, as she said, "that if we don't have it, we don't miss it." Anything they bought on credit they paid, without fail, within two years, pledging that nothing new could be purchased until the previous debt was off the books. They were almost brutally frugal. Barbara bought powdered milk for her daughters, forgoing fresh milk, and she and Walker didn't even tip waitresses.

Walker was not going to be like his father, he said.

In July 1966, the couple took a step that plunged them into a pit. They bought a 5.6-acre piece of ground in Ladon, South Carolina, south of Charleston, and built a house. Walker and a friend, Bill Wilkerson, a radioman who had worked for Walker, had often talked of becoming business partners, but could never agree on what the business was going to be. Finally Walker decided on a bar, but nothing about the project seemed to have been well thought out. Everything was haphazard, accidental, and lacking in harmony, proportion, and orderly sequence. What would be the cost of liquor licenses and permits? Real estate taxes? State taxes? Who would do the staffing?

The remodeling for the House of Bamboo bar wasn't completed before Walker was again assigned to sea. Wilkerson had dropped out and, in desperation, Walker had convinced his brother Arthur to come in as a partner. Walker saw Arthur as a weakling, not the kind able to persist in the face of difficulties for the sake of realizing a goal. But he had the money and that was enough. Except new complications occurred when Barbara and Arthur got to spend time with each other. To Barbara, Arthur seemed a man more considerate, tender, and caring than her husband, and one day after painting in the bar, Arthur and Barbara found themselves alone. They had drinks, danced together, and suddenly found themselves in a state of raw excitement. Arthur went home, but the next night both were irresistibly drawn together, and after drinks, talk, and dancing, the two of them began an affair that she claimed lasted for ten years.[5]

That Arthur, who was married, would betray his brother by sleeping with his wife speaks for itself, but Barbara's role is troubling and attracts pity. She loved Walker. There was about her an attitude toward him that seemed to say, "For me there is no other." Writer Albert Camus once movingly likened love to two beams of light "painfully searching for each other in the night and finally focusing together in a blaze of illumination," and in her there seems to be a certain degree of that noble feeling.

But Walker was not looking for someone to love, he had already found that object in himself. For Walker, happiness was a transaction—the man gave the woman what she wanted, and she gave him whatever he wished. Over and over again, Walker seemed to estimate Barbara's value solely by the return she offered him, which he construed as her ability to keep him pleased. "She was contributing nothing to my life at the time," he said of her.

Unfortunately with the passage of time, Walker had become more callous and more full of selfish calculation. The health of his marriage or the welfare of his wife were not on his agenda of self-advancement. Larceny was.

The bar opened in September 1967 and was an immediate failure. It was a failure that hurt. Walker was trying to maintain two households, raise four children while living in a trailer, and struggling to pay off a second mortgage taken out to afford the bar, all on a navy salary of $120 a week. When he returned from a cruise, Barbara informed him that a creditor had shown up asking for money, saying that if she didn't have it to pay, "he was going to take it out in trade with me in the trailer for an hour." Cold and uninterested, Walker's only reply was, "Do what you have to do. But I'm not closing the bar."

In December, he would cross the Judas line.[6]

4

★ ★ ★

JOHN WALKER JR. almost got caught stealing his first classified document. He had been working the evening shift, but waited until he was rotated to the morning shift, which meant that he was the watch officer, the highest-ranking person in the message center. Turning his back to the other six men in the room, he put the document in the pages of a magazine that another sailor had left on his desk. Walker waited almost an hour, then at last stood and went to the copy machine in a small, glass-enclosed office. No one had been near it all night.

Walker had always figured if he were going to get caught, it would probably be during his first attempt at theft. He was almost right. He placed the magazine facedown on the copy machine, closed the plastic cover and made a copy of a page. He looked around. No one. He took out the stolen document, put it facedown on the glass, and closed the cover. A voice froze him to stone.

"Hey, skipper you can get in a lot of trouble for what you're doing," crowed a voice. Walker had the sickening feeling of a man surprised slipping money out of his mother's purse.

He turned around. A sailor who worked for him was standing there, coffee cup in hand. "You know better than to copy personal items on the machine," the sailor, with a chiding laugh, said. "Naughty, naughty, naughty."

And Walker gave a strangled chuckle.

In Washington, the taxi dropped him at M and Sixteenth Streets, a block north of the Soviet embassy. The embassy is a four-story mansion built by the widow of George Pullman, the railroad magnate. It is mock French eighteenth century in style, its sidewalk entrance blocked off by a black iron face, its transomed first-floor French doors closed tight by louvered shutters. Walker had driven to Washington in his MG sport car, looked up the embassy address in a phone book, and then hailed a cab. Now he was scanning the street, looking alertly for FBI, which was known to keep the place under constant surveillance. Walker went on past the drab, gray, shuttered old building, then turned around and came back, realizing he'd just given the C-4 division of the FBI a second chance to identify him. (It hadn't.)

A car was just coming out of the embassy driveway, and a burly, broad-shouldered security man was closing the gate shut behind it when Walker slid in, one shoulder first, startling the man.

Walker asked to see the director of security. The Russian's face stayed blank. "Embassy security," Walker said, beginning to panic. The man just stood there, and Walker strode to the front door. He opened it and stepped in, frightening a woman staffer seated at her desk.

"I want to see the man in charge of your security," he said.

The main door behind him opened and closed, and the man at the gate stood blocking the way out.

The nervous receptionist disappeared into a door on the right.

When she came out, she showed Walker into a small office and beckoned at a desk chair. Finally, after a wait of several minutes, a slender Russian in his twenties entered the room. This was Yakof Lukashevich, a security officer.

"Why did you come here?" he asked Walker in accented English.

Walker stood up. "Are you with Embassy security?"

"Why did you come here?" the man repeated.

The burly man came up to stand behind Walker.

"I am interested in pursuing the possibility of selling classified United States government documents to the Soviet Union," Walker blurted in eager expectation.

But not a shade or suggestion of change showed in the young Russian's face.

"I want to sell you top secrets. Valuable military information," Walker said excitedly.

"I've brought along a sample," and he removed a keylist from his jacket's front pocket and handed it to the Russian.

The Russian looked it over with care, then turned and left the room.

To intelligence officers walk-ins are a problem. They may be a "dangle"—someone with information that is enticing but bogus, designed to smoke out the Soviet operatives assigned to handle walk-ins and get a sense of embassy security procedures. By this method, U.S. counterintelligence experts can add pieces of information to a portrait being assembled of Soviet counterspy tactics.

This Russian was clearly no novice. He knew by heart the secret procedures of the U.S. National Security Agency (NSA) because he came back very upset with Walker's document. Why wasn't the keylist signed, he asked.

Walker explained that NSA keylists always had a letter of promulgation on the back that identified them as keylists, but sometimes they weren't signed. The lack of signature meant sloppiness, nothing more, he said.

The Russian, watchful, asked Walker his name.

Walker was momentarily stunned. He hadn't anticipated this. "James Harper," he said, because, like Johnny Walker, it was a brand of whiskey.

The Russian asked to see his identification.

Walker balked. Was this necessary? It was, the Russian said.

The Russian took Walker's billfold and read aloud his real name, and then said, droll, "Thank you . . . Mr. Harper."

Then he got down to business. Lukashevich wanted to buy the document Walker had brought, and he wanted more documents like it. As the Russian went to copy his identification, Walker kept looking anxiously at his watch, filling with anguish. He would be late for midnight watch back in Norfolk. He had been late once before, and the officer he was to relieve had been mad as hell. Walker dreaded angering the man again.

When the Russian returned to the office, Walker complained. He was in a rush. The Russian was calmly smooth. It was necessary to proceed slowly, Lukashevich said.

"The hell it is," Walker snorted.

They talked. Was Walker's motive for coming political or financial, the Russian asked.

"Purely financial. I need the money," Walker said.

It was the right answer. No Americans spied anymore for the sake of ideology. The KGB had an acronym for recruitment motivations of spies, MICE—Money, Ideology, Coercion/Crime, and Ego. If someone, especially an American, said he or she was doing it for ideology, they were lying. It was money and ego that mainly drove post-1940s Americans to spy, and the Russians knew it.

Walker rudely interrupted Lukashevich, who seemed to be trying to conduct a job interview. Walker had rushed for time and was blunt: what he wanted was a lifetime contract for spying. The fee was negotiable, anything from $500 to $1,000 a week. Lukashevich was utterly disconcerted. A lifetime contract?

Walker handed the Russian a copy of his upcoming monthly schedule so that they could select a date for another meeting.

The Russian balked.

It would be better if there were no face-to-face meetings, the Russian said, but Walker disagreed. They would need to set up another to work out details of dead drops and payment arrangements, plus agree on the kind of documents he most needed to steal. Lukashevich and Walker talked, then the Russian left the room and came back with an envelope full of smooth, fresh $50 bills. The total came to $1,000. The Russian placed a sheet of paper on the desk. "What is that?" asked Walker.

"A receipt," the Russian said.

Walker signed the receipt, and the dog's collar snapped fast around his neck. That signature alone would guarantee his continued performance and compliance with whatever the Russians desired for he could be blackmailed into submission.

"We always used to make our agents sign receipts," a former senior CIA agent handler said. "You always want something on your agent."

When Walker arrived home, he had a billfold stuffed fatly with cash and Barbara was suspicious. Where had all the money come from, she asked. "I got a second job," Walker said. And, of course, in a sense, this was perfectly true.

5

★ ★ ★

THE KW-47 MACHINE was one of the oldest in the navy, in service since the days of World War II. It resembled an ordinary typewriter with a large bin full of rotors. Each rotor had a number or letter of the alphabet at its edge, and by setting predetermined instructions in the machine, the code maker printed those letters and numbers at random, in a kind of gibberish.

What acted to sort out the gibberish was a keylist and that was what the Soviets wanted. To make sense of any message, an operator would have to possess the current keylist, which would translate the transpositions by disclosing that, for example, the letter "k" in the message actually denoted the letter "a," and so on. The keylists unlocked the secrets closely held deep inside every U.S. military base, ship, and intelligence installation around the world. That's why the keylists were changed daily—their importance of their security was absolutely paramount.

A keylist would give the Soviets nothing they could immediately act on, but a keylist would enable them to examine past U.S. operations to see what had really happened, how ships and planes had been deployed, and perhaps get some sense of how U.S. Navy vessels and aircraft operated in emergency conditions so that Moscow strategists could form counter-strategies and exploit tactical and strategic weaknesses. The Soviets would

even be able to infer how the top U.S. leaders made critical decisions under pressure. Turning a batch of keylists over to the Russians would be a
catastrophe of unprecedented magnitude, especially if they got one for the
KW-7. The KW-7, used widely by the U.S. Navy, Air Force, State Department, Army, and Marines, was the most important piece of cryptographic
equipment in the United States because daily the most critical and vital intelligence in the U.S. military establishment came over it.

Two disasters would occur that would fulfill the long-held dreams of
the Russians to acquire keylists to the KW-7. The first was John Walker Jr.

To validate a grandiose self-image, Walker had to show the Russians
that they had hired not just a spy, but a spy of astounding talents who
would loom in their minds as a gigantic figure of legend. "I decided that if
I were going to be a spy, and I was clearly going to be one, then I would be
the best damn spy there ever was, and that meant giving them everything,"
Walker said, somehow making his embrace of criminality sound like a feat
of productive accomplishment.

He met with his Soviet contact at a Zayre store in Alexandria. Terms
of employment were agreed on, and he was given dead drop instructions,
ways to contact the Soviet embassy in an emergency, and other information. Walker was paid $4,000, plus an extra $1,000. After Walker went to
National Airport to retrieve his stolen documents from a locker, the Russian appeared behind him. "Did you bring your shopping list?" the Russian asked.

Walker handed him a piece of notebook paper and the Russian's interest grew intense as he spotted the last item: the KW-7 keylist.

In January 1968, in the bottom of a trashcan, Walker left a KW-7
keylist at a dead drop in a Virginia suburb.

The second disaster that would occur to fulfill the long-held dreams of
the Russians to acquire keylists to the KW-7 happened in late January
1968 when the U.S. spy ship, the *Pueblo,* was captured off North Korea
on a mission to monitor electronic intelligence. The crew of twenty-nine
NSA technicians had no time to destroy all the highly sensitive coding documents and machines. Much of the NSA gear that crammed the ship, including a KW-7, were taken intact. The North Koreans then allowed the
Russians to examine what they had captured.

It would take fifteen years for the dimensions of the disaster to emerge.

6

★ ★ ★

FOR YEARS, THE Walkers had avoided thinking "big." They had lived in a way that embodied the idea that the good things of life are obtained by patient stages. For both, having adequate money signified having a decent life, a means of avoiding unfavorable comment, and a method of gaining your neighbors' esteem while building up and preserving your own. Yet the flood of new rogue money appeared at first to have floated John Walker Jr. free from Earth. First he allowed Barbara to spend over $10,000 in cash redecorating a posh three-room apartment. Then, amazingly, it spawned in him a sudden obsession to appear socially proper. He wanted his children schooled in the finer graces, and Barbara abruptly began teaching the daughters to walk across a room with a book balanced on their heads. Wearing fashionable clothes, having good grooming, and making a favorable impression became supremely important. It was a long way from the days of resoled shoes and powdered milk, when the family's dreams barely transcended its needs.

Barbara suddenly transformed herself into the ideal wife, meeting Walker each evening at the door, decked out in a cocktail dress, carrying a martini and a folded newspaper. Walker would go and drink and relax by himself, then come to dinner, presiding magisterially at the head of the table. At the finish of dinner, each child was called on to tell of something of significance that they had learned that day.

But the elaboration of outward forms didn't arrest the inner rot racing through the marriage. In fact, Walker's personal problems quickly multiplied. First, he unaccountably lost his will to work at his navy job. The young sailor who in the beginning had tried in everything he took up to attain such success and perfection as to provoke praise and surprise now acted as though his job was only a boring form of selling himself. By July of 1968, Walker's boss, Bill Metcalfe, labeled Walker's performance at work "abysmal." Metcalfe resentfully described why: "My boss and I would go to sea from time to time," he said, "and when we got back we never knew what the hell was going to be wrong because Johnny Walker had been left in charge." Walker had also developed a smart mouth, and his loose attitude toward women put Metcalfe off: "The guy just didn't have any moral standards as far as I was concerned . . . if a woman looked twice at him, why he'd be unzipping his britches."

Shirley McClanahan, a navy dental technician, had observed the same thing. She called Walker "Mr. Crude." She explained, "If you were a woman, all he wanted to do was get into your pants. That was his thing. Women had one use for him. He tried to go to bed with every woman he met . . ."

Endless sex seemed a strange pursuit for a man who basically disliked women and whose habitual description of them didn't range much beyond the phrase, "Dumb cunts."

WALKER'S TREASON HAD been the dividing ridge of his life, and from that time onward, all his rivers began to flow another way. He had wanted success on the cheap, but hadn't fully counted on suffering the consequences, on having to endure the awful, haunting fear of capture. Like a dime store Macbeth, Walker became moody, unable to concentrate, vague, and full of unconquerable restlessness. During a dead drop, he had gotten into the habit of leaving the car in drive, keeping it in place by putting on the emergency brake. One time Walker, holding a trash bag filled with KGB cash, had to sprint madly after his unoccupied rental car, rolling along empty, after the emergency brake had given way.

"I couldn't sleep," Walker said later. "I was miserable and seriously considered killing myself again, my life was such a nightmare."

Only coarse pleasures seemed able to engage the deepest energies of his personality and move him to action. He bought a sailboat and invited friends and their girlfriends aboard. One woman that Walker took out was Elizabeth Thomas, a nineteen-year-old student, nicknamed "Jimi-Jet" because "She lived her life like a jet propelled aircraft." She would say later of Walker and herself, "Alcohol turned out to be a predominant part of our relationship," helping both to portray an enhanced idea of themselves.

Barbara felt jealous and uncertain, full of unnamed distressing anxieties knowing that Walker was seeing other women, but not knowing who they were. She was deeply hurt, and yet Walker retained a strange, almost sinister hold over her. When it came to Walker, she found her heart could still melt like snow. For her, there was no one else in life. Arthur Walker was there at times for sex and consoling comfort, but only Walker was deeply rooted in her heart.

One matter that did gnaw at her was the source of the extra money, and one afternoon in 1968, a gloomy, suspicious Barbara began to search Walker's desk. She had searched the desk before, but Walker had left a syringe in the desk, implying that he was selling drugs for extra cash, and she had left off looking for a while. But now she was more thorough, more determined, and more patient in her search, and finally, in a bottom drawer, she found a metal box. Having pried it open, she discovered in it drawings of dead drop locations, $2,000 in cash, and a handwritten note that said, ". . . information not what we wanted, want information on rotor."

When Walker came home, Barbara was quick to confront him. "Tell me about the box," she said. "What does it mean?"

Walker did not hesitate. "I'm a spy. That's where I get all the money," Walker said.

Eighteen years later, before a grand jury, Barbara, under oath, claimed that she had called Walker a traitor and that he had given her two black eyes by punching her in the face. Walker vigorously denied this, saying there had been no quarrel about anyone's patriotism. Barbara didn't care about that. Instead, it was the usual, "Why didn't I love her anymore?" His reply had been scathing and cruel, full of the strength of utter and weary indifference. "You want to know why I don't love you anymore? Let me count the ways, Barbara," he said.

And it was Walker's account, rather than Barbara's that has the ring of truth. Reporter Pete Early, who has done the best work on the Walker case, tends to believe Walker's version of the event. Barbara, he said, "rarely mentioned patriotism" in their talks.[7]

And if Barbara truly felt Walker to be a traitor, her horrified repulsion expressed itself in an extremely bizarre form. According to Walker, she said, "Can I get involved with this with you?" She was oddly excited, he said. When Walker asked why she wanted to get involved, she said, "Because I want to prove my love for you. This is something we can do together." Barbara does not admit to this statement, but she acknowledged that she offered to go with Walker on a dead drop, and, in fact, would end by accompanying him on two. On the first, he sat beside her on the front seats of a rental car while he used his powered binoculars to scan for FBI agents. She watched him drop his trash bag of stolen documents, pick up his KGB payment, and when she got home, she pressed flat on an ironing board the tightly rolled-up $50 bills after Walker asked her to.

She was thrilled at the romantic interlude, but all Walker was thinking was that she was a traitor too and that a wife couldn't testify against her husband.

Meanwhile, Walker's navy work continued its descent into the slipshod and halfhearted. Finally, he asked for a transfer, thinking he would feel less nervous if he could live and continue to spy farther away from Washington where there would be fewer FBI. To his delight, he was assigned to San Diego to radioman school at the Naval Training Center. His parting fitness reported he had made "numerous serious mistakes" and noted that his performance had fallen below "his previous level," but his new post was a real plum. At San Diego, Walker was appointed director of the navy's basic radioman school. He then became director of the Practical Applications Laboratory of the communications school. Since his recruitment by the Soviets, he had showered down on them a blizzard of technical manuals, key cards, keylists, and rotor readings for such systems as the KWR-37, Adonis, and KW-26. The material was so voluminous, it was more than the Russians were able to analyze, and they requested that Walker slow down and deliver material only every three months.

But at San Diego, Walker's torrent of stolen data suddenly shrank to a paltry trickle. The chief Soviet interest was in acquiring keylists, and Walker would see few of these in his new job. He had access to some cryptographic material relating to aircraft, brief intelligence reviews of U.S. Naval operations around the world, some secret messages, and some monthly intelligence digests, but that was it. The KGB cut his payments by half—to $2,000 per month.

And Walker's own character was undergoing a sinister change. By choosing to be a thief and a criminal, he had closed the path to other, more promising selves that were open to him to become. Activity is always movement toward an end, and all Walker's energies were now completely absorbed by the hunt for gain. It encouraged a fresh callousness in him. "I got into a what-the-fuck-is-happening mode. . . . There was a certain thrill to it all and a metamorphosis was taking place," he said. He had gone from a fear of being seized at any minute to beginning to feel invincible. He realized that the FBI weren't the tireless, intrepid bloodhounds they were supposed to be, but that they were just inept bureaucrats.

And he faced a perplexing problem. Walker was always craving more and more money, and if he didn't have access to the materials the Soviets required, then he would have to recruit as a subagent for a U.S. Navy man who did. And now came the beginning of a long-term and unparalleled national security disaster for the United States because Walker already had the man in mind. His name was Jerry Whitworth, a sincere, insecure, almost meek man who would prove easy prey for a loud, humbugging, confident man like Walker. In July 1970, Whitworth had become an instructor at Walker's school. Walker was thirty-three, two years older than Whitworth when they met. Walker was drawn to appearances and he liked Whitworth's looks. Although a chief petty officer, Whitworth was the exact opposite of the man with a cigar in his teeth, a fat belly hanging over his belt, and a coffee cup waving from his hand. Whitworth was professorial. He wore heavy framed glasses, had a black neatly trimmed beard, and liked to talk about Ayn Rand's "objectivist" philosophy. He was six feet two and 180 pounds.

In talking with anyone, Walker's mind was always alertly cocked to pick up any signs of moral weakness. Walker soon understood what Whitworth's was. Whitworth had been a poor farm boy, from a one-stoplight Oklahoma town, who had picked soybeans and been the high school class clown. His family life had been profoundly unhappy, he lacked the energy of inner will, and he harbored an inner emptiness and defeatism that was woven very deep in his spiritual fabric. Yet within him lurked a twisted desire to succeed, to amount to something, to be special, and to be admired by people in compensation for having been so unhappy. The things wrong with Whitworth were wrong all through. He was a kicked dog in search of a master, and he found that master in Walker.

Walker sensed this instantly. Walker did not make friends of strong personalities and did not tolerate equality in his relationships. He had to wield the power, and supply the wisdom to be the deciding voice of insight and guidance. He had apprentice disciples instead of friends. The door to genuine friendship is appreciation and liking and its soul is sympathy, which is why the lonely respond to an offer of friendship. At times, Walker appeared able to open his heart to the misery of others and to be uncondemning of their defects and shortcomings, almost as if he shared them as his own. He seemed to be accepting friendship, and in many cases, his deceit worked its magic on its victims. Walker, of course, had his own explanation. "I think it was because I was always doing something interesting and exciting, and they weren't. I was the high point of their lives because they didn't have anything else going for them," he said.

Some were dismayed to see Whitworth fall under Walker's influence. To them, Walker was "a flake" and "a jerk." Michael O'Conner, an instructor and friend of Whitworth's said he was surprised "that someone with Jerry's knowledge, attitude, education and general wherewithal, meaning that he was a squared-away individual, a cut above the street" would associate with "a dingdong" like Walker.

To Bob McNatt, Whitworth's supervisor at the school, Walker was a commonplace and obvious type. "I had been in the Navy eighteen years by then, and I had seen a lot of people like Walker," he said. "(Walker) just didn't seem to care about the job that we were doing, and he never demonstrated to us that he had any special skills or that he knew about anything that we were doing professionally. The truth is that Walker spent all of his time talking about and looking for sex."

By contrast, Whitworth liked Walker: "He was clearly one of the best in our profession. He was smart, clean-cut, a good thinker, and very serious."

It was sailing that brought the two friends together. Walker had bought a new, bigger boat named *The Dirty Old Man,* and Walker started teaching Whitworth how to handle it. Walker was careful to be patient and to treat his pupil as an equal. "I liked Jerry and wanted him to like me," he said later.

Walker had a diabolic ability to sense, and to see into the innermost thoughts of the people near to him. As he talked with Whitworth, he kept an ear cocked for any weakness, waiting to see if Whitworth had any "larceny in his heart." And Walker began to ask what appeared to be innocent questions designed to bring to the surface indiscretions. One night both men were aboard the sailboat returning to San Diego from Mexico. Both had been drinking heavily. They talked of films they had seen, and ventured onto *Easy Rider*. Walker detested the film, boasting he was the only person in the theater "normal enough to cheer when those idiots got shot by rednecks."

When Whitworth said he would like to ride his motorcycle across the country, Walker quickly said, "You going to finance it by selling drugs as they did?"

Whitworth said thoughtfully, "You know, I might do something like that if I only had to do it once. You know, make one big score and end up with a large sum of money so I could do whatever the hell I wanted to for the rest of my life."

With an acute, shrewd instinct of knowing when to back off, Walker didn't pursue the point. But in further conversations, he discovered Whitworth was a thief. Whitworth had divorced his wife years before, but hadn't notified the navy and had continued to collect extra pay for housing given to married sailors. He'd already defrauded the government of $6,000.

Walker began to flatter Whitworth's self-esteem by tokens of special regard and precedence, softening up his prospect, when suddenly, in 1971, Walker's own career prospects brightened like someone turning up the lights in a dim and shuttered room. Because of his unforeseen good fortune, Walker delayed his final "pitch" to recruit Whitworth. He had just become CMS custodian aboard the *Niagara Falls,* a fast, sleek, modern supply ship, loaded with cryptological equipment, whose voyages ranged widely across the Pacific. She contained priceless prey. Aboard her, still in use, were the KW-7 and the KY-8, the latter a new system that allowed an admiral to speak securely to the White House or chief of Naval Operations. There was also the KG-14, the KWR-37, and KL-47 as well as three months' worth of keylists and technical manuals.

Walker spent three years aboard the *Niagara Falls*, and what had been a trickle of data had exploded like a gush from a burst sewer. Soon the Russians were reading U.S. Navy secret messages as easily as U.S. ships were reading them. One voyage lasted fourteen months, another ten, but Walker stayed busy. Working with the industry of a bee, he supplied the Russians with nearly a hundred percent of the crypto data aboard the ship. With a Minox camera attached to a chain that placed it just the right distance from a document, he snapped away at each day's keylist. Every three months, he went through six to eight rolls of film, each containing thirty-six exposures. He hid the rolls in an attaché case until the ship reached port and then made plans to fly to Washington to make his dead drop.

Like jobs and marriage and life itself, spying is a monotonous practice. Walker's procedure for his dead drops were drearily invariable. He would wait until a Saturday to drive to Washington in a rented car. The Russians assigned him six separate sites to go to. A 7-Up can left by one meant they were ready to go ahead, one left by Walker at the second site signified he was ready too, and at a third site, he'd left his documents. At the fourth site, he would pick up his payment and instructions for another meeting.

By 1972, Walker was passing to the KGB "in-country" keylists that were being used in Vietnam only. In spite of Walker's insistence that the Soviets would never pass intelligence to the North Vietnamese, it's clear that they did. Beginning in 1968 through 1973, a CIA station chief (COS) in Saigon, Theodore Shackley, recalled that somehow the North Vietnamese had forewarning of B-52 strikes, and that even when the planes were diverted to secondary targets, the North Vietnamese seemed to know in advance which ones were to be hit. The effectiveness of the strikes was eclipsed, and Shackley said later, "It was uncanny. We never figured it out."[8] U.S. intelligence officials insist to this day that the United States lost planes shot down because of alerted North Vietnamese air defenses. These losses were especially devastating for the Nixon administration, which in 1972 dropped more bombs in Indochina than had been dropped on any enemy in any other war.

The U.S. Navy knew nothing of any of this. It continued its deep sleep. Walker was swimming in money, the KGB had restored his $4,000 per month salary, and he had even redeemed his reputation as a fine navy officer. His fitness report at that time described him as "intensely loyal, taking great pride in himself . . . possesses a fine sense of personal honor and integrity."

But then the world is always taken by the outside aspect of things.

The disintegration at home, meanwhile, accelerated. When Walker once called Barbara "a pig," she replied, "You made me what I am," and he exploded in furious rage. Violent fights began, and Barbara, when Walker was gone to sea, began to turn mean. Parents are supposed to be warm, fructifying suns, allowing their children to blossom in their nourishing light, but the worse Walker treated Barbara, the more Barbara turned on her children.

One time Michael and Cynthia had bought two pet mice at a pet store. Michael loved animals. But when they arrived home, Barbara, who'd been drinking, told them they couldn't keep the mice. Little Ben was the name they'd given one of the mice. Barbara suddenly snatched it up and the children were forced to stand in the bathroom as she dropped it into the toilet and gave the handle a twist. "I saw little Ben swim like crazy, then he was gone," said Michael.

On another occasion, Barbara, annoyed at how long Cynthia was taking to do the dishes, rushed with the energy of hatred into the kitchen and grabbed her by the back of the hair, then plunged her face into the dishwater and held it there. "She held her face under the water. I was afraid, really afraid, that she was going to drown her," Michael said. When Barbara finally let her daughter up for air, she began hitting her.

Yet as much as she hated Walker, and as empty as her life was of anything worthwhile, Barbara still loved her husband enough to go on another dead drop. "I was still trying to keep the marriage and my family together, and I thought if I kept showing him how much I loved him, things would be all right," she said.

7

★ ★ ★

AFTER HIS TOUR ended with the *Niagara Falls* in 1974, John Walker Jr. knew he had to retire from the navy. A few years before, he had, with great ingenuity, forged his own security clearance, but he knew now he would fail any lie detector test. He needed a subagent. The year was 1974 and Jerry Whitworth had already retired from the navy, but his retirement had been a ludicrous fiasco. Whitworth had tried night school and failed. Between June and December, he had then tried to learn to fly and make money spotting swordfish in the Gulf of California. He had no civilian profession, no vocation, and, at bottom, wanted a life free of hardship, not requiring great physical effort or a great degree of concentration. After four months of floundering in civilian life, Whitworth reenlisted in the navy reserves, then, a month later, left the reserves and reenlisted for four more years.

He would become Walker's partner in treason, but in his final pitch, Walker led Whitworth into it carefully, like someone leading a blind man from one dry stone to another as they crossed a rushing brook together. Whitworth had to first promise he wouldn't go to the authorities, even if he refused the offer and didn't want to get involved. Whitworth solemnly promised. Then came the flattering compliments from Walker—how he was only telling Whitworth all this because his friend was the only person he would ever trust, and how he was "putting my balls in your hands with this."

It was all premeditated. "I had thought about this for a long time, and wanted to touch all the right spots," Walker said. He employed a clever device, called in the spy trade a "false flag" recruitment. Rather than tell Whitworth he was selling information to the Soviets, a fact from which Whitworth might recoil, Walker made Whitworth think he was selling material to Israel, which Whitworth saw as a beleaguered ally of America. It didn't matter that Walker disliked Jews.

Walker had been a good spy, but Whitworth would steal the navy's "crown jewels." Whitworth was assigned to the small, desolate island of Diego Garcia in the Indian Ocean, a seven-mile-square coral atoll owned by the United Kingdom. There were forty odd code machines on the island and Whitworth had access to all of them. He and Walker arranged a primitive verbal cipher, to avoid any alerting words. Whitworth liked to scuba dive, and if he had photographed a top secret document, he was to call the theft a "dive." Three months after his first theft on the island, he wrote to Walker, "I finally made my first dive. It was real good."

The evil machine was in motion. After Whitworth completed his tour at Diego Garcia, he was assigned to the USS *Constellation*, an aircraft carrier, which traveled the Pacific. Whitworth operated the crypto and communications equipment aboard the ship, whose code room processed as many as 2,000 messages per day. Whitworth had photographed the technical manuals for three of the navy's most heavily used code machines, the KW-7, KWR-37, and KY-36—almost the equivalent of giving the Soviets the actual machines! In July 1978, he left the *Constellation* and went for a tour aboard Walker's old ship the *Niagara Falls*. By then he and Walker were making $4,000 to $6,000 a month spying. It was while aboard the *Niagara Falls* that Whitworth made the greatest theft in his entire traitor's career. The take included complete diagrams and manuals for the KW-7, KY-8, KG-14, KWR-37, and KL-47 cipher machines plus keylists for fleets deployed in both the eastern and western Pacific.

When Whitworth completed that tour, he again talked of retiring, but Walker persuaded him to ask for a shore assignment, and Whitworth was assigned to a position that would be, for the KGB, a place without price for a spy—the telecommunications center at Alameda, California, which processed 1,300 messages per day. There Whitworth was promoted to chief petty officer in charge of the Naval Training Communications Center, not only serving as CMS custodian but also in charge of the AU-TODIN message center. He was able to secure a whole month's keylists by removing them in an attaché case, taking them to a van parked in the lot by the docked ship, photographing them, and then returning them to their safes. Two aircraft carriers were based at Alameda, and all their communications were channeled through Whitworth's office. The take was beyond belief. It meant giving away to the Russians future assignments, operational plans, and even prospective ship modifications.

Another incredible Whitworth coup was soon to occur. In October 1982, as chief radioman, Whitworth was assigned to the *Enterprise* as communications watch officer. He was at this post during FLTEX 83-1, a three-carrier training exercise involving forty ships and 250 aircraft in the northern Pacific. His position meant he could monitor and steal messages passing to and from the units, the carriers, the planes, the participating Air Force, and the Canadian units, and he could pass back to the Soviets records of intrusions by U.S. planes into Soviet airspace to see what radars came on and what other defensive reactions took place. The Whitworth data could give the Soviets a good picture of the entire architecture of U.S. Navy communications. Giving the data to the Soviets meant that Whitworth saved the Russians at least fifty man years of analytic labor, according to U.S. Navy intelligence officials.[9]

Whitworth began to be rich, and his greed was growing the more it was fed. Walker had retired from the navy in 1976, and two years later, Whitworth had been assigned to Walker's old ship the *Niagara Falls*. Walker, in the meantime, paid Whitworth $28,000 and $100,000 in $50 and $100 bills, and another $110,000 in 1981. Whitworth—the man who had once told a girlfriend that he never wanted to own any more possession than could fill a Volkswagen bug—began to amass possessions. He bought $20,000 worth of personal computer equipment, and during one shopping spree, ran up a bill of $1,218.90 at Mohad Adid Abdallah's television store. And there was the Fiat convertible, the Mazda sports car, "his" and "her" motorcycles, big tabs at the better restaurants, the two sculptures, and a painting purchased for the house.

In fact, both master spies were succumbing to the desire of successful men to put their prowess in evidence by exhibiting some durable results of their exploits. When it comes to rating and grading people, the eyes of most go first to what we observe them owning or using, and Walker and Whitworth, by displaying their wealth, were legitimizing a life based on fraud, seeing their expensive possessions as proof of superior ability and a way to achieve a height above their peers.

IN FEBRUARY 1975, Barbara, who had been incapable of action or putting together a plan, finally served Walker with divorce papers. Their empty husk of a marriage had buckled in ruin long before. The couple had separated, and Walker moved to the Beachcomber Motel and Apartments in Norfolk, a few blocks away from his home. His idea of being a father at the time was, ". . . there was no problem so big it couldn't be run away from." As a result, the children grew to be totally out of hand. Laura, defiant and indocile, was twice sent to juvenile detention homes. Margaret and Cynthia were chronic runaways. Michael was addicted to sex, smoking marijuana, and drinking. Barbara was increasingly drunken, threatening, and erratic, displaying some deep-seated reluctance to contend with everyday life. We see it in her not being able to steadily hold a job, in her addiction to alcoholic torpor and television, in her letting her children buy her airline tickets, and in her borrowing hundreds of dollars from her daughter Laura that she never repaid. Barbara remained inert, scorning even the basic exertions without which most human characters begin to decay and their energies expire altogether.

BUT SLOWLY, OVER time, she began to harden, especially when it came to money. When Walker was served the papers, he flew into a perfect fury of self-righteous vexation. Then he tried to appeal to practicalities—Barbara was going to lose all her medical benefits, a divorce might damage the children emotionally. He even asked her, incredibly, what was wrong with the way they were living now?

But again, his anxious concern was only for his own safety. He had long ago discarded any feeling for Barbara or their marriage and harbored little affection for their children. Now he worried about being betrayed. "I didn't want her blabbing things to her relatives and having them tell the FBI," he said.

But Barbara remained adamant about getting the divorce. When it came to money, Barbara had a hard, unforgiving mercenary streak that couldn't be trifled with, even by Walker. She wasn't simply going to fade into vapor as he wished. No. She wanted Walker to pay her $10,000 in cash, $500 a month in child support, and $1,000 a month in alimony. Walker, completely staggered by the steep financial demands, retorted that there was no way he could afford those amounts—his navy salary at the time was only $18,000 per year.

And then there occurred something baffling and astounding.

Like Walker, there was about Barbara something of the child that is unable to develop beyond a certain point. Recoiling from the finality of complete adult independence, she agreed to accept $1,000 in spy money under the table for alimony. She had mustered the backbone to break up with Walker, to end the marriage, only to immediately relapse into dependence on him and reinvolve herself with him, not as his wife, but as his criminal accomplice. She was like a drug user who wants to end an addiction but doesn't dare to endure the pangs of immediate and total abstinence and so squirrels away a few more pills in case of relapse or weak need. For Barbara, Walker remained a fall-back, a sea anchor to windward, out there just in case.

The divorce became final in June 1976, the same month Walker retired from the navy. The first week of July, Barbara received an envelope that contained $1,000 in cash. In addition to the cash and child support, he gave her three lots in Florida that he'd bought for investments, worth $40,000.

Barbara was satisfied. She bought a brand-new Ford Monte Carlo and moved to Maine.

8

A BLEAK, BAFFLED Richard L. Haver could only sense that the U.S. Navy was confronting some fresh, unknown, and cunningly malignant force. As he reviewed the failed missions, the compromised programs, the strangely ominous changes in Soviet submarine strategy, he fought down the dark premonition of disaster slowly building inside him. Haver was a former intelligence officer who had worked in operations in Vietnam. While serving there, he had met Bobby Ray Inman who, in a twenty-eight-year navy career, had risen through the officer ranks to become a three-star admiral. Inman was boyish, with a large head, a toothy, winning smile, and thick glasses. Under Jimmy Carter, Inman would head the National Security Agency (NSA), America's largest and most powerful intelligence outfit. It was Inman who would also play a critical part in convincing Haver to forgo law school and remain in intelligence work.

It's hardly a surprise that Haver would heed Inman's advice. Inman was a man of special, arresting interest. He was described by a reporter as "the only intelligence specialist to serve as an executive assistant and senior aid to the Vice-Chief of Naval Operations" in the early 1970s when he had monitored some of the navy's most secret intelligence programs.

"Ivy Bells" had been one such program. Approved in the early 1970s, the plan was to use a U.S. Navy and NSA team, operating from a submarine, and place a telephone tap on a Soviet cable that ran from the Russian missile submarine base at Petropavlovsk on the Kamchatka Peninsula and under the (mainly) ice-covered Sea of Okhotsk, where it joined landlines that ran to Soviet Pacific Fleet headquarters at Vladivostok, and on to Moscow. In August 1972, in a tense, risk-ridden mission, the NSA spooks aboard the submarine *Halibut* had successfully placed the tap that "violated every soul of Soviet secrecy."[10] A renegade former employee of the NSA would later compromise the program, but for a time, the tap had given the U.S. planners priceless information on new Soviet cruise missiles, details on how the Russians moved troops, details of fleet plans and operations, and the like. It was a tireless, producing gold mine that gave information far beyond what any dead drop or defector in place could produce—all through access to high-level military messages too important to be sent by radio or any less secure means.

Because of such programs, Haver understood and appreciated the combat and intelligence value of the U.S. submarine. With their future, he saw, lay the nation's fate. To him, they were truly wonder weapons.

Nuclear submarine duty was always demanding duty. The crew usually numbered 150, divided into three teams of fifty. Patrols lasted seventy days, preceded by thirty days of preparations on shore and followed by another hundred days of training and leave while another crew took over for a hundred-day schedule.

Life aboard was a trial. The crew work consisted of an unvarying schedule of six hours on, twelve hours off, sleep to be taken in a three-tier bunk bed. Life was quiet. There was nothing to disturb the silence of the night watches except the creaking of the bulkheads as the craft rose or sank in the depth of the sea. Off duty, the crew watched movies or played penny ante poker or studied correspondence courses. There was no TV, no mail, and no newspapers.

This was due to the vessel's secrecy. Its invisibility was priceless, its reason for being. The sub kept in contact with its headquarters by means of wire antennas that were allowed to float near the surface, attached to a squat torpedo-shaped "kite" so that the crew could pick up twenty-word messages from the crew's families, transmitted from Cutler, Maine, or North West Cape, Australia, by VLF (very low frequency) radio waves, capable of penetrating water. These transmissions were backed up by messages from Lockheed C-130 Tacamo communications aircraft. The sub never responded, never identified itself, and rarely even used its identification friend or foe (IFF) system, since the device would give away its presence.[11]

The whole strategy of tracking Soviet subs quietly in order to destroy them before they could salvo their missiles in time of war rested entirely on the U.S. Navy's codes remaining secure and on U.S. subs retaining the lead in undersea quietness, a lead the U.S. Navy had always enjoyed over its enemies.

Yet something had gone horribly wrong. By the late 1970s, the Soviets seemed to have somehow become aware that the United States had the ability to detect and trail its submarines. Moscow suddenly sent out fast attack subs to accompany its Yankee and Delta strategic missile submarines that represented a truly frightening leap in technology. Nor was that all. The Soviet attack subs were behaving in unpredictable and abnormal ways, abruptly circling back on the Yankees and Deltas like a wary cat sizing up a strange, unfriendly room—almost as if they knew someone might be there behind, following. The Yankees were quiet but quite easy to track, but the Soviets attempted to remedy this by fielding a new, even quieter submarine called the Victor III attack boat—again, almost as if Russians had been warned to mend their noisy undersea ways and had been cautioned that more silence beneath the sea was absolutely critical to any success in combat.

Within the U.S. Navy, a feeling of profound anxiety began to spread. The undersea craft had always been given top secret rendezvous points with other U.S. subs, the location held in the strictest security. Except now, when the U.S. subs arrived on spot to retrieve new command messages, there were other hostile, shadowy presences hovering in the waters nearby—Soviet subs or spy trawlers unaccountably loitering on the scene. Startled out of their wits, like a horse that bolts at the rustle of a snake, the U.S. sub commanders would quickly abort the rendezvous and flee, but there were other unexplained, unaccountable menacing occurrences, such as Soviet subs that recklessly hurtled right through U.S. fleet exercises as if to provoke reactions that could be electronically recorded, or the Soviets would appear at a place scheduled for a U.S. fleet exercise that had been canceled by Washington at the last minute. What had brought the Russians there?

The shock at first strangled the minds of some U.S. intelligence analysts in a kind of nightmare. It was almost as if the Soviets could foretell the moves American vessels were going to make. Everyone in the U.S.

Navy leadership had for years found comfort in the confident conviction that the Soviets' sixteen-missile strategic subs were their only good chance of surviving a preemptive U.S. attack, and suddenly they felt like men stranded in the middle of a tightrope that had just been given a profound shake.

Hard eyes and tough minds began to reassess the situation. Intelligence officers hate coincidences by instinct. Too many coincidences violated a decent sense of odds, the very laws of probability. Some U.S. officials smelled a plot and suspected a spy behind the new occurrences. Others simply knew that essential elements of the crisis were being miscalculated, but which? No one knew.

The navy had already redoubled efforts to gain fresh intelligence partly in an attempt to discover what was going amiss. New and daring intelligence-collection missions were undertaken almost in a mood of desperation. There were moments of towering audacity, of breathtaking hazards, of brushes with death, of narrow escapes from discovery, of harrowing difficulties. The *Parche,* for example, in an epic mission that lasted 137 days, used untried, devious routes to avoid any chance of enemy surveillance and was able to plant taps on Soviet cables on the bottom of the Barents Sea because U.S. spooks believed the taps would give access to direct exchanges between Soviet fleet officers and shore installations. The taps would not only show how the Soviets planned, moved, and did business, but also might give U.S. analysts a clue to what had gone so wrong with U.S. Navy security.[12]

In a tiny compartment behind the torpedo room, the spooks on the *Parche* were packed as close as sheep in a pen, while the sub loitered in grave peril of Soviet discovery. On an earlier mission, it had taken the spook specialists two weeks to sort through the hundreds of lines running through each cable to choose which ones were to be tapped and at what specific time. While it remained on station for a week to listen to the tap, the *Parche*'s officers knew that if Soviet listeners somehow detected the sub's prowling, all would be over. Discovery threatened grave disaster for the ship, and far in the back of a few officers' minds, there moved visions of ghastly catastrophe—of sudden gushing inrushes of water, of clawing, scrambling, frantic figures, and of dreadful panicked cries. It was a fear that officers felt but never made specific to the crew. As a crewmember said, "Here you've got some one hundred some-odd guys willing to die, and they don't even know they're truly in a situation where they might."

From then on, every nerve was strained. No one in the operations spared himself or herself any stress of exertion or any agony of peril or weariness. The U.S. Navy could not afford to make anything less than the utmost exertions because at stake was the nuclear balance of power.

THE SOVIET COLOSSUS cast no spell over the new president, Ronald Reagan. With the new administration came a sense of urgency, an imperative to regain a military superiority and to restore U.S. prestige, which the new group felt had been carelessly squandered. The years under Richard Nixon and Jimmy Carter had been years of détente, to both men a process that had been merely a matter of recognizing the fact that, however reluctantly, the United States shared the planet with the Soviet Union, and that by developing new cultural and commercial ties, the United States could better extend its influence with the Soviet leadership. There is a whole school of diplomacy, derived from commerce, that emphasizes that it is chiefly through trade that human beings first learn compromise, toleration, and common sense in their dealings with each other. The minds behind the détente were an expression and outgrowth of that school.

But the Reagan administration belonged to a second school that saw the purpose of diplomacy as victory and victory alone. To this school, the denial of complete victory meant defeat. Diplomacy was ". . . an unremitting activity directed towards ultimate triumph . . . an endeavor to outflank your opponent to occupy strategical (sic) positions . . . to weaken the enemy by all manner of attacks behind the lines; to seek every occasion for driving a wedge between your main enemy and his allies," a British diplomat Harold Nicolson neatly put it.[13]

To Reagan's new crew, Moscow had been emboldened throughout the 1970s by American timidity and flabbiness. Those days were over. In early 1983, Reagan had called the Soviet Union "the evil empire" and challenged the Kremlin's legitimacy as a government. He also called for internal policies to be changed inside the USSR, the first time any American president has done so since Harry Truman.

Under Reagan, there was going to be a titanic military buildup that would expand the U.S. Navy from 450 ships to 600 ships. There would also be more appetite for head-on collision as well. The new policy was enunciated by Navy Secretary John Lehman in 1981. Lehman's idea was to use the U.S. Navy to show the Soviet Union who was boss, and no one doubted he would. The new Navy secretary was known as brilliant, brazen, tough, able, and mean. He was a cocky operator who simply dealt with opposing opinions by shouting them down. He was also a man of charm. In his early forties, Lehman displayed strong, tan, shapely hands, and was a compact 170 pounder that stood five feet nine inches. He was a man who liked wearing wide-shouldered double-breasted blazers. He was also a man who believed that someone who was modest had much to be modest about, and in the navy public relations officer's room, all four walls displayed framed newspaper articles and magazine covers showing Lehman in an aviator's helmet, in a flight suit (he was a qualified A-6E Intruder pilot), or in a dramatic debating pose. A navy officer explained, "This is secretary's I-love-me room. Every once in a while he comes in here. It's an ego trip for him."[14]

When Haver gave the Reagan group his gloomy briefing about the Soviets appearing to be massing the bulk of their attack subs, ships, and planes to protect Soviet ballistic nuclear subs being held back in bastions, Lehman was there listening, chin set, an alert, flinty look in his eyes. Under Lehman, who once called Henry Kissinger "an outright communist,"[15] the navy was going to have a new and more aggressive forward strategy, which meant moving U.S. naval units into "high threat areas" near the Soviet Union.

In April 1983, the navy dispatched an exceptionally powerful battle group, including three aircraft carriers, part of a forty-two-ship armada manned by 23,000 men, Air Force B-52 bombers, and F-15 fighters, and 255 shipboard planes, to head for the Kamchatka where the armada began operating within the accepted patrol area of Soviet submarines.

The three-carrier formation was critically important because if the U.S. Navy were ever to attack Soviet shores, it would use the aircraft carrier, the most powerful ship in the U.S. Navy, savaging the Soviet Union in its home waters and ports. The Pentagon had taken a year to carefully prepare in detail for this exercise, and the carriers enacted an incredible range of intricate maneuvers to be used in wartime as part of a dozen or so actual attack scenarios. Navy and air force planes engaged in mock attacks and reconnaissance missions, while U.S. subs, playing the part of the Soviets, tried to penetrate carrier group defenses and Anti-Submarine Warfare warnings.

An important part of the mission was to gauge the Soviet degree of defensive response and to carefully track any electronic emissions crackling across its extensive surveillance networks. Throughout the Cold War, both superpowers played a dangerous game of chicken in which both sides dispatched flights of bombers or fleets of ships toward each other in a manner that suggested they were going to attack. The purpose was to make the mock attack seem so real that the enemy would "light up" its communications—its radar warning and defensive targeting systems. It was dangerous because the side being attacked wasn't always quite sure until the very last instant whether the attack was real or simply a drill. What the United States would see, in the words of former CIA official George A. Carver, would be "patterns of command subordination, organizational tables, location of units, movement of units, signature characteristics of certain types of message, such as attack orders . . ." without having to read a word of Soviet code.[16]

As the exercise went on, navy officials felt their dark uneasiness deepen to apprehension as they realized the Soviets weren't reacting much at all. In fact, they stayed eerily inert. When a similar exercise had been directed only a few months earlier at North Vietnam, the response was everything the navy analysts could wish for. The Vietnamese turned on everything, allowing the United States to identify missile sites, airfields, and anti-aircraft batteries, and even to isolate the emergency frequencies used by different units. But this time, the Russians didn't stir at all. It was especially puzzling because Russian electronic reaction to smaller and less important exercises in the past had been emphatic and intense. But now it was almost as though they had "known the Navy was coming and possessed a copy of the operational plan . . . ," as if they knew "exactly what the Navy was attempting," commented intelligence writer John Barron.

They had.

Whitworth, having been persuaded by Walker to stay in the navy, had been assigned aboard the aircraft carrier *USS Enterprise* as radioman when it had been in a mission off of Vietnam that obtained critical intelligence while performing a similar mock attack. In that exercise, the U.S. carriers had operated just the way they would in an actual attack, and Whitworth was privy to all of it.

The radio room of the *Enterprise* processed 2,000 day-to-day operational radio messages, sent out in exactly the same order they would have been in the event of actual war. All the objectives of the exercise had been collected in thick books that had been given to all the participants.

Whitworth would sell the books to the Soviets, plus he had also selected a twelve-inch stack of messges that he felt would earn him the most money. The result was to give the Soviets a step-by-step breakdown of how the U.S. Navy would proceed to deploy a U.S. joint carrier group in an actual wartime attack. Since the exercise had been done in coordination with Canadian forces, the Soviets now had a clear idea of how America's northern neighbor would operate as well.

By 1983, however, Whitworth was no longer the ardent spy he once had been. He had been a strange choice for an agent. Walker believed he could lead and manage Whitworth like a child because Whitworth was an amiable muddler with a weak and intermittent will. In addition, perfectly vacuous ideas were always arching up like rockets inside Whitworth's head to burn out in darkness almost as quickly as they came. At various times, Whitworth would tell Walker he was thinking of retiring from the navy to become a stockbroker (for which he failed a qualifying test and had no talent), or saw himself a computer salesman (for which he had less talent), all of which would send Walker into a panic.

After the *Niagara Falls* had gone into dry dock in 1978, Whitworth again thought of quitting, but was persuaded by Walker to ask for shore duty instead. He ended up at Alameda where he was promoted to chief petty officer in charge of the Naval Training and Communications Center, serving as CMS custodian and chief of the AUTODIN message center.

But Whitworth was a man who scared easily. When a security breach occurred at Alameda, swarms of investigators had appeared, and Whitworth froze, thinking that the bottom had suddenly fallen out of the cask. He wasn't a suspect, but Whitworth's milky mind at last grasped that he was a player in a game that had harsh and terrible penalties for failure. He was transferred to Stockton for three months to help install a communications system and there had no access to codes. He then returned to his work at Alameda, but Walker saw at once he wasn't the same man. Walker had persuaded him to ask for duty aboard the *Enterprise,* but even that was only a temporary expedient.

Whitworth, like Walker, still dallied with a kind of pitiful, twisted wish to be heroic. In Norfolk, Whitworth had remarked to Walker, "Doesn't it bother you that we both will probably die without anybody knowing how good we were?"[17] But to Walker, Whitworth was clearly losing his fire. One time, when he talked of retirement, Walker had sternly warned him, "Look, Jerry, this is big-time espionage. You don't just walk out. Who do you think you're dealing with? Some little guy in western New York?" By this time, Whitworth had known that the Soviet were his real employer, not the Israelis.

Whitworth did perform admirably aboard the *Enterprise,* but he was getting both grandiose and greedy. He complained to Walker that he wasn't getting paid enough, and to demonstrate to his employers that he was playing an indispensable part, he deliberately withheld two-thirds of the documents he had stolen aboard the *Enterprise,* and, on purpose, fogged some film of secret documents that Walker had taken with him on a trip to the Soviets in Vienna. When the Russians saw the film, they bared their teeth and refused to pay Whitworth.

When Whitworth was told he was not to be paid, his face instantly turned quite white. Inwardly, he smarted with wounded rage and, for revenge, he began to toy with the idea of betraying Walker, writing coy letters to the San Francisco office of the FBI about an undiscovered spy ring that was passing codes and technical manuals to the Russians.

WALKER WAS A man given to looking ahead, especially when it came to securing his espionage income. If Whitworth was like the car that you never were certain would start, then Walker had to ensure he had an agent in place who would have continued, guaranteed access to codes and crytpo and who could provide him with a steady supply. He began coldly eyeing his offspring.

Walker had always viewed his children without affection. Like his friends and contacts, they were simply expendable capital. They were only objects of assessment, of thought, even of faint interest, but only objects. They touched neither his heart nor his intelligence. He called his wife "bitch breath," and his children "little bastards," and after moving out, he hadn't maintained any contacts with any of them. Now, with chilling ruthlessness, he began to assess which one of his kids would be the best to advance his schemes. His daughter, Laura, was the first. Walker picked her because his daughter Margaret "was a total loser," and "Cynthia was destroyed."

Laura had joined the army, a service Walker didn't like because it had too many blacks, and Laura hated blacks too. But Laura was tough and independent, and she craved attention, always liking to be "in the center of the spotlight." The "E" for ego in the KGB acronym MICE just might be the key that turned in her lock, Walker thought.

The porch lights of Walker's fatherly charm switched on, and the warm brightness was sudden and dazzling. Walker took Laura out on his boat, took her out to dinners, and took her on dates together to bars. He bought her several hundred dollars worth of clothes and told her a bit about why he hadn't been around much as a father. Sitting head to head over drinks, Walker, in an apology, acknowledged he had abandoned his family, but then he hadn't really had a choice, for he had only sought some sort of peace. Laura had never heard her father's side of the breakup, and as she listened, she felt her heart soften toward her father: "I was his child. . . . I felt for the first time a closeness to him."

They smoked marijuana he'd brought in a bag, and they got stoned together, impressing Laura even more. Soon she was describing the KG-27 cipher machine she operated as a member of the Signal Corps.

But like her mother, Laura was a creature entirely captive to momentary impulse. She had met an army man, Mark Snyder from Lanham, Maryland, and soon, like her mother and grandmother Peggy, Laura found herself pregnant and unmarried. She and Mark finally got married in September 1979, but faced a meager and precarious existence.

Walker assessed how much Laura's predicament may have worked to weaken her resistance, and having shrewdly taken her measure, began pitching her, telling her how she and Mark could "live very comfortably and afford the nice things in life they deserved," like cushy apartments and fun sailboats.

"It was exactly the same bait I used with Whitworth," he said. "I mean, why would I change it when it worked with him?"

Laura at first agreed to steal classified documents for Walker,[18] but when she protested she was pregnant and it would be difficult, he curtly suggested she get an abortion. She flatly refused. But Walker took Mark and Laura to a new car dealership in Norfolk and put down $500 for a brand-new Mazda GLC for the couple. Laura knew it would put them deeper in debt and under new obligation, but she still wanted the car, regardless. Walker always acutely and shrewdly gauged the seductive power of mere things on people of hot blood and dull brain.

Laura's life soon unraveled even more. Many love stories aren't about love at all; they are stories of promising opportunities, and Laura and Mark had none in prospect. When Walker flew to visit her on the army base, he found the couple living off base in a dilapidated trailer. Mark was a pothead, the car wasn't working, and Laura had quit her job.

With his daughter, Walker was quick to drop the pretense that he was equally sweet in any company. He said to her, "Laura, you're worse than some nigger bitch. At least niggers have their babies and stay in the army but you're so fucking stupid you didn't get that right." He abused her for several hours, adding, "I can just imagine what an asshole this baby is going to be."

Walker slept that night on the sofa and, at breakfast, Mark sat in a self-absorbed daze smoking pot at the table. When Mark left, Laura's despair spilled over like a bucket overturned. She said she would never have married if she hadn't been pregnant.

At this Walker grew gentle. He called her "Honey," and explained that working for him would net her $500 to $1,000 a month. All she had to do was get back in the army. He gave her $500 in cash on the spot, and Walker would later say Laura took the $500 as a retainer for being a spy. She would later deny this, saying that Walker had put such pressure on her that she would have said anything just to buy some room to breathe. She spoke of her father's approach as "brainwashing." "He'd break you down and make you feel like the lowest form of life," she said. "He'd say you're never going to be successful. You're not very bright. You're just not anybody very special."

Later Walker talked of recruiting his daughter with that sense of innate, haughty blamelessness that is characteristic of him: "I was her father and wanted to help her out of the mess she was in. I merely did what any father would do," ignoring that he never attempted a real rescue of her or tried to be a truly redeeming influence.

When Laura still proved troublesome, Walker quickly switched his focus to Michael, the family favorite. Michael's chief activities in life up to that point included getting high, getting laid, and going surfing. Like his father, he had learned at an early age that dishonesty paid and deceit was profitable. He had gone to work for his father's detective agency, Confidential Reports, a firm that investigated adultery cases and insurance fraud and where Michael had discovered in himself a liking for playing roles and being able to deceive people. He had a character incapable of any energy of effort. He was a poor student, inattentive, restless, and feckless, but, like his father, he had cunningly ruthless social skills, combined with the same sinister talent for getting other people to do what he wanted.

"I'm going to be a private investigator like you," Michael said. "My dad was a neat guy. And I wanted to be like that," he said later.

"No way," said Walker. He wanted his son in the navy.

Finally, Michael yielded. He liked the uniform and he liked the status. And he liked pleasing his dad.

Michael brought his unscrupulous street smarts to the navy. As he explained later to a reporter, "The Navy is just like everything else in life. You have to play by their rules. But once you learn the rules, you can move around them." He was already making money, confronting new recruits with offers of how to iron their clothes so that they would pass inspection. The charge? Five bucks.

Like his mother, Michael was always gentle and undemanding of himself, always making exceptions in favor of himself, always a shunner of what was difficult because he had too much solicitude toward his person. Like his father, Michael wanted economic self-advancement without exertion and desired to reap rewards for which no useful function had been performed. When he was a chief yeoman, he had a class of sailors who were facing a test, and Michael went and stole fifty copies of the answers, then told the group to raise $50, saying he would show them how to pass.

"I was learning how to manipulate the system," he said jauntily.

Michael was assigned to the USS *America,* an aircraft carrier, and one day Walker asked Michael to come by the house. He led his son into the den and closed the door: "Michael, you may know this already because your mother may have said something about it to you, but if you make copies of those documents you work with, the classified ones, and you give them to me, I can get you some money. Some big money."

Michael felt born aloft by a vivid elation: "I felt proud, really proud, and I felt so cool. I could hardly wait to meet some beautiful blonde Russian agent."

When Michael left on the USS *America* for a cruise in the Caribbean in the fall of 1983, his father said, "Get what you can. But be careful." Later he would say, "I knew in my heart, he couldn't refuse me. . . . It's natural for a son to want to please his father."

Like his father, Michael's sole standard of value was money. For example, he didn't see why his wife, Rachel, who was going to be a doctor, worked so hard at getting good grades. "So you can get a C instead of an A. What's the big deal?" he said. He liked to surf and party with his punk rock friends.

Michael began to steal his first documents within days of his being assigned to his post. "I decided I was going to drain that ship of every secret it had," he said, echoing his father.

With his son in place, Walker, in the meantime, tried to recruit Gary, his brother, who later didn't remember being approached. But that was okay—his older brother Arthur was already working as a spy for him.

9

★ ★ ★

THE CALL HAD come to a fifteen-year FBI veteran Walter Price in the bureau's Hyannis office, and it didn't seem anything worth bothering about. It was from a scorned wife full of unappeasable spite, reporting that her ex-husband of nine or ten years was a spy. In his report following the interview, Price noted that the woman was an admitted alcoholic (she had downed a glass full of vodka as they talked in her West Dennis, Massachusetts, apartment), and she felt very slighted. She claimed her husband owed her $10,000 in unpaid alimony, and she'd just come from seeing him and was stung to the quick to notice he had such luxuries as a young girlfriend, an airplane, and a houseboat.

To Price, the story of this woman's husband having been a spy (for she spoke of it in the past tense) seemed a clumsy attempt at revenge. But like other FBI field agents, Price had to report to regional headquarters every 120 days, and in February, he went to Boston and told his supervisor about the wife's charges. The FBI Boston office sent a report called an "airtel" to its Norfolk office. It arrived on February 22nd, 1985, and was handed to Robert Hunter, a member of the Foreign Counterintelligence Squad.

Hunter, aptly named, had come from a small Pennsylvania town where his father had worked in a steel mill. The family had moved to

Florida, and he had entered college only to flunk out. He had later gone to a junior college and then to a state university where he had worked hard enough to graduate with honors. Hunter, forty-nine, was a friendly man who had unbendable principles and who kept himself very fit. He also possessed the patient endurance and sharp wits of the born spy catcher.

One of Hunter's chief satisfactions of his job was the thrill of discovering a meaning where before there had only been random, senseless fragments of fact, the intense pleasure that lay with searching and discovering new material to use as evidence, and the challenge in examining the material and determining if an account by a spy was the truth or a lie, and, if a lie, why he or she had lied, again, in order to produce even more evidence. The most superb and final satisfaction was putting the evidence together to produce not only an account of what happened, but a connected account illuminating the ideas and motives of the actors and the influence of circumstances.

As he ate lunch and read Price's report, Hunter had a prodding hunch—that alertly animated feeling of being on to something important that often engulfs an experienced investigator. Where Price had simply felt cold, Hunter sensed some faint heat, and where Price had felt dead blankness, Hunter had sensed some hidden significance. Their minds were of an entirely different cast. For example, Hunter didn't worry about the wife being a drunk. Sometimes a person had to get drunk to get up the nerve to call the FBI. It was the details of her story that arrested him and aroused his interest. The details of the dead drops Barbara said she had made were uncannily accurate, matching to the letter the methods of KGB tradecraft.

But serious questions gnawed at the agent. Was John Walker Jr. still active? And how could he be caught? *The FBI had never caught an American suspected of espionage in the act.* Hunter was quick to see that the case would require a full field investigation (FFI). Only an FFI could give him the ensemble of tools he needed to pursue Walker, including wiretaps, telephone toll records, and actual surveillance of the man. Hunter and fellow agents quickly gathered the information for a supporting affidavit, and, utilizing the input from the bureau's Legal Division, they finally submitted a request for the wiretaps to the attorney general of the United States.

By the time of her call to the FBI, Barbara Walker was burnt down to the wick. The roles of parent and child had been reversed. She had visited Norfolk, her airline tickets paid for by her children and her daughter-in-

law Rachel, who was forced to work extra shifts to do it and had wondered why she should have to work to help pay for her mother-in-law's
trip? Barbara spent her first week with Margaret, then moved in with
Michael and Rachel and quickly unloaded her tales of woe. Her own
mother, Annie, had died, and Barbara had borrowed $500 from Walker
for the funeral, and Walker had said curtly he expected to be repaid. Barbara had then quit her job at a shoe company in Massachusetts, even
though she had no new job in prospect. For hours, she sat alone in Rachel
and Michael's house, smoldering in resentment over her ruined, thankless
life and drinking a bottle of triple sec, the only liquor the young couple
had in the house. Then Barbara suddenly announced she wanted to go and
see Walker. Right now, she said.

Barbara brushed right past Walker's startled secretary, and, standing
before his desk, said, "I need $10,000." Walker's snakelike temper lashed
out, and he irately ordered her out of his office. When Barbara returned to
Michael and Rachel, who were waiting in the car, she began chain smoking, squashing her cigarettes when they were only half finished, in a grim
fit of furious rage. "I'm going to fix him," she said.

It was spring of 1985. In March, the FBI interviewed Laura who told
of her father's efforts to recruit her. At the time, Laura was trying to wrest
custody of her son from her estranged husband, Mark, but Mark had
countered all her previous efforts by threatening to expose her father as a
spy. Laura realized the arrest of her father could be put to advantageous
use. At the bidding of the FBI, she placed a call to her father to whom she
hadn't talked to for a year.

As the agents listened in, they experienced bewildered disgust at what
they heard. Walker was filthy, vulgar, coarse, and uncouth. There had always been a gigantic streak of tastelessness in his character, but when
Walker bragged about being in good shape, weighing 150 pounds "naked
and wringing wet," they could hardly believe it was a father talking to a
daughter. Walker then began to roundly, thoroughly, and methodically
curse out Laura for not having kept in touch, using the world "fuck" two
or three times per sentence. Laura said that her life was in the toilet. She
was broke all the time, and profoundly unhappy and miserable.

She then set out with great cunning a bait that brought to light her father's hidden, dark, sinister side. She told him she'd thought of going back
into the service, adding, "I thought of going into the CIA, but I didn't
think I could pass the polygraph." The agents' breath was checked, but

then Walker replied, "You had a legitimate problem there." Hunter felt a rush of jubilant blood.

The probe gained speed.

By March, the military records of John and Arthur Walker arrived. As the agents bent over them, a thousand dark and gloomy possibilities sprang alive in their brains. The records told one story, but within them, they knew, there lay concealed another. The first story, in the records, would hopefully lead them to the origins and beginnings of the second. An agent, Steve Carter, read Walker's file and looked up visibly shaken. He glumly shook his head, concluding, "If these people gave the Soviets the information they had access to, the damage will not only be grave, it will be catastrophic."

Soon Hunter and his fellow agents had taps in place on Walker's phones. They got to know the man, his foul mouth, his humor, and his compulsion to deceive.

But Hunter was not only keeping an eye on John Walker. The bureau had also begun a quiet probe of Michael Walker. It was prompted by only a speck of knowledge: Barbara had once told the bureau that the previous fall Michael had urged her not to turn John in because it would hurt Michael's navy career. That bothered Hunter a lot.

By late April, the agents had listened to Walker's phone calls for twenty days, and had come up with nothing. The effort seemed wasted. Boredom reigned, but they went on, and suddenly one conversation made them sit up. Rachel had called Walker to ask about his encounter with Barbara and said, "I talked to Maggie a couple of times and I understand Barbara was upsetting Maggie a bit with her problem. You know what I mean."

Hunter, hearing this, instantly decided Rachel knew that Walker was a spy. Better was quick to come. When Rachel invited Walker to attend her graduation ceremonies on May 18, he replied, "Oh lordy, I can't believe it. I know I'm going to be busy that weekend. Can you goddamn believe it?" When his favorite aunt died, and her funeral was scheduled for that same weekend, Walker begged off having to attend, saying he had business in Charlotte, North Carolina.

Hunter's heart began to beat faster. What errand was so important that it couldn't be rescheduled, Hunter thought. He circled the date on his office calendar.

One thing Hunter was surprised and dismayed to hear was how

Walker brought out the worst of the family members he talked to, even his aged mother, Peggy. As Hunter heard Walker and Peggy viciously run down and jeer at the faults, shortcomings, and defects of family members, Hunter concluded, "It wasn't only the profanity. There was something that went beyond the gutter. John Walker had a nasty, rancid, sneering side to him. I was beginning to see that this man was not only devious and untruthful, but also evil. . . . He was a truly evil person."

In early May, Hunter and his boss Joseph Wolfinger went to Washington for a strategy session. The case was now officially called "Windflyer." The Washington agents' proposal to put a tracking bug on Walker's van was inflexibly rejected by Hunter. Walker was an experienced private eye, knowledgeable in surveillance techniques. The Washington agents grudgingly agreed. Before they adjourned, Hunter asked what they should do if they got a chance to catch Walker making an actual dead drop. Hunter was met by skeptical smirks. It had never happened before.

THAT WARM MAY Sunday opened with a sense of approaching climax felt by the FBI. The dead drop of a spy is always a complicated, highly hazardous choreography in which neither party ever meets the other—the peril is too great. The purpose is to exchange stolen documents, and to be successful meant the transfer of documents must go totally undetected by any hostile eye. The spy and his handler must never catch sight of each other. Their paths must never cross.

Usually a dead drop operation covered only a few miles, but today would be different, thanks to an extremely complicated set of Russian operational instructions, very expertly drafted by the KGB. In the end, the chase would end by covering sixty square miles of suburban Maryland countryside—a record, the FBI would say later. The sixty square miles would allow for a lot of surveillance by Walker's Soviet handlers to make sure their top spy had not blundered into a trap.

The agents on Walker's trail were tense and serious. From now on, they were on the knife's edge. Whatever happened today would be decisive. Walker continued west, driving in an erratic manner, designed to detect surveillance. He would keep to the speed limit, then suddenly speed up, then as suddenly slow down, drifting, looking up in his rearview mirror for any vehicles that were doing the same.

Special Agent Bev Andress said, over the radio, "Hey, Hunter, are we having fun yet?"

"Not yet," he said, somber. He was waiting to see if Walker would turn south for Charlotte, or north for Washington.

But after Walker approached I-95, he turned north. When he made that turn, Hunter felt a thrill of anticipation, a joyous surge of resolve. The FBI was going to have a shot at catching a spy in the act. He got Andress on the radio. "Now we're having fun," he said. With grim satisfaction, Hunter thought of how this Sunday would be Walker's last day as a free man.

Walker's Russian instructions were in color and in an original document. This was exceptional by itself. Usually instructions for dead drops were issued in the form of photocopies because photocopies left no fingerprints or disclosed any indentations from erasures. According to tradecraft rules, the Soviet doing the pickup did not know the value of the material he was retrieving from his agent, just as the Soviet who took the fourteen photos for the dead drop did not know who or what they were for. An operation was safer and more secure if each person was provided only a small piece of a puzzle and kept in the dark about the rest.

At 4 P.M., Hunter's team had turned the surveillance over to the Washington teams. The agents were calm, clearheaded, sure of themselves, composed, and intent. The FBI knew it was dangerous following Walker in daylight, especially on empty roads in an isolated area so they hurriedly parked in driveways and gas stations, always keeping in contact with the FBI plane that flew obliquely on Walker's tail at 3,500 feet.

Walker continued his leisurely drive, and agents knew he was memorizing the roads, familiarizing himself with two sites: one where he would deposit his stolen documents, and the other where he would retrieve his KGB cash payment. The tension of the agents tightened to a new and painful pitch when they realized that for now, only Walker and his handler knew where those sites were. Hunter and the rest also knew that Walker was not going to make any real attempt to pass documents and retrieve payment until darkness had come down to cloak and conceal his actions.

Disaster hit without warning at 4:45. Hunter was at the FBI field office in a run-down neighborhood four blocks away from headquarters where a command center had been set up. He was standing with fellow agent David Tzady when they heard the radio crackle excitedly, "Does anyone have the eyeball?" No answer. And then, as time prickled with empty, tense silence, a voice said suddenly, "We lost him."

The plane no longer had him in sight.

When he heard the news, Hunter almost swallowed his cigar. Szady flew into fury, his incensed comments on the incompetence of the Washington crew like a rain of sharp hammer blows on wood. Darts thudded into Hunter for having argued against putting a tracking beeper on the van. But soon an edgy calm descended on the teams. They had to brush aside their swarming anxieties and think things through to a solution, and the solution demanded a clear head. The agents stood and gazed greedily at the road maps put up on the field office walls.

The clock ticked away. With each minute, the suspense grew more acute.

The agents were tired, anxious, strained, and their nerves were frayed to ribbons. Suddenly at 7:48, the voice of a female agent exclaimed over the radio, "I've got him!" A great cheer of rapturous joy went up in the field office. In an instant, the heavy, stonelike load of worry had lightened, and once again, the agents were all business. Walker was seen getting out of the van at Circle Drive and Ridge Drive, between Rockville and Poolesville, Maryland. Night was coming on. The land was dark, the sky still held some beautiful spring light, and the lights in houses were brightening. It was the bureau's single-engine plane overhead that had picked him up. The airborne agents couldn't see what Walker did, only that he got back in the van and drove back to Quince Orchard Road where he had pulled the vehicle into the curb.

At 8:23, the agents suddenly spotted a Soviet car. The man in the blue 1983 Chevrolet Malibu could have been a father taking an innocent drive with his wife and son, but the license plate made one wonder—it was a red-white-blue diplomatic plate reading DSX-144. The SX signified the Soviet Union. Running the license tag number through the FBI computers, the agents learned that the man in the blue Malibu was Aleksy Gavrilovich Tkachenko, the third secretary of the Soviet embassy. The wife and child were strangers being carried as props. Tkachenko was carrying $200,000 and instructions for Walker's next dead drop and would have had a hard time explaining what he was doing with all that cash. Unfortunately when Tkachenko drove by, the ready-for-action signal, the 7-UP can, was missing, an FBI agent having mistakenly picked it up for evidence. Tkachenko needed no further urging, he fled the scene at 9:08 P.M. Walker had no means of knowing what had happened. He had delivered his materials, a large grocery sack, containing a mass of secret documents, and then he'd returned to another site where he was to pick up his payment. He went to the area between two trees designated in the instructions as the place where he would find his money. It wasn't there. Walker returned to where he had left his materials. They were gone. In a frantic disbelief, Walker buzzed back and forth between the two sites unable to understand what had happened.

Worried and utterly worn out, Walker finally pulled into a Ramada Inn in Rockville a few minutes after midnight. As he rested, the FBI examined Walker's package. It contained 129 highly classified documents placed inside another grocery bag that was neatly folded shut, encased in plastic to keep it dry, and mixed in was a carefully washed Coca-Cola can and rubbing alcohol bottle, an unused crumpled Kleenex, and other washed objects. All of the documents came from Michael's duty station on the *Nimitz*.

The agents got ready. At 3:30 A.M., field agent Billy Wang, posing as a room clerk, phoned Walker's room from the lobby, notifying him that a drunk driver had just crashed into his van. As he hung up the phone in Room 763 at the Rockville Ramada Inn, Walker's thoughts spun round in a blizzard of confusion. If the FBI were on to him, why hadn't they arrested him after he'd put down his package? Maybe the Russians had simply screwed up and left his money at the wrong spot? Maybe it was true that some drunk had hit his van and badly damaged it. The foul-up at the drop site and the phone call from the downstairs desk could be coincidences, couldn't they? Besides, the FBI never worked weekends. He used to joke about it with his Russian handlers.

Walker went and tensely peered out the window, then picked up the envelope that contained the hand-drawn maps of the dead drop route. They were incriminating. He had to get rid of the maps and instructions. But then a reluctance tugged at him. If he did, then he wouldn't be able to find the place to pick up his cash.

Walker's room door opened warily. He came out, cautious as a cat, checked the stairwell, and then skipped back into his room. FBI agents Hunter and James Kolouch, wearing white Kevlar vests over their shirts, were concealed in a corridor near an elevator bank, guns drawn. A few minutes later, the hidden agents heard Walker's door open, but Walker didn't appear. Anxieties mounted. Where had he gone? But then the door opened again, and Walker materialized, walking very quickly, a .38 in one hand. As he reached for the elevator button, the agents Hunter and Kolouch barreled round the corner to confront him, shouting, "FBI! Drop it!"

Distressed confusion suffused Walker's face. For five seconds he did nothing, still holding the gun. For the agents, it was one of those critical moments of life where time is compressed to an explosive *now,* and there is only that *now,* and what may come after is too abstract to think about.

Walker let his pistol slip to the floor.

Hunter and Kolouch rushed in. There was a loud, sucking sound as Kolouch ripped off Walker's dark toupee. They yanked off Walker's running shoes, knocked off his glasses, and stood while he was thoroughly searched and his pockets emptied.

"Fucking spy," Walker heard someone mumble.

Walker, his face congested, sulky, angry, still mustered enough bravado to jeer at his captors: "Quite a crowd you got here. Don't you have any consideration for the taxpayers? And that phony call. That's the oldest trick in the book."

Hunter grinned at him and said, "I know, and it still works."[19]

As he was being led out to be taken to Baltimore to jail, seventy or eighty agents were lined up outside to get a look at the most damaging traitor in the history of U.S. espionage.

Walker was taken aback by the hedge of crowd standing there to catch a glimpse of him, stony hatred in their faces. Under his breath, he said, "All those people—My God, I had no idea."

10

FIVE HOURS AFTER John Walker Jr. was arrested, two FBI agents arrested Jerry Whitworth in his trailer in Davis, California. Michael Walker was arrested aboard ship with 1,176 stolen documents in his possession. In jail he would refuse to see Barbara Walker and wrote to her in a note, "Mother, you are the biggest BITCH I've ever met!" Arthur Walker was arrested on May 20th, 1985, and he and Michael both joined John in jail by the end of May.

The jockeying for position within the legal system began.

It was a time of pitiless calculation. The bonds between the ring members quickly shredded to tatters and fell away. The government planned to put John and Michael on trial in Federal District Court in Baltimore. The case against John was strong: the FBI had recovered a large amount of incriminating evidence from his Norfolk home that included a naval warfare publication titled "Threat Intelligence Summary, Naval Air Forces" and a satellite communications manual with Whitworth's fingerprints on it.

In the meantime, Michael had waived his rights and confessed, as had Arthur.

Which left Whitworth. The case against him was circumstantial, and there was within the government a relentless, vindictive lust for his blood. Even though many FBI agents felt the blackest cravings for taking revenge against John, different parties were in full chase for different things. High-ranking Pentagon and Justice Department officials wanted retribution and justice, but they had to pick their path with care. They wanted a plea bargain with Walker, which meant they would offer a specified sentence to him in exchange for a plea of guilty. They wanted certain information to be kept out of court. But they also wanted Whitworth: he was to be an owl, nailed to a barn door as a warning and a threat.[20]

Walker went on trial on October 28. He had pled poverty after his arrest so he could get a public offender, but then the court found his net worth to be $182,785, and the IRS put a lien of $252,487 on Walker's possessions. Soon, his house was auctioned off, plus $25,440 worth of his things, including his navy medals and an oil painting of him in a navy uniform.

The only reason the government was dealing with Walker at all was to enable it to crucify Whitworth. If Walker would cooperate and testify against Whitworth at a big show trial, then the government promised it would go lighter on Michael.

Walker agreed to plead guilty to espionage and conspiracy because he secretly believed that he would one day be paroled. He received a life sentence in return for a twenty-five year term for his son. Arthur had received three life sentences and was fined $250,000.

All eyes now turned to Whitworth.

He had plied Walker with stolen documents for a decade, and the Pentagon wanted to know how much chaos he had personally caused. At first Whitworth blithely claimed he was innocent and apparently naïvely believed he could beat the charges. But once he heard Walker would testify against him, he was a shaken, different man.

On the government's side, every care was taken to make the case complete. From Walker's testimony came details of forty meetings, income tax violations, and the $332,000 Whitworth had earned as Walker's top spy. The jury also heard of Whitworth's spending sprees and listened as IRS accountants spoke of the shop clerks and automobile dealers who talked of Whitworth's lust for showy possessions. The jurors would also hear of keylists and coding machines, and blackest treachery.

As the evidence piled up around him like trash in a blind ally, Whitworth throughout sat in the courtroom looking oblivious and detached, never seeming to move, his thick beard hiding any expression on his face.

The verdict hit Whitworth like a hammer blow that crumples up a tin can. Whitworth was forty-six years old when Judge John P. Vukasin Jr.

sentenced him to 365 years in prison and fined him $410,000. The judge, in a cold fit of temper, described Whitworth as "a man who represented the evil of banality . . . a zero at the bone. He believes in nothing. His life is devoted to determining the wind direction and how he can make a profit from the coming storm."

Because of the intensity of the drive by government officials to discredit Whitworth, Walker was spared a trial, and, unfortunately, much secret information involving his case was never revealed or resolved. For example, FBI officials said they suspect that Arthur became a spy when he was serving on U.S. submarines, before his brother joined the navy. "Art was definitely more involved in espionage than he told us," Hunter said. The FBI agents believe that Arthur may have recruited his younger brother.

According to Hunter, Arthur never could pass a polygraph with questions about when his spying career began, nor could Walker. When asked by the FBI about how and when he'd begun his career as a spy, Walker trimmed and embellished, and tricked out some tale that always ended up flunking the polygraph test. The FBI knew Walker had been in the Soviet embassy, but not at the time he later claimed. When had his criminal career begun? After forty-three debriefing sessions with Walker, no clear answer had emerged.

Did the FBI get all the members of the ring? FBI officials to this day said they don't believe they did. The KGB handlers, who grew nervous when they heard Walker saying out loud the names of ring members, had set up an alphabetic shorthand: "S" would stand for Michael, "K" for Arthur, Whitworth would be called "D", "F" would be for Walker's brother Gary. But there was an "A" whose identity the FBI was never able to discover. Nor was the FBI able to trace all of Walker's money. The feds believed that "Jaws" had earned as much as $1.5 million from spying, and while some of it was traced and recovered, every attempt to locate and impound all of it ended in flat failure.

A more interesting unanswered question is this: did U.S. intelligence suspect Walker was a spy long before Barbara's belated tip? Over and over senior CIA officials involved with the Walker case insist that Barbara was the source that turned over the stone that exposed him. But under cross-examination of FBI agent Dave Szady by Walker defense team lawyers, startling and tantalizing new facts emerged. When Szady was asked by an attorney whether the FBI began investigating Walker before March 1985, Szady said the information had come from Barbara and Laura. But the defense attorney asked, "So it wasn't until you got the information from Laura that you actually started the investigation in earnest, is that what you're saying?"

Szady replied yes, but added, "We had other information that confirmed what Barbara was telling us was correct."[21]

In fact, a court document disclosed that Walker may have been under investigation as early as August 1983. In a 1986 affidavit filed in pretrial proceedings pertaining to a Whitworth defense attorney's questions about wiretapping, it emerged that John J. Dion, the Justice Department official who had authorized the arrest of Walker that balmy May night, said that he had checked wiretaps dating back to August 1983! This clangs loudly like a shovel striking rock. It was in August 1983 that Whitworth's tour of duty abruptly ended aboard the USS *Enterprise*, and there are U.S. intelligence officials who believe that it was a U.S. mole in the KGB who alerted U.S. counterintelligence to Whitworth and eventually Walker. U.S. officials have said that Walker and Whitworth were being fed disinformation that the two passed on to the Soviets for at least two years.

What is wishful in one's character hopes that this is true.

WALKER, NOW IN JAIL, was not a man to accept the consequences of his acts with anything like good grace. The man who had been comfortable playing so many roles now assumed another: that of victim. In prison, he would at times wallow in great troughs of self-pity. In one typical outburst, he said, "What has happened to me is unfair. I've been destroyed by the government for no real reason, and so have Art and Mike. . . . If they let us out now, what do we do? They've taken all our money. Do you think anyone would hire us? It's really unfair."

What prompts him to this extraordinary conclusion?

That he believes he did no damage. In one breath, Walker is all bragging, pompous bravado, declaring himself to be the most important spy of all time, and in the next, he claims that betraying communications secrets to a hostile power locked in deadly all-or-nothing rivalry with the United States was basically harmless. "I keep reading about how I'm the worst spy since the Rosenbergs gave away the bomb," he said. "Okay, show me. Where's the damage? Where's the invasion by the communists? Where is the Red Dawn?" Arguments like this show Walker to be a man with no intellectual grasp of the Cold War, including its ten million casualties in proxy wars.

To Walker, whose mind was always buzzing with scams, the Cold War was simply another, bigger one. "Everyone has an angle," he said. "All you fucking stupid Americans who sit around all day watching the boob tube—(the war) ain't gonna happen. . . . That's all a game, man, to keep the defense contractors rich."

But if the Cold War was a fake and a scam, then Walker's spying was pointless, futile, and lacked any importance and impact whatever. If it were merely a scam, then he is relegated to history's sidelines. But in talking to the FBI or the press, Walker's protests of harmlessness always end by being routed by his vanity. This was the case when he told Hunter that he, Walker, had been "the best spy that ever was" and "invaluable."

Walker's importance could only be taken as fact if the question of real war—the possibility of dire, ferocious armed conflict—had been a serious matter looming in back of all the propaganda. And in spite of Walker's haughtily stubborn assertion that no war would ever occur between the United States and Russia, the days of the Reagan presidency brought the old postwar confrontation of the world's two chief powers to fresh levels of insufferable anxiety and danger. First there was the incredible, astonishing U.S. military buildup—3,000 combat aircraft, 3,700 strategic missiles, and about 10,000 tanks purchased in Reagan's' first six years. But other movements were afoot that were to have a decisive effect on the Soviet Union's fate. For example, the Pentagon had a secret plan to bankrupt the Soviet economy, America was waging another secret "economic war" on the Soviets, and there was a secret U.S. deal with the Saudis to bring down oil prices, which would boost the U.S. economy and cost the Kremlin billions of dollars per year. Plus there was also the dangerous gambit to use the Afghan mujahideen in the Soviet-occupied Afghanistan to conduct military strikes on Soviet soil. In addition, using an underground "rat line" or intelligence network in Poland, the Reagan administration was busy undermining the Soviet hold in Eastern Europe.

The Soviets did not know all of these things, but they knew of some, sensed others, and were engulfed by gloom, doubt, and self-questioning. Suddenly the Kremlin's world had become uncertain, mysterious, frightful, and full of the unexpected and unsettling. Russian fears soon grew into premonitions of disaster. Intense anxiety and near panic made the Russians credulous. As the relations disintegrated between the two powers, there came a series of incidents, small in themselves, that ended by producing a crisis of extraordinary peril. First, on August 31, 1983, the Soviets shot down a Korean Airlines passenger plane, Flight 007, which had strayed into Soviet airspace near military installations in the Sea of Okhotsk. All 269 people aboard the plane were killed, and a wave of warlike feeling swept over America. Reagan and Secretary of State George Shultz said the shooting was deliberate murder. It was a lie, but the damage was done.

Then on October 6, Lech Walesa, the Solidarity leader in Poland, won the Nobel Peace Prize, and the Soviets complained of a Western-Zionist plot to destabilize Poland, the largest and most prosperous contributor to the Warsaw Pact. (They were right. There was a plot, and the Israelis were involved in running the rat line.)

Anxiety mounted on October 26, when the United States invaded Grenada to rescue some American medical students, and in the process, dismantled the infant communist government there.

By then, a deep, anxious gloom had settled on psychologically shaken Soviet leadership. Already in 1981, Yuri Andropov, head of the KGB, was so convinced the United States was planning a surprise first strike that he instituted a series of special war alerts. He also began something called "Operation Ryan," which was tasked to look for any signs that the United States might be preparing a nuclear sneak attack. The fact jittery, over-stressed nerves almost caused a small, inadvertent incident to get out of hand occurred in November 1983 during a NATO exercise called "Able Archer." NATO forces were practicing tactical nuclear weapons release procedures, moving through all the stages from readiness to general alert.[22] But the Soviets thought this merely a cloak for something far more sinister. The Soviet leaders had almost always used military exercises to conceal any real military movements as they had in their 1952 invasion of East Germany and their 1968 invasion of Czechoslovakia. Thus the Soviets expected the Americans were doing the same thing, and in London, the Soviets began an all-out push for new information about a first strike, using GRU and KGB agents. A wild-eyed Andropov frantically ordered preparations in Department 8 of the KGB for terrorist attacks on NATO and American targets in Europe, including letter bombs to be sent to British Prime Minister Margaret Thatcher's office and dead drops of explosives to be placed behind vending machines or under sinks at restaurants near American bases in West Germany. Other Russian specialist teams were to use biological and chemical weapons on designated targets. Soviet anxiety grew so great that a frightened Soviet embassy actually began to burn sensitive documents, believing nuclear war to be imminent.

A later generation cannot easily appreciate the excruciating nervous strain of this potentially catastrophic time, and it's clear that Walker did not.

It was during dark and threatening days that the Soviets used Walker's information to tear up a bunch of SOSUS hydrophones in order to clear an avenue for decapitating nuclear attacks on the continental United States. Millions and millions of dollars were later spent to replace the hydrophones, nor was that all. Damage caused by Walker continued into the early 1990s as Russia continued to be able to read coded radio transmissions among American military units, according to very senior former CIA officials.[23]

Even though the United States spent over a billion dollars to put in place new code systems on its ships to end Soviet access, damage may continue to the present. It was chilling to read, in December 2001, the headline "New Russian nuclear sub catches U.S. by surprise" on a website. The story said that Russia's newest nuclear-powered submarine, to enter service in January 2002, was quieter than the U.S. Los Angeles–class attack submarine, "giving it greater survivability." Called the Akula II-class attack sub, it was launched years before it was expected to be.

U.S. officials said it was more of Walker's work because it had been Walker who, above all rivals, had made the Russians aware that quietness for submarines was the key to their effectiveness in war. It was Walker and Whitworth who had "passed crucial secrets about U.S. techniques for quieting subs, such as cushioning engine equipment to prevent vibrations for resonating through the hulls."[24] At the time Walker was arrested, U.S. sonar operators on subs were still being startled out of their wits by remaining unable to detect some of the newest Soviets subs until their enemies were right on top of them.

Yet there is an irony.

It was during the truly sinister crisis of the early 1980s that Walker's treachery acted to help quell the fear and panic in Russia that could have detonated a war. One of Walker's handlers, Boris Solomatin, who had been the KGB official in charge at the Soviet embassy in 1967 and who was later awarded the distinguished Order of the Red Star for his handling of Walker, told a senior CIA official that he, Solomatin, had been summoned to the Soviet Presidium during the explosive period of Operation Ryan to assure the Soviet leaders that the United States was not going to attack them. How did he know? Solomatin told the Soviet leadership that, thanks to Walker, Soviet intelligence knew the *exact position* of every U.S. Navy SSBN and they "were not in an attack position."

He was forced to appear before the Soviet Presidium *three times*, he said, adding to the agent in a guttural growl, "Your government owes me a medal."[25]

How did the Soviets know what the U.S. SSBN attack positions were?

Walker, of course. Apparently, the crowning theft of the spy ring had been Walker's selling the Russians the repair manual for the KW-7 code machine, the U.S. Navy's workhorse. This proved priceless for the Russians. Quickly and deftly, they reengineered it so that when Walker and Whitworth stole a month's worth of keylists, the Russians were able to read U.S. Navy fleet messages and communications to Washington in real time.

Reassured by Solomatin, the Soviets gradually grew less alarmed, and the dangerously wicked, flaring flame of the threat of war finally flickered and went out.

But what if war had come?

KGB General Oleg Kalugin described Walker to Hunter as "the number one agent in the history of the KGB," adding, "He was much more valuable than Ames, especially if war had erupted." But U.S. intelligence had known this in 1985, ever since a blond, dashing, high-ranking KGB officer Vitaly Yurchenko, forty-nine, had defected and given the FBI information that made a cold shudder pass down its back. Yurchenko was the highest-ranking KGB officer ever to defect, and he had been assigned the job of discovering why Walker had been blown. The Soviets did not believe Barbara had turned him in, but that the FBI had been tipped off from an American agent on the Soviet side, as evidence now would indicate.

During debriefings, Yurchenko told Hunter that Walker was the best agent the KGB ever had and stated that "Jaws" had provided so much information that a special building had to be built in Moscow to house the analysts who worked on the material. Walker's information was "the most important operation in the KGB's history," Yurchenko said. According to the CIA official who interviewed Solomatin, thanks to Walker, for over a decade, the Russians gained the ability to read 1.2 million classified U.S. military messages. Two handlers of Walker had received the highest honors from the Soviet government: Yurki Lenkov was awarded an Order of Lenin medal, Vladimir Gorovoy was given a Hero of Russia award. Solomatin, in addition to getting the Order of the Red Star, had been promoted to deputy chief of Soviet intelligence. Walker himself had been given the honorary rank of admiral in the Soviet Navy.

Yurchenko had made clear how dangerous Walker's disclosures were for

U.S. security when, in talking to the FBI in 1985, he made the chilling remark that in the event of war, the U.S. Navy would have been "annihilated," thanks to the edge given Moscow's military by Walker and Whitworth.

The now former CIA official who had spoken to Solomatin angrily agreed. Because of Whitworth and Walker, "the Soviets had one leg of the strategic triad cocked and locked for ten years," he said. The whole U.S. idea of "a graduated response in the event of attack" had been placed in jeopardy, he said.

"WHY HAVE I always been surrounded by weak people?" Walker asked an FBI agent after his arrest. "It was this group of misfits and weaklings (his wife and family) that brought me down."

By then, Walker's world had shrunk to a six-by-eight-foot cell that was bare, hard, hateful, and ugly. But the spy's pretensions to greatness were as unbounded and outsized as ever. His chief contacts by then were convicts. Since the main motive of Walker's social life had usually been to prove other people inferior to himself, he continued to think of himself as some colossal titan of spying.

Bragging about one's criminality is the most tiresome form of conceit; Walker's conceit was overpowering. In his interviews, reliving the tawdry adventure of his life, Walker again and again depicted himself as a hardy spirit that decides, approves, and achieves. But is this accurate? Is he a forceful, admirable character that somehow took the wrong turn? We admire any life that is given to a striving to improve. We admire the heroism of hard work, the eager expenditure of strength and strenuous will in the service of the worthwhile. We are in awe of people capable of the most patient endurance of pain who exert themselves to the fullest extent of their powers even though racked by dreadful fatigue and plagued by the urge to quit in order to accomplish a task. We have only to think of Benedict Arnold's unheard of exertions in the Maine wilderness to know what made Arnold great. His actions there define the heroic.

But with Walker and Whitworth, what do we see?

There is nothing respectable about these men. In character, they are not the titans they claim, but monumental pigmies. Walker once boasted that "K-Mart has better security than the Navy," but the remark is typically unkind and self-exalting. The navy simply couldn't imagine beforehand a scoundrel like Walker. The Navy had placed its faith in the scrupulous honor and conscience of its enlisted men. This wasn't a weakness, but a generosity, and a kind of extending of moral credit. The great Dutch historian Johan Huizinga said that "every community, even one of animals is based on the mutual trust of beings who could destroy each other." Without mutual trust, a community of human beings is impossible. But Walker saw trust as gullibility because he was a soulless predator. He always acted as though honesty was a species of weakness that only he was smart enough to perceive and exploit. With Walker and Whitworth, there was never any sense of seeing a bit of themselves in others and being reluctant to inflict any hurt or humiliation or harm. The ethical impulse that in most people makes them feel they owe something to society and that prompts them to want to serve it is simply absent from their makeup. For Walker, an institution like the navy is not something to which you feel an obligation; it was simply a machine for secretly lining your pockets and securing additional property.

We are all imprisoned in the limits of our own consciousness, but Walker is so subjective that he sees no world outside himself or his petty aims. He is responsive only to what impacts him personally. He likes to say repeatedly, "I was surrounded by some dumb shits," but his ignorance of his employer, the Soviets, is truly astounding. With a straight face, he told reporter Peter Early about a conversation, he, Walker, had had in Vienna with his Russian handler about Watergate. "I mean, the (Soviet) press follows the party line because of principle. It believes what it says is best for the country, but the press in America doesn't give a damn about anything but making money. A reporter will print anything to get ahead and get his promotion."

Here Walker is simply measuring the journalist by himself, seeing in another his own ruthlessness and lack of principle. Not only can he never admit to doing wrong, but he seems to think his actions somehow stand outside of ethics and are not bound by the normal moral standards of human society. "I was living every fantasy I had," he once said exultantly of his lifestyle based on the fraudulent prosperity from his spying.

Even for his family Walker never seemed to feel any real feeling of considerate sweetness or any savoring of their qualities. To him they were tools to use. In fact, his egoistic unkindness acts to cut the stems of all living things close to him so that they weaken and wither away, just as his wife, Barbara, had. In the earliest phases of all our lives we are conscious of owing things to other people. In almost all of us this takes the form of caring and providing with some conscientiousness, but Walker is unmoved by his human contacts, whether they be parents or his wife or his children. When, in prison, Walker's daughter tells her father, "Daddy, I still love you. I want you to know I will always love you!" it enrages him. He calls her "stupid," and adds "who needs that bullshit? Tell me something useful, information I can use. Tell me how Barbara and Laura are going to screw up my life."

To be emotionally stirred is to be concerned and to care, but when Walker looked at his children or his friends, nothing stirred in him. He exploited their will to survive, knowing that all people tend to wait silently and submissively for better times, clinging to whatever small blessings they still enjoy. But at heart, he felt nothing for his children or his friends. That is, unless he needed them. Then Walker was a whirlwind that swept up everyone into its greedy force because his friends and family were of lighter weight than himself and were necessary to complete his purposes. To attain their aid, any approach was morally right as long as it succeeded. Think of Whitworth, or Walker's approaches to his daughter Laura. Whitworth and Laura had a duty to perform, efforts to make on Walker's behalf, a contribution to make to his welfare, and any means was justified as long as it convinced them that serving him would be as big a benefit to them as it would be to himself. He made them feel understood and made them feel needed, important, or sympathized with, catering to their pitiable inner craving for increased significance by dangling before them the bait that the whole gross world held in awe—more money. That they were to Walker merely expendable capital to be used cleverly, cunningly, without scruple or hesitation and to be tossed away the minute they displayed any desire to prosecute independent purposes of their own, didn't matter. Nor did it matter to Walker that when he tried to reduce his friends and children to the level of accomplices that he was preaching a doctrine of utter irresponsibility, and that when they accepted his enticements he had not simply placed them on the road to ruin but had ruined them already.

Perhaps the most troubling thing about Walker and Whitworth was that they appeared to have no adequate idea of what human life is for. They were creatures who have simply ceased to develop. Of course, Walker had a mind, but its activity was simple, consistent, and invariably set in one direction: the pursuit of self-gratification. He was never able to muster a fight against the lesser, more worthless claims of his nature. Orgeta y Gasset once said that the essence of life is to be stirred by what is estimable—in other words, that the world is moved forward when we give our admiration and attention to the best things, the most substantial, excellent, and great. But Whitworth and Walker had minds that were closed to noble impulses. What enthralled them, and what they chose to give their energies to, were the flimsy, decorative aspects of life, such as the phony prestige and spurious glory of mere costly indulgences and empty display. Whitworth used his spy money to have his wife pick him up dockside in a silver Rolls Royce, or to throw extravagant parties at the Hotel Coronado in San Diego. Walker wasted his life imprisoned in puerile pastimes, including sailboats, airplanes, the deluding enhancements of alcohol, and the endless pursuit of indiscriminate sexual pleasure or "a toy in the blood," as Hamlet calls lust. As a man, Walker never stood on scruple, never clung to any virtue. He was never honest according to his lights. There was nothing of the strong or steady or admirable in his life. He was the opposite of heroic because the heroic is always indifferent to material advantage. Walker was enslaved to material advantage. He exhibited no extraordinary talent. He accomplished nothing of value, and pursued nothing that added to a fuller, richer sense of human existence. He had seen other people rise from modest positions in life to places of money and power, but did not have the confidence in his own abilities to try and do it honestly and to persist in the face of difficulty and setback. Instead, he turned to fraud and theft.

The impression I got spending so many hours on his life was this: we may think we make choices in life, but in the end, they make us. Both spies found out, to their ruin, that a desire fulfilled is a desire made stronger. By satisfying a wrong desire, you have gained something evil only by lessening your good. You may have more, but you have gained it at the cost of being less. When enough wrong choices have been indulged in long enough, pleasure and fraud prevail over conscience, and that ideal self, the deepest, truest, strongest self of which we all once had an image of, is lost for good.

Walker was the first of the truly catastrophic spies, but then a germ can kill many people and not be impressive in appearance or size. Aldrich Ames and Robert Hanssen would come after Walker, but even Hanssen would not do the damage that Walker did.

In his spiritual cheapness, in his greedy mediocrity, in his low aims, in his reckless chase for his own pleasure, in his helpless, childish addiction to money as the greatest good, we see in Walker someone who carried in himself a concentrated dose of all the worst poisons of our own recent times.

His is a tale of great sorrow and great waste, and in reading it, one stops staring at Walker and turns to look and see how it is with oneself.

The Traitor as Proteus and Government Agent:
ROBERT HANSSEN

*Society is a body in which no member may be diseased
without endangering the whole.*

— FRIEDRICH NIETZSCHE

*Work of the enemy! Such deeds he loves, loyalty divided
in confusion of hearts.*

— J. R. R. TOLKIEN

THE FACE THAT stares out of the photograph could be that of an old, maidenly aunt. It is docile, tame, and flaccid. It has a pleasant oval shape with dark, bland eyes set wide apart, large, fleshy lips, and hair that curls over the brow in that short cropped style old women like to wear. Hard wear has washed all intensity from the expression. But then you notice that the aunt is holding a sign that displays a date of birth and the date of arrest, and you realize, with sick shock, that you are looking at the booking photograph of FBI mole Robert Hanssen, the "most damaging FBI agent in U.S. history," as one book proclaimed.

Hanssen's career, dominant instincts, and habitual forces of character are not singular, but manifold—mixed together in a disturbing and contradictory ensemble. A former CIA counterintelligence official remarked that Hanssen reminded him of William Gladstone, Britain's nineteenth-century four-time prime minister described by the great British biographer Lytton Strachey as having a personality that was "a confusion of incompatibles." Hanssen was a devout Catholic who went to mass every day and who joined an elite, severe Catholic order, and yet who served with equal devotion a pitiless, atheist regime that he claimed at heart to despise. Hanssen was a puritanical, prudish man who would not allow homosexuality, abortion, or birth control to be discussed at the dinner table, yet he gave an American Express club card, $8,000, a Mercedes, and other gifts to a Washington stripper, and took her with him to Hong Kong where she performed on him something his wife would not—oral sex. Except for this incident, he was a devoted husband and at the time of his arrest had been married for thirty-three years to one woman, his beloved Bonnie. Yet Hanssen sent nude photos of his wife to Jack Hoschouer, a friend from high school and even allowed Hoschouer to watch while Hanssen and Bonnie had sex, Hanssen deliberately positioning his wife so that his friend could see better. At one point, Hanssen suggested to Hoschouer that they drug Bonnie unconscious so that Hoschouer could also possess her and have Hoschouer's child.

Hanssen was a master counterspy, yet he sold his expert counterintelligence skills to protect himself while he put up for auction to the Russians incredibly sensitive U.S. secrets that earned him $1.43 million in KGB money, diamonds, and foreign bank deposits. To ensure his own safety, Hanssen betrayed Russian defectors in place working for the United States, sending some to their deaths. Much more ominously, Hanssen also betrayed U.S. plans for World War III and incredibly secret U.S. plans called Continuity of Government measures that ensured the orderly political succession and functioning of the U.S. government in the event of war, a gem of such priceless value that the Soviets could have seriously jeopardized U.S. national security except for the fact that the Soviet system had collapsed. As it was, in betraying all he did, Hanssen wasted "hundreds of billions of dollars" of American money, ruined careers, killed agents, and reduced to gutted ruins many top secret U.S. government programs, according to a former very senior CIA counterintelligence official, now retired, who was working on the Hanssen case.

That same observer, an experienced veteran of many high-priority counterintelligence cases and possessed of great instinct and insight, found Hanssen baffling. It was this former agency official who made the reference to Hanssen's resemblance to Gladstone, and he added that Hanssen made him also think of Elmer Gantry, having the word "hate" tattooed on one hand and "love" on the other. It is hard not to agree. A mercenary moral idiot like John Walker Jr. is not hard to figure, but Hanssen is rare in that he seems to have bewildered even trained professionals who examined him, and perhaps Hanssen remained a mystery even to himself.

His particulars of life are unspectacular. His father, Howard, and mother, Vivian, were from a working-class mainly white suburb of north-west Chicago called Norwood Park. They had met when both were work-ing at a department store at the start of the Great Depression. Howard be-came a Chicago cop and resigned to serve in the navy as a petty officer and was away when his son Robert was born on April 18, 1944.

Howard was a coarse-grained, self-centered man who liked to bet on the horses and on a family vacation would manage to stop at every place that had a racetrack. His son Robert was a shy boy, who was uncomfort-able around people, earnest, thoughtful, and withdrawn. He brought out the hard-boiled, brutal side of his father. It was a side that enjoyed inflict-ing humiliation and watching another squirm, whether it was rolling up his son in a navy mattress until the boy couldn't move or grew frightened, trying to toughen his son up by spinning him around and around in blan-kets until he threw up, making the boy sit for hours with his legs spread open, or, one time, lifting his son off the floor by a leg, which hurt him so much that he involuntarily urinated on himself.

And with the physical abuse came verbal belittling and sneering ridicule. The mother of Hoschouer remembers mainly that Howard was always down on his son. One time she ran into the father at the Jewel Gro-cery Store in Norwood Park. "'Oh my son, my son, is he ever going to amount to anything?' Always something about Bob. No matter what Bob did, it wasn't right. I've never seen a father like that. He never had a kind word to say about his only child."[1]

The malice was not confined to words. Howard arranged in secret for his son to fail his driver's test. On another occasion, after Bob and three friends planned for weeks to go backpacking in Colorado in celebration of graduation from Taft High School, Howard and Vivian refused at the last minute to let Bob make the trip. "Howard liked to fuck with Bob," said a friend. "It was just like him to let (Bob) plan that trip and then not let him go."[2]

Hanssen never fought back, but secrecy is the eroticism of the young, and Hanssen suffered in secret. But the brutalizing hostility did terrible damage. As a young man, Hanssen was an ill-nourished and stunted plant. He lacked social polish and in the presence of others always hung back, nervous, awkward, and self-conscious. But if he didn't know how to enter a room or lacked the self-confidence to strike up a conversation, he was gifted when it came to mechanical things, which is often a lonely child's aptitude. Hanssen built radios and became an amateur radio operator. He liked to fix things and around them became fearless and enterprising.

After high school, Hanssen attended Knox College, a small liberal arts school in Galesberg, Illinois. Hanssen was six feet tall and very lean. Like many parents who despise their children, Howard sought to gratify his own vanity through his son's accomplishments, and Howard had sternly resolved that Hanssen was to become a doctor. However, after finishing Knox, Hanssen again failed his father. Hanssen lacked grades good enough to gain admission to medical school and won only a "conditional admission" to dental school at Northwestern University where he studied for three years. Hanssen appears to have hated it, and his father was far from delighted. Howard was soon complaining of his son, "He won't amount to anything. I'm spending all this money on dental school."

Hanssen had met his future wife, Bernadette "Bonnie" Wauk, while working a summer job at the Chicago State Mental Hospital. She came from a large Roman Catholic family in Park Ridge, Illinois. Her father was a psychiatrist. In his senior year, Hanssen had begun writing her, and she had loved his letters. Bonnie would soon marry Hanssen, the twenty-four-year-old Lutheran, in a ceremony the violent summer of 1968 just days before the Chicago street riots.

Bonnie in her photos is a striking creature, radiating a supple animal health, the unspoiled freshness of youth, and the unblemished expression of someone with a completely untroubled conscience. She had dark, rich, full hair, with bangs almost down to her twinkling eyes, a fair oval face, a strong chin, and a mouth with a large smile displaying ranks of white, even teeth. She was almost a beauty, with an ample-breasted figure and great legs. She brought to the marriage a liking for giving and receiving sensual pleasure.

But as one looks at photographs of her through the years, what dawns is that at forty Bonnie bears the same expression that she did at eighteen, and her innocent expression has become a kind of mental vacuousness. Nothing of thoughtful intelligence had developed in it over all that time.

Her family was large and Catholic, given to a worldview that stressed transgression and repentance and that saw virtue as the will to refrain, natural drives as enemies, freedom consisting of emancipation of the senses, and Truth as being identical with the teaching of priests. But Bonnie's parents saw that Hanssen adored her and treated her as his queen, and that was enough. Like Islam, Catholicism is an authoritative religion that requires converts, and it wasn't long before Hanssen decided to convert to

Bonnie's church. In most matters, both Hanssen and his wife seem more comfortable obeying than questioning, and since she belonged to Opus Dei, a very stringent, rigorous Catholic order, it seemed natural that he would follow her and belong to it as well.[3] As the marriage began, Robert Hanssen seemed a petty, peaceable mediocrity. Both he and his wife fell easily into predetermined roles, like people who buy their clothes ready-made off a rack. Bonnie became the mother and housewife, and Hanssen turned into the dominating man of the house who paid the bills.

In 1971, Hanssen graduated from Northwestern with an MBA in accounting and information systems. By then he had become ultrareligious, and he had joined the Chicago police and was sent to counterintelligence school to learn how to install bugs and high-tech surveillance equipment, mainly to spy on fellow officers. In 1976, he set his sights higher and tried to join the National Security Agency (NSA), but missed, and instead became an agent of the FBI.

He still could not muster the moral courage to confront, rebuff, and defy the father who still governed him with such a stern and terrible hand. When Howard came to visit the couple, Hanssen would stay upstairs and be sick to his stomach from nervousness before he finally and reluctantly came down to the usual inquisition of scorn and sneers. It was Bonnie who rebelled against Howard's ferocious pitilessness toward his son. She bluntly told him, "If you are under this roof, if you cannot be respectful to Bob then you are not welcome to come."

Hanssen first did duty in Indiana covering white-collar crime, then was assigned to a field office in New York in late summer of 1978 where, as an accountant, his natural spot was in the budget unit. What Hanssen had not counted on was New York's exorbitant cost of living. The family couldn't afford to live in the city itself, and Hanssen bought an ordinary house in the suburbs of Scarsdale, New York. Bonnie joked grimly to her mother that she lived in the "Scarsdale slums." But Scarsdale was not really a slum, but a very expensive place to live, and Hanssen was earning the same salary as a sanitation worker. The family was growing, the bills piling up, the responsibilities multiplied, and the funds weren't there because he was working as an unglamorous accountant in the criminal division, making a long commute each day. As Bonnie was poised to give birth to their fourth child, the money shrank to a trickle.

With the child on the way and with only a mediocre salary to show, the humiliation of failure stared Hanssen straight in the face. If there was anyone in whose eyes Hanssen wanted to loom large and appear an impressive success, it was his wife's.

In 1979, not long after his transfer to New York, Hanssen walked into Amtorg—the outfit where Elizabeth Bentley's lover, Jacob Golos, had worked—and he offered his services to the GRU, Whittaker Chambers's old outfit. By then Hanssen was working in the Soviet Intelligence Division of the FBI's New York office. His motive for turning traitor? "I wanted to get a little money and get out of it," he said later.

Counterintelligence people are by nature and training very calculating and cautious, and Hanssen was no exception. Hanssen craved the money but sought at all costs to avoid any personal risk in obtaining it. He would create the occasion that offered him safe ground where he could reveal his wares without risking challenge. The FBI had an intelligence source of supreme importance inside the GRU. His code name was "TOPHAT," and his real name was Dimitri Fedorovich Polyakov. Recruited by FBI agents in 1962 at Grant's tomb in New York, Polyakov's material filled twenty-seven file drawers at the bureau, and his importance to the United States could not be surpassed. He had been a source of the first distinction.

Hanssen's fear was that Polyakov would somehow stumble across Hanssen's identity, and this meant that Hanssen had to secure his position by betraying Polyakov before Polyakov could betray him. Hanssen set right to work. First he put out his baits—information to whet the Soviets' interest and convince them that they were dealing with someone who had access to extremely sensitive U.S. documents. In his first theft, Hanssen revealed to the Soviets that the FBI was bugging the Soviet residential complex and also gave them a list of Soviet officers suspected of working for the United States. He utilized his tradecraft to ensure his secrecy, using onetime pads or encoded radio transmissions when talking to his new employers. To better have them take him seriously, in a letter of complaint about the paltriness of his payment, Hanssen even showed a little leg, coyly disclosing he was an FBI agent.

Polyakov had a barrel chest, piercing eyes, and a kind, round, applecheeked face. He was a decorated Soviet war veteran, "a jewel in the crown," as former CIA director James Woolsey described him. Polyakov sent the United States detailed data on the Vietnam War, on China's military, and on the widening split between Moscow and Beijing. He would provide one of the first warnings about the John Walker Jr. ring when, in

1979 or 1980, he told a CIA handler, "I think your military communications are penetrated."

Hanssen knew the fate of Soviet agents in place who were caught: they got a bullet in the back of the head and an unmarked grave. The CIA had taken over handling Polyakov since the 1960s, calling him "Bourbon." Hanssen reasoned that if Polyakov were snared, accusing eyes would turn toward the Russian agency handlers, not the FBI. And if he wanted to spy, Hanssen had to get rid of a Soviet general with such wide access to sensitive data that he might accidentally stumble upon Hanssen's name. The Soviets paid Hanssen $30,000 for the information for Polyakov's life.

But Hanssen was not as clever as he thought. There are several versions as to what happened next, but it appears that Bonnie found Hanssen scribbling on some papers in the basement of their house and suspected he was having an affair. A rush of anxious unrest settled on her. Only days after their marriage, an old girlfriend of Hanssen's had called up and said they had just made love, and that she, not Bonnie, was his real wife and woman. Any confrontation is tense and Bonnie asked Hanssen for an explanation and he had abjectly begged for her forgiveness. But now Hanssen was behaving oddly again. For one thing, he had begun to miss mass and now, out of fear, he tried to hide the papers from his wife. She flew at him, badgering him with questions, and he admitted that he had sold data to the Soviets, but claimed he had flimflammed them and had sold them only junk.

Bonnie's agitation and dismay were extreme. Religion was her touchstone, almost for her an alternative brain, and so she turned to the church, compelling her husband to see a priest from New Cannan, Connecticut, Robert Bucciarelli, a member of Opus Dei. To Bucciarelli, the course was clear: Hanssen had to turn himself in to authorities. But the priest pondered and spent a tormented and restless night, and his attitude softened by morning. The next day, he told Bonnie and Hanssen that the affair could be made right if Hanssen gave the money to a worthy charity. His priestly vows forbid him to do anything further, he felt.

Soon Hanssen was claiming that he had given the money to Mother Teresa's Missionaries of Charity, and Bonnie stamped her suspicions underfoot, but no one knows to this day what he really did with the money.

As for Polyakov, his doom would not be made final until June 13, 1985, when, at Chadwick's restaurant in Georgetown, Washington, a CIA traitor, Aldrich Ames, who had no idea of Hanssen, gave the Russians a complete list of the CIA assets contained in a seven-pound bag. Ames was paid $2.7 million by a grateful KGB. As a result, priceless Soviet agents in place were shot, and many others were put in prison. Polyakov was arrested in July 1986, and intensely questioned for twenty months. At the end of his interrogations, he was then led into a room, ordered to kneel down with his back to his executioner, and then shot in the back of the head so that the emerging bullet would so disfigure his face as to make it unrecognizable.

Sandy Grimes, a CIA handler of Polyakov, was heartbroken and incensed. "I felt he was part of my family because I knew so much about him and his family, even his father-in-law's pants size. He had a forty-two inch waist," she said later.

She had had to schedule her vacations to coincide for Polyakov's return from his posting in New Delhi to Moscow so that she could take a break when he did.

Her admiration for the man was immense: "He had fought in World War II and was aware of the great human sacrifices made by his country—All for nothing—because only a handful of people in Moscow were benefiting. He was worried that the United States did not understand the Soviet mind or what a dangerous threat communism was."

She had warned her superiors at the agency that she would resign if anything happened to Polyakov: "That's how strongly I felt about him and our obligation to protect him. When someone you worked with that closely is caught and executed, it really destroyed you."[4]

After Polyakov's murder, she hardened in her mind, however, vowing to capture whoever had betrayed him and ended by playing a major role in the downfall of Ames. Hanssen she never knew.

Hanssen's feelings about betraying Polyakov aren't known, but they are very probably similar to what Ames felt after he betrayed some of the same people and American agents. "All those people on my June 13th list knew the risks they were taking when they began spying for the CIA and the FBI," he told a reporter. "If one of them had known about me, he would have told the CIA, and I would have been arrested and thrown in jail. Now that I was working for the KGB, the people on my list could expect nothing less from me. It wasn't personal. It was simply how the game was played."[5]

To Ames's mind there was apparently no difference between imprison-
ment and violent death as penalties for being uncovered as a traitor.

Hanssen himself would conceal his 1979 act of treachery from
everyone except his defense attorney. The official federal indictment listed
1985 as the first year of Hanssen's employment by the KGB. One professional who didn't buy it was Paul Redmond, the chief CIA officer on the
Ames case. We met at a lunch where he was introduced as "America's
George Smiley" by former CIA Director James Woolsey, but Redmond, a
good-natured man famous for his intellect and his blunt speech had a style
described by a colleague as "Fuck you! Strong note follows." Feigning being grumpy, Redmond said, "I'm not as fat as Smiley."[6] But after the
lunch, we were talking and he said, "The 1985 date is wrong. Hanssen
went to work for them before that." I looked at him as though I had just
heard a flowering plant sing opera. But it's a federal document, a court
document I said. They weren't liable to make mistakes. "Well, they have,"
Redmond said. "Why do you think so?" I said. "My instincts as a case officer," said Redmond.

And he, of course, was right.

Plato Cacheris, the defense attorney, would use the knowledge of
Hanssen's earlier years to bargain leniency and prevent him from getting
the death penalty.

By 1981, Hanssen was working at the FBI's headquarters budget unit
and within that unit, the Dedicated Technical Program. Every human being has a character, a history, and a career, and is a struggling being whose
future happiness and success depend on the reactions to it on the part of
the people in the work place. Hanssen was awkward, shy, reserved, un-
confident, and his knowledge of these defects only made them worse. To
compensate, he adopted attitudes, seeing work as simply the dreary do-
main of the mediocre. But Hanssen did not have a conquering temperament or one that is able to fire and capture the imagination of his
colleagues because of his confidence and flair. Around other people he always felt oppressed and contracted. But he was very intelligent, and his
being very, very bright led him to make a fatal mistake that many bright
men make—of attempting to win the applause of a group without first
earning its approval. His attempts at socializing fell flat and he abandoned
his efforts to make friends because nothing came of them. Unlike his peers,
he was not garrulous, cordial, accessible, cocky, familiar. He was not

boastful. Hanssen, who felt he possessed a vast field of mental vision, smarted under incessant disfavor, always conscious of being a man missing something that other men had, always the colleague who managed to hit the wrong note. And so he fell back on acting haughtily superior, almost as if he thought that towering above his colleagues would compensate for not being liked by them. Eager to increase his knowledge, Hanssen's technical talents took him forward all the same. He moved from the budget unit to the Soviet C-3A unit at FBI headquarters, the counterintelligence group that targeted the Soviet Union.

The budget assignment was an important one for a future traitor, because one cannot know about secret moneys without seeing how they are being spent or will be spent in the future. A treasure of secrets spilled out before Hanssen's eyes like gems from a split purse. What boded worse for U.S. security was that Hanssen's promotion gave him access to an even greater range of sensitive, compartmentalized information that would enable him to do devastating and savage damage to the system he served. In his budget job, his seat at the drams of spying was central and down front.

Spying would soon come to be the dominating interest of Hanssen's life, but to all he was doing or would do, the bureau remained remarkably blind. For starters, it did not harbor the remotest inkling of a senior Soviet mole moving freely about in its ranks. In fact, a wave of excitement had risen like a cheer in 1983 when the FBI recruited its first two spies inside the Soviet embassy. At that time Bonnie was teaching at Oakcrest, an Opus Dei school in Washington, and the boys went to another Opus Dei School in Potomac, Maryland. The family lived frugally in Vienna, Virginia. Outwardly, Hanssen remained pious, upright, foursquare, seldom missing a chance to go to mass.

At work, Hanssen still remained an outsider, a man out of tune and always at odds with his social group. Yet more upward career moves came. He soon went back to New York, moving Bonnie and the five children into a modest three-bedroom house in Yorktown Heights, a location that required a daily commute of ninety minutes on a good day. This time Hanssen's job was to supervise the counterintelligence squad, and it was sometime during this period, before he left Washington, that he decided to resume his career as a Soviet spy.

Money and the ability to appear a superb husband and provider to Bonnie lay at the root of the decision. She wore the final authority in the marriage and was the person who had to be pleased and get her way if there was to be any peace in the home. She was strict, particular, severe toward others. She was a moralizing prig with a streak of the bully, always eager to show others what she thought was wrong. For example, she was dismayed by society's laxness when it came to sex. In the 1960s in Chicago, when some hippies ignored her warning to stop parking their car in her outside space, she shoveled sand into the car, inserted a hose, and then turned on the water. Then she waited on the balcony for them to discover what she had done, brandishing Hanssen's gun and shouting, "It only goes downhill from here." In the supermarket, she would turn the covers of *Cosmopolitan* magazine backward in an act of self-appointed censorship, and she once berated a female clerk at Victoria's Secret for displaying pictures of women in lingerie. In brief, Bonnie seems to have been a petty, cramped spirit that oppressed. Hanssen was only earning $46,000 a year and needed more because a sixth child was on the way, so now it was need that drove him on. But surely Hanssen's failures in human relations at work also figured in. He labored always with the painful knowledge of harboring superior talents while being seen as a social inferior by purblind peers who to Hanssen only stumbled along, with only intellect enough to feel their way blindly from point to point. He worked always under the sense of embitterment that comes with social eclipse. Scornful rejection by peers drives even mediocre people to desperate decisions.

On October 1, 1985, on a trip to Washington, he contacted Soviet intelligence offering to betray "documents . . . of the most sensitive and highly compartmented projects of the U.S. intelligence community." In the first communication, he betrayed three Soviet agents, not knowing that Ames had already given the KGB their names. One, Valery Martynov, a Soviet employee, is still believed by CIA officials to have tipped the FBI off to the precise identity of John Walker Jr.

The Russians might be killed, but giving up their names would more solidly lay the foundation of Hanssen's credentials as a spy. They would also bring him badly needed money, and indeed they did. On November 5, the KGB left a $50,000 payment at a Nottoway Park dead drop in suburban Virginia, and another payment for the same amount would follow. Martynov was recalled to Moscow on November 6, and the tall, big, jovial Russian who adored his family would be shot by a firing squad.

In March, Hanssen was soon busy alerting the Soviets to the fact that the NSA had learned how to intercept coded government traffic from Soviet satellites, wrecking a program that had cost untold millions of dollars to set up. By giving away which frequencies and channels were being listened to and which codes had been broken, they could shut down the circuits or, worse, feed back through them disinformation to mislead U.S. analysts. NSA expert James Bamford said the betrayal "was one of the worst blows to NSA since its founding."[7]

Hanssen now adopted a codename with his handlers, "Ramon Garcia," a fictional name for an undercover agent when Hanssen had spied on fellow officers with the Chicago police. Soon, in return for destroying a $100 million NSA program, and after giving details on Soviet defectors and having betrayed four U.S. agents, sending some to their death, Hanssen had collected $60,000.

He did not distinguish himself with the FBI in New York, although New York was the Holy City of Soviet spying, with over 200 Russian agents very active there, many using a UN cover. Instead of being assigned to a major counterintelligence operation, Hanssen ended up spying on Amtorg, only a secondary target. His old defects dogged him. He smarted under a sense of incessant disfavor, always conscious of missing something others had, of falling short, of having to suffer a sense of eclipse and failure.

He returned to FBI headquarters in 1987, a GS-14, assigned to his old counterintelligence unit on the fourth floor. To his colleagues, Hanssen's return signaled not an upward move but a shunting to one side and meant his tour in New York had been a bust. But it was a welcome move for Bonnie and the family because it cost a lot less to live in the Washington suburbs than New York, and the family of six children was not a small one after all. Hanssen bought a ranch house with four bedrooms on Talisman Drive in Vienna not far from his and Bonnie's earlier home. Although doing the dead man's float at the rank of supervisor with no hope of reaching shore, Hanssen was finally given an exciting new assignment. He was to examine past penetrations of the FBI by hostile agents. He was to rummage through the huge, weighty FBI counterintelligence (CI) files and study the case of every potential traitor. "He was at the center (of the program)—he saw everything," said former FBI counterintelligence official David Major.

On September 14, Hanssen once again took up his career as traitor, leaving documents from the National Security Council at Nottoway Park in Virginia and receiving $14,000 in payment. The unfortunate thing now was that he had begun to gain wider access to more various kinds of sensitive national security information. One program he betrayed was called

COINS-II (for Community-On-Line Intelligence System) and involved the classified intranet the U.S. spook community employed. For betraying this, Hanssen was paid $20,000. Other items followed, including details on a Soviet defector from the KGB's equivalent of the NSA and the work he was doing for the United States. There was also a highly classified assessment of Moscow's nuclear arsenal, details of warheads, numbers, data on what the United States believed Moscow knew about U.S. nuclear capabilities, a CIA counterintelligence study, and a comprehensive FBI review about allegations from various CIA and FBI Soviet assets about penetrations of U.S. intelligence that described FBI sources, not by name, but in enough detail to provide devastating clues for canny and determined hunters of men. For betraying these, Hanssen got $25,000. He also gave away documents filled with data on MASINET or measurement and signature intelligence dealing with the network of secret U.S. intelligence collectors around the world. SOSUS, which measures the electronic signature of Soviet submarines, would be included in this.

He would go on to bigger game. By 1989, he would betray Project Monopoly, a tunnel the United States had dug into the new Soviet embassy.

The new Russian embassy on Mount Alto in Washington was built on a sinister height that enabled Russian intelligence to intercept the whole network of calls from the White House to the State Department, the Defense Department, and to other sensitive government departments. The United States had learned some very sophisticated methods for waging electronic warfare. Back in the 1970s, they had realized that training a laser on a window meant you could re-create any conversation taking place inside from the minute vibrations registered. The United States had also learned how to enter emissions from an installation or device like a telephone or computer and travel back up through a web of connections to gain entrance to the interior of a facility by that means.

In the late 1970s, a West German military electronic genius by the name of Major Franz Dwinger, a major in the German Air Force, had once stealthily crept into the electronic emissions of a MiG-23 fighter sitting on an airfield in East Germany. Working from a keyboard in West Germany, he was able from that plane sitting on the runway to work back through all the electronic systems to which the plane was connected and produce an image of the base and its aircraft and installations that was so clear, sharp, and detailed that his commanding officer asked what aircraft had taken the photograph when no plane had taken it at all.

The United States was into much advanced versions of this, and the place from which the methods could have been used to the greatest effect would have been this tunnel under the Russian embassy. After millions and millions of dollars and years of labor and planning and correcting the design, just to gain an edge, Hanssen betrayed the program. The Russians simply countered by building a "bubble," a secure room that was sealed against emitting any emissions and that even stood on rubber wheels as extra insurance.

Bad people support each other, using systems of mutual aid, which is why so many of them thrive and are hard to topple. It is a reflex of all traitors to warn their handlers of the danger of other key spies. When master British traitor Kim Philby heard of Elizabeth Bentley's having gone to the FBI, he instantly alerted the KGB. Philby did the same thing when he heard of Gouzenko's defection. Act quickly and limit the damage—that was the rule. It is ironic that only a month before betraying the U.S. underground tunnel under the new Russian embassy Hanssen would set in motion the events of his own destruction by attempting to help another alleged U.S. traitor under federal investigation.

The case would involve a State Department official named Felix Bloch who had just returned to the United States after serving seven years in Austria where he had been an economic officer in the American embassy there. Like Hanssen, Bloch, a proud and ruinously touchy man, felt that somehow he could never make his full significance felt and was resentfully jealous of others who had gained promotions that Bloch felt his superior merits had better deserved. After he was assigned to Vienna in 1980, Bloch had just begun to take his first steps out of the general background, and in 1983, gained praise for his handling of the visit to Vienna of President George H. Bush, a very prestigious assignment. Bloch was just beginning to be thought special by the people who mattered. The problem was the CIA suspected that the diplomat might be disloyal, possibly recruited by the East Germans when he was assigned to that country in 1974.

Certainly a shadow seemed to follow Bloch's tall, bald compact figure in Vienna, and it belonged to a man from an alien and hostile universe: the KGB. According to authors David Wise and Elaine Shannon, the FBI suspected that it was a KGB officer named Reino Gikman, a phony name lifted from the birth certificate of an actual Finn who had been long dead, who was Bloch's control in Vienna.

But according to Wise, when U.S. agents and the Austrian federal police searched high and low for proof of the connection, no evidence could be found that the two had ever met.

Then, in 1986, Bloch made a misstep that would prove worse than unfortunate: it would be fatal. According to Wise, Austrian military counterintelligence caught a glimpse of Bloch slinking through the back door of the Soviet Embassy. This information was quickly passed on to the CIA, and the scrutiny of Bloch gained a new intensity. Bloch returned to the United States in 1987, and for two years all was quiet. Then on April 27, 1989, Wise recounts how alert CIA agents listened in on a telephone call between Bloch in Washington and Gikman in Vienna. The FBI opened its file on the case the next day, and, because Bloch was on U.S. soil, the FBI had jurisdiction.

For days federal agents watched and listened in. Nothing. Then in May of that year, Bloch suddenly made a trip to Paris. According to Wise, the FBI alerted the CIA station in Paris who alerted French counterintelligence. The latter allegedly tracked Bloch when he met a man named "Pierre Bart," and alias for Gikman, in a posh hotel bar on the right bank. Although in an interview with Wise, Bloch said he didn't know Bart was Gikman, Wise makes clear the FBI and CIA both suspected he did. On May 22, only days after this meeting, Robert Hanssen disclosed the Bloch-Gikman probe to the KGB, according to Wise, whose account was substantiated by FBI agents interviewed by the author. The Russian reaction was swift. On June 22, a man who called himself "Ferdinand Paul" made a call to Bloch's cozy Kalorama apartment in Washington. Paul said he was calling on behalf of Pierre Bart who could not see Bloch in the near future because Bart was sick. The caller then added a bit ominously, "A contagious disease is expected." He then told Bloch that he was worried about him and cautioned Bloch to take care of himself.

The FBI agents listening to the call went sick and numb with shock. The call was clearly a warning by Gikman to Bloch that he was under close surveillance. Any doubts of there being a Soviet mole in U.S. intelligence vanished in an instant. Someone with access to highly sensitive information had betrayed the case. Now that someone had to be found.

For three years, the agents swept through files, made endless lists, inventoried documents, compared facts, drew up lists and charts. Nothing surfaced; no new connections appeared. They began again, and although Bloch's alleged spying could not be proved, Bloch was fired from the State Department for making false statements to the FBI, forfeiting a $50,000 a

year pension and ending up working as a bus driver in Chapel Hill, North
Carolina, according to Wise. Glum and defeated, the grim-faced investigators began again to comb through their information with relentless
thoroughness.

Hanssen in the meantime was beginning to exhibit the symptoms of a
man who has lost his will to work. He had lost that zest for wholehearted
activity. His wife had birthed six children and had three miscarriages, and
they seemed a perfect couple, yet he seemed unable to find the power to
tense his will to the utmost in activity. He was tired all the time, devoid of
energy, lacking active purpose and vestige of determined, effective drive.
Plus he had begun to be sloppy with money. It was Bonnie's sister, Jeanne
Beglis, who first noticed the huge wad of cash Hanssen had simply left sitting out on the dresser. Or had Bonnie seen it first and been so upset that
she had run across the street to report the money to Jeanne? Versions differed.

Mark Wauk, Hanssen's brother-in-law, brought up the matter to his
superior, Special Agent Jim Lyle. Lyle was not overly alarmed. In fact, he
hardly seemed alarmed at all. Weren't there innocent explanations possible? There were. Hanssen's father sometimes helped the family with
money. Or couldn't the cash have come from Opus Dei or some other
charitable outfit? Lyle said to Wauk that if Bonnie had questions about the
sources of her husband's money, why didn't she ask him about it? Lyle
seemed to avert his face from the matter because the less innocent explanation of the money implied something so ugly and horrible that he
seemed not to want to ponder and absorb what it meant. The meeting was
inconclusive. Lyle didn't write up the meeting, didn't report it to anyone,
and nothing further occurred. Wauk was left to fume in frustration.

Hanssen would run free for another ten years. (It was true he broke off
all contact in 1991, but while idle, he was not inactive.)

The FBI's search for a mole continued, tireless, unremitting, and utterly pointless. Driven headlong by frantic determination and a desperate
craving for a result, the FBI had fastened its focus on the wrong man. The
man's name was Brian Kelly. It is profoundly ironic that it was Kelly who
had first unmasked Reino Gikman. But the disease of partiality had put
the FBI on Kelly's trail and kept it clamped there for three utterly fruitless
years. There is a tendency in all organizations to confuse the unpleasant
with the improbable. The possibility that the FBI itself was home to
the mole seemed to bureau agents so outlandish, that they refused to seri-

ously consider it. This moral prejudice produced a serious intellectual mistake. To the bureau, it would provide vindictive pleasure if a CIA agent would turn out to be the traitor rather than one of their very own brightest, even if he wasn't among the best. Kelly lived where they thought the traitor would live—he had all the right accesses and had been in crucial places at critical times. Thus, the bureau men tailed Kelly, opened his mail, tapped his phones and computer, even seized his jogging map that the jubilant bureau experts at first were convinced contained a layout of secret dead drop sites. Yet nothing panned out. Hopes, like new leads, withered to ashes.

In 1994, the cunning Ames had finally been caught, but an examination of the cases he compromised showed that the state of affairs remained incomplete. Not all the betrayed programs had been accounted for. There remained someone else, another mole still at large. Their hearts sank like bags of lead in water.

And then the miracle happened. It was like the breaking of dawn, the falling away of fetters, the restoration of sight, the finding of a huge gift of money found in the mail. A former agent in the Russian intelligence service (SVR) indicated that he had a dazzling secret to sell. By now Kelly had taken and passed polygraphs, had been officially cleared, and had received an apology from the FBI, but, about to tumble into the FBI's laps would come the evidence that would enable the bureau agents to close the cage door on Kelly with a punishing clang!

Using every precaution and employing every plausible pretext, the former KGB man came and met the FBI in New York. It turned out he had a sensational gift to give—the former agent had a KGB file on a star American mole. The Russian had removed the file from Russian foreign intelligence headquarters and carefully hidden it away. For a steep price, he would part with his prize. But immediately unforeseen difficulties cropped up on every side. To get paid, you had to produce, yet the Russian wanted the money before he showed the FBI anything of value. Was it a devilish scheme? A clever, subtle swindle? Some kind of crude scam? Was the bureau being manipulated, aroused, brought to a pitch of interest, only to be cheated out of funds and any view of solid proof?

The waltz went on. The agents advanced, the Russian withdrew. He returned, they scrutinized and argued and kept their own counsel. He offered, they counteroffered. Dealings stalled completely. Then the Russian dangled something absolutely tantalizing before the FBI's wide eyes. The

Russian claimed he had a tape recording of the American mole actually talking to the KGB. The hearts of the agents bounded and leapt with ripe joy. Here was a chance to finally crucify Kelly beyond any doubt or objection. So what if an FBI exoneration had already been placed in Kelly's file? What weight would that have if his voice turned up on the Russian's tape?

Mike Rochefort, heavyset, calm, soft-spoken, was the key FBI man handling the Russian's case. After agreeing to pay $7 million for the file, the Russian turned it over to the CIA in Moscow in November 2000. The CIA brought it well guarded from Russia to "a city on the East Coast." All of the file's items went to the FBI lab on the third floor of headquarters. There were the letters of the mole on computer disks and the titles of the documents he'd stolen, including a complete inventory and description— a total of 6,000 pages!

And suddenly there it was: a conversation labeled July 21, that was between Aleksandr Fefelov, a KGB officer, and the mole. The bureau brought in one of its most talented counterespionage agents, Michael Waguespack, a gray-haired, cordial Louisianan who had worked major CI cases for twenty years. With Rochefort and another agent, Tim Bereznay, the three went to a secluded room in the basement of headquarters and closed the door.

The agents licked their chops and turned on the tape, waiting to hear Kelly's voice, waiting to hear the vindication of so much dogged effort, so much relentless grit, so much methodical care and conscientiousness. And then, like men made of old stone, they simply sat stunned. It was not Kelly's voice that floated out on the closed air. It was another voice, a strange voice. Rochefort was like a man who'd been struck on the head. He was like a dazed duck. It wasn't Kelly at all. He'd spent three years chasing the wrong man. It wasn't Kelly. But then who in the hell was it?

Waguespack almost had it. The name of the voice fluttered like a jittery butterfly just out of his grasp. Waguespack knew he knew the voice, even knew the inflection, but he couldn't make his mind name the name.

The trio adjourned in perplexed frustration, absolutely dashed down.

It was a few days later while working through some of the file material that FBI agent Bob King's eye fell on a strange quote from the mole. Twice in the KGB file, the mole had quoted General George S. Patton as saying, "Let's get this over with so we can kick the shit out of the purple-pissing Japanese." With a swoop of sick shock, King recognized where he had first heard the phrase. "I think that is Bob Hanssen," he told Waguespack.

King hastened and hurriedly gathered the group. Again they listened to the tape. King burst out, "My God, that's him!"

On February 18, 2001, while making a dead drop in a Virginia park near his house, a SWAT team and a crowd of FBI agents, pointing machine guns, arrested Hanssen. After a trial and seeing her husband sentenced to life in prison, Bonnie, having found out about the stripper and Hoschouer being allowed to watch her perform as a wife, exclaimed bitterly, "My husband is a traitor and a pervert."

AT THIS POINT, the reader I hope will forgive me if my narrative becomes autobiographical, but as the Intelligence Correspondent for UPI, I was already covering the Hanssen case when the September 11, 2001, attacks occurred. In the anxious aftermath, the Hanssen story became entangled with attacks and the fears those attacks awoke in the senior levels of the U.S. government about the ability of terrorists to deliver nuclear weapons to the continental United States.

"It's the job of administrators to plan for nightmares," said Dick Murphy, former Middle East diplomat and senior Middle East fellow at the Council on Foreign Relations, and on September 11, 2001, a bright, fall Tuesday, America experienced one. It was the most horrifyingly unexpected and savage terrorist attack in U.S. history, which saw hijackers crash two airliners into the World Trade Center, toppling its twin 110-story towers, as a third plane slammed into the first three rings of the five-ringed Pentagon and a fourth aircraft crashed outside Pittsburgh after its passengers, using cell phones, became aware of what their fate was to be and fought back.

The attacks were a masterpiece of savage slaughter. The initial casualty estimate was 6,000 Americans not simply killed, but reduced to grisly, gruesome little bits of body parts—a piece of an ear, a tooth, the part of a hand, a finger with a ring on it. The onslaught was typical of the style and savagery of Osama bin Laden, a Saudi exile who had declared war on America in 1998. Bin Laden was fascinated with low-tech high-impact attacks that caused indiscriminate mass casualties. He had been involved with the 1993 attack on the World Trade Center towers, and he had killed Americans in Somalia and Yemen. In 1998, he had bombed almost simultaneously two American embassies in Kenya and Mozambique, killing over 200 and wounding 4,000.

The sickened, dazed horror that stole over America was uniquely distressing and intense. In a mere forty-five minutes, the explosions had brought the huge continent of America to a standstill, with the president stranded in the air on Air Force One, U.S. fighters aloft with orders to shoot down any other commercial planes that strayed from their scheduled flight paths, and the vice president sheltering in a bomb-proof cave below the White House.

The attacks sent an unmistakably grim message. "Look at the headlines," said a former senior CIA official who spoke to the author on the condition of anonymity. "'U.S. Under Lock Down;' 'High Alert, Evacuations Nationwide;' 'Attack Paralyzes New York;' 'California Near Standstill . . .'"

His next words were chilling: "It's not a large group of people who have made this happen. But they closed all the airports, paralyzed New York City, and made everybody fearful. And they are saying to themselves, 'We are just a handful of people who did all this, and, make no mistake, we can do it again—and we will.'"

Only minutes after the attacks early Tuesday morning, the most dreadful and persistent nightmare to haunt mankind since World War II now vividly awoke in the minds of Bush policymakers: the fear that terrorists were attempting to topple the government by killing its senior leadership. Within five minutes of the Pentagon attack, the Secret Service bundled Vice President Richard Cheney off to the Presidential Emergency Operations Center, dug deep beneath the elegant White House grounds. Cheney was a man who kept his head calm in a crisis. He had gotten a call from the president saying, "We're at war," and told Cheney to brief the leaders of Congress.

But Cheney's mind was focused on forestalling any more attacks. He called the president back and asked for permission to authorize U.S. fighter aircraft to shoot down any commercial planes being used as cruise missiles by hijackers. It was a hard-minded, merciless decision to have to make, but President George W. Bush wasted no time. "You bet," he said, and gave the authorization.[8]

At about 10:30 A.M., Cheney called the president with some disturbing information. White House intelligence sources had received a message: "Angel is next." Since Angel was the code name for Air Force One, still on its way back to the capital, listeners felt their blood harden to ice. The terrorists appeared to have inside information about the most sensitive U.S. security procedures. It was then that the idea of a decapitation strike hit

Cheney with full force. He got on the phone to Bush. "Don't come back," he said.

Bush, of course, did come back. He had the kind of unflinching energy and character whose courage rose with the amount of demands circumstances made on it. But the uncertainty centered on what the terrorists knew and how far in they had penetrated, and this was unsettling to many. Said another former CIA official, asking not to be named, "There were some speculations out there that (the terrorists) had insider knowledge of the president's travel logistics."[9]

The Bush administration immediately went to Continuity of Government measures, and this is where Hanssen's betrayals rose to take their place on the scene.

Since Hanssen had betrayed those security procedures to the Russians, the question that arose was, had the Russians, by chance, made the information available to terrorists, not as an act of official government policy, but because of an underpaid employee who had enough access to the data to want to seek to profit from its sale?

No one knew.

Continuity of Government procedures dealt with the chain of succession in civil authority in the event of war. Set up during the days of the Cold War, these were designed to secure the orderly functioning of the U.S. government in the event of a president being killed. It was a procedure worked out over decades designed to help the U.S. government survive in the event of salvo of Soviet ICBMs and designated the succession of political authority. Successors to the president were to be tracked at all times. One system, the "Central Locator System," ensured that the successors to the president are never in the same place at the same time. During the State of the Union address, for example, one cabinet member is still kept in a classified location in case of a disaster on Capitol Hill.

A major change of approach to the issue came in the 1980s, when U.S. intelligence analysts realized that though they could be hardened, huge bunkers could not escape surveillance by Soviet satellites. There was also a rebellion against "being hunkered down and bottled up in a fixed site."

It was decided to use national parks or resort areas as sites from which to conduct nuclear retaliation measures. As military and intelligence expert John Pike said, "It was a hide in plain sight idea."

The president and his advisors would be put in a regular van or all-terrain vehicle, followed by eighteen-wheeler trucks that would look like any other traffic on any typical American highway. Once they reached the special campgrounds in the national parks, they would enter a hardened site and operate from there. Several such sites are located in the Shenandoah Valley and were built in the 1980s.

Such tactics were called "Presidential Survivability" measures, and the United States had gotten the idea when U.S. intelligence discovered the Soviets building all sorts of resorts and recreational areas along the Black Sea in or around Moscow. A former senior CIA official said that the Yamanr-tau Mountain, near the Urals, is clearly such a Russian site and work continues on it to this day.

In any case, the chain of succession would move from the deceased president to the vice president to the speaker of the house, to the president pro tempore of the Senate, and then down through the cabinet secretaries in order of their creation—State, Treasury, Defense, Justice, Interior, and so on.

In the 1970s, when Hanssen began spying, Continuity of Government plans involved two helicopter squadrons, one operated by the marine corps, Squadron HMX-1, which was alert at Andrews Air Force Base, Maryland, twenty-four hours a day, seven days a week. In the event of an attack, a souped-up H-2 helicopter, followed by a heavily armed gunship, would have barreled in to land on the south lawn of the White House taking the president and his advisors to huge bunks called "wartime relocation centers." One of these, called Site 2, Ravenlock, is located near Camp David, Maryland, while the other, Mount Weather, is located on the West Virginia border. There is also Site 7, in rural Pennsylvania, which was where Cheney would be taken.

A second squadron, HS-1, tracked presidential successors. The squadron would swoop into areas where the presidential successors would be going to and take them into hardened bunkers or silos. The Secret Service and military practiced their pickups. "The deal was that any new cabinet member, within six months of being appointed, was to be actually picked up and flown to these sites so that they were familiar with the infrastructure," a former pilot of one of the units said. "They got to know our faces, and we got to know theirs."

The squadrons often did simulated passes over the sites to familiarize themselves.

Then, in the late 1980s, when Hanssen was going through his most intensive period as a spy, Bush changed the Continuity of Government label to "Enduring Constitutional Government" measures. It was the same horse with a different saddle. There was also the National Security Reorganization Act that set up a decentralized system consisting of primary and secondary command centers. Since major command centers could easily be destroyed by Soviet ICBM attack, the attack would isolate the secondary centers from orders needed to launch retaliatory strikes against Moscow. "Only the variable functioning of a presidential command center would enable the United States to retaliate against attack. The presidential command center would also act as a brake on secondary centers pre-delegated by the president to release nuclear weapons," John Pike said.

In any case, the president had given nuclear weapon release authority to several commanders of the North American Air Defense (NORAD) system and to six or seven three- or four-star generals.

There was one more weapon the United States could use: the Post-Attack Command and Control System, a secret network of airplanes capable of launching a U.S. retaliatory strike in an emergency.

The day of the attacks on September 11, 2001, came to an end. In New York City, the grieving began, but in Washington, the entire town was gripped by fear. What if bin Laden had somehow acquired a portable nuclear weapon? It was not as outlandish as it sounded. From British intelligence, the Bush administration had learned that bin Laden was much closer to being able to build a radiological bomb or "dirty bomb"—a conventional explosive encased in radioactive waste—than had been previously thought.

A further touch of dread and doom was added the first week of October when Israeli security forces arrested a Pakistani attempting to enter Israel with a radiological weapon concealed in a backpack. The report said that the would-be bomber had gotten to the territories via Lebanon. That was the initial report. A radiological weapon doesn't kill many people, but it scatters radiation and makes some areas uninhabitable. The asphalt on the streets must be taken up, all computers would be contaminated and have to be destroyed, and the psychological damage would be incalculable. Information about the arrest went straight to Bush and a close circle of advisors.

I was in Washington the second week of October and had meetings in various hotels, some lasting two to three hours with spooks or members of the U.S. intelligence community. A joint command center had been set up and two sources of mine had been in it when they saw a report of the Israeli arrest. I was the one who broke the story. Even those intelligence operatives and analysts who had not seen the report communicated a great fear that reigned in the White House about the danger of a sudden nuclear explosion. It could come from a portable nuke or a radiological bomb. No one was sure, except it was feared as a real possibility.

If there was any ungovernable panic at the unfolding of events, it lay inside a few souls honest enough to admit its presence, like the CIA consultant who told me he wanted to move his family out of New York for a month or so.

Representative Chris Shays, a republican from Connecticut said to me, "If you asked me if bin Laden had (a portable weapon) I would say, probably not, but, on the other hand, I wouldn't be the least surprised if there were a nuclear explosion in Israel or the United States."

Jim Ford, a former Department of Energy intelligence official who had dealt with nuclear smuggling said, "The big, big fear is that nuclear weapons have been sold" to terrorists or nation states that sponsor it.

A portable nuclear weapon, put in a backpack, could only come from one place: Russia. U.S. intelligence officials had first learned about the Russian backpack device from Russian agents in place in 1995. There were things called "suitcase bombs" as large as two footlockers, which the Russians had designed for Soviet Spetznetz Units, which resemble our Delta Forces and which would use the weapons to assault and destroy NATO command and control centers in the event of a NATO-Soviet war. The devices could not be detonated without matching codes held in strictest security in Moscow, former CIA officials said.

But the backpack was more sinister. It needed no such codes, but it too had been designed for Spetznetz forces, and if any comfort was to be had, it lay with the fact that the weapons had such an intricate and complex system of activation that the ability of a terrorist to detonate one "would be incredibly limited," an agency official said.

That was some comfort, but not much. Senior Arab intelligence officials had told the CIA in the early 1990s that bin Laden had obtained one or two suitcase bombs from a Central Asian republic in return for $30 million in cash and two tons of heroin, a deal brokered by the Chechen mafia. That story was discounted but there were additional possibilities that were even more disconcerting. "What is torturing us is what we don't know," said an administration official who would speak only on condition of anonymity.

Shays told me, for example, that at least forty-eight small nuclear weapons had disappeared from Russian arsenals and still remained unaccounted for.

Bush quickly dispatched one hundred senior administration workers to the protected sites with Cheney in his bunker acting as their chief. High-ranking officials numbering between seventy and a hundred began rotating in and out of the sites, grumbling, afraid that being away would undermine their jobs. They were drawn from every Cabinet and every major agency, the concern being to prevent disruption of telecommunications and energy networks, water supplies, transportation links, and the like. Only the executive branch made up this shadow government.

The sites were supplied with twin rotor transport helicopters, escorted by F-16 fighters, and followed by a chain of government buses.

When they arrived, they thought they would remain there for only two or three days, until terrorism assessments allowed them to return, but they underestimated the fear and uncertainty in the air. The backpack weapon was a special worry because as one senior former CIA official said, "It's probable that bin Laden has been able to obtain this system."

According to intelligence experts, the system consisted of three coffee can–sized aluminum canisters that had to be connected before detonation. In wartime, the system would have required a Russian crew of five including a commander, a radio officer, and three army non-coms.

The weapon was formerly in the custody of the 9th Directorate of the KGB, responsible for protection of Russian leaders, very much like our Secret Service. Assigning the weapon to that directorate probably meant that the teams were close to the Russian leaders. According to U.S. sources, the detonator was about eight inches long and was to be inserted in a "knife-like sheath" in one of the units. The weapon had a three- to five-kiloton yield, or about a quarter of the yield of the Hiroshima bomb.

The fact that the United States had accurate information about the system was due to brilliant intelligence work by both the FBI and the CIA in running a Russian expert on the system who remained an agent in place in his country. The Russian defector in place had been very blunt in telling the Clinton administration that its knowledge of the system was totally wrong and inaccurate. After he gave his corrections, they were put in a top secret blue border report—a report so sensitive that President Bill Clinton and Sandy Berger, his national security advisor, were only allowed to sign it and not even allowed to keep a copy before it returned to the CIA.

And here Hanssen's treachery casts its shadow directly across our story.

The CIA and FBI viewed the Russian source on the backpack bomb to be invaluable. They wanted him to remain in Russia as a producing source. But after Hanssen's arrest, agents from both agencies began to scan computer log-ins and an alert agent in one of them began to check in to see which computer sites Hanssen had visited and where he had loitered. Hanssen was a computer whiz and had browsed files using keywords to try to discover any inquiries that might reveal he was under scrutiny and being tracked. But as the agent gazed over the logs, he suddenly found that Hanssen had happened on to the expert source on Soviet portable nuclear weapons and apparently found him fascinating. Hanssen had returned to the site more than once, and each time spent more time there.

The CIA/FBI agents quickly concluded their agent in place had been betrayed and could well end up like Polyakov.

Events began to move with accelerating speed. Certain that their agent in place—America's best Russian expert on the building and operation of portable nuclear bombs—had been betrayed, and could face execution, the FBI and CIA conferred about how to best whisk the treasured agent out of Russia.

There were several ways to go, and the options were debated. Finally one was decided on, and the man who had taught America a new thing to fear was whisked away in deepest secrecy and safety and set up with a new life in America.

DO WE KNOW what damage Hanssen really caused? There was a damage assessment, but as Stuart Herrington, a former master military counterspy said, "They are never very accurate. A damage assessment is a report card to the enemy. You tend to massage it a bit."

There were allegations that Hanssen spied for Israel and China as well as for the Soviet Union, but they have been generally discounted although not entirely disproven. And we do not know what the damage assessment found. Redmond headed the team that did the digging.

Certainly we do not know the full truth about the file and the $7 million deal to get it. For one thing, the Russians knew Hanssen was going to be arrested before we in the public did. I was told that at the time by CIA officials.

The other puzzling fact is that Hanssen was no longer doing his best work for the Russians. A former Soviet CIA expert said, "Why did this guy (the Russian) . . . why did this guy come out neat and clean with his file and to give away a has-been." He added, "Instinct tells me there's more to it than that. There is another deal there that is being disguised."[10]

I have been able to confirm the $7 million figure that was used to purchase the file, to be paid out in small increments over time, but have not obtained further details to advance the story.

Which leaves us with Hanssen. It is our own habitual use of language in describing a traitor that in part prevents us from seeing more clearly a person like Hanssen. We say (because others do) that he lived a double life. But what if, in fact, he led several lives, simply because he had several selves lying side by side, just as layers of different species of rock lie peacefully adjoining each other in a boulder or a cliff? There was certainly an unexpected depth to the man, a series of layers of which no one seemed to have any knowledge. Perhaps the self that denounced communism was just as earnest as the one that served it. Perhaps the loving husband was just as sincere as the husband who disliked his wife and felt revengeful satisfaction by displaying her nude on the Internet or allowing his friend to watch her performing sex.

I do not find Bonnie an attractive character. Of course, we must distinguish between what is her misfortune and what is her fault, but she seems a willful, narrow-minded, conservative woman, not at all interested in unconventional ideas—someone who was all decorum and who liked sticking to the respectable and proven. Hanssen appeared to be under the thumb of his wife, and so he probably saw his conformity to her rules and her little laws as a kind of positive accomplishment, an achievement of humility, instead of another weak failure on his part to get himself put on an equal plane with another human being. Hanssen certainly never trusted his wife. He approached her not as something to love, but as a problem to solve and avoid. Hanssen had a theory that to control a woman you had to tell her a certain number of positive things, and if you did, then things would be good and peace would descend. It's a theory of escape, rooted in defeat and cowardice. According to a friend, Hanssen said that in a woman's brain "there is a counter, and they count up the good things you say to them and the positive strokes you give them."[11] It is not always the stronger mind that dominates in a marriage. The more intelligent of the two partners is often more open to compromise, more apt to see what the relation must have to endure than the mate who simply plants their demands in the sand and stands there with their arms crossed.

But Hanssen also appears to have harbored a dislike and hostility toward women in general. He hated women being agents because he deemed them weak, inferior, and incapable. He was aggressive toward them, once touching the exposed breasts of one of Bonnie's sisters as she sat breast-feeding her baby and causing her to flee in repulsion from the room. He also assaulted a co-worker at the bureau.

As for Hanssen himself, what can we say in assessment?

It is clear he was as much of a spiritual as a social misfit. Our progress in life—the things of worth we are able to accomplish—show us the stuff of which we are made, and yet when Hanssen assessed himself, what did he see? His adult life is a repeat of his childhood relationship with his father. Human judgment always found him an object of ridicule. He made the bitter discovery as an adult that in human relations he always lacked equal footing and acceptance and was always rated below his peers. He was always a subordinate doormat to his wife, and always less than others, except when he resorted to underhanded deception.

No person in life is simply content to remain at the level at which they began. Every individual wants to strengthen and perfect their capacities, to expand their dominance over vital areas of their lives, to win the battle between duty and appetite, inclination and development. But no one wants to do this alone. People crave, above all things, unity with their peers, to have their favorable notice, their hopeful expectations, their attentive sympathy and warm applause and praise for solid performances. But although Hanssen sorely desired these things, he had defects of disposition that denied them to him.

And why? Because everywhere he looked, Hanssen saw that mediocrity had found its home in groups and cliques where it reigned enthroned with terrible power. Hanssen had no social gifts. He couldn't make himself stand out in a crowd and so turned to being a criminal, choosing rather to count as a traitor than to count for nothing at all. At some point, Hanssen, a weak, shrewd creature instead of an impressive one, appears to have resolved to use deception and treachery, to make himself master of the stronger, but stupider forces that surrounded him, to damage and upstage them, and to revenge himself on the human collective that had acted to exclude him.

In all of the cases discussed here, the fathers were failures, drunks, and victims of a huge weakness of will and in some ways weakness of wits. Think of Benedict Arnold's father having to be dragged by his wife from taverns or John Wilkes Booth's father and his periods of wandering madness. John Walker Jr.'s father, like Arnold's, was an alcoholic and an abuser of his wife. In all cases, the childhood of these men was a hell of horrors.

The mistreatment of a child unfortunately carries over into its adult life. A parent that is always unfair and cruel creates a huge fund of mistrust that the abused child will apply to all people who come after. An unfair and cruel parent destroys the social compact since the child discovers that nothing in his childhood is experienced in the way that it is commonly known and described. The child learns that the terrors of punishment, intimidation, and unjust attack exist even in the safest of havens—in the home and at the hands of the parents he loves and depends on.

An abused child will always be wary of the world, but its vanity does not relinquish its claims to crave to count for something even if it takes to criminality in order to reach some kind of accomplishment.

If one cannot excuse Hanssen's treachery, one can sympathize with his social agonies. He did have gifts. He saw that distinction and excellence are a kind of force that none dare criticize in life, but he was excellent only in limited areas that were looked down on by many and to which he was confined. Worse, it was only to those areas that he could live fully because socially he was clumsy and cross-grained and was always borne down by the burden of knowing that he attracted no sustaining sympathy or interest among his peers.

Hanssen is a tragic figure, a lost ball in the tall weeds, lonely and forgotten and despised. It is a vicious, unsettling irony that he could only attain a sense of triumph by betraying his country, and that the only genuine acclaim he had in life, the only vestige of acceptance, was given him by his country's enemies.

Notes

THE TRAITOR AS HERO: BENEDICT ARNOLD

1. Information about Arnold's importance as a military figure is from Willard Sterne Randall, *George Washington*, New York, John McCrae/Owl Books, 1998, p. 397.

2. Bruce Catton, *A Stillness at Appomattox*, New York, Pocket Books, 1958, p. 311.

3. Some accounts say he was fifteen.

4. James Kirby Martin, *Benedict Arnold: Revolutionary Hero*, New York, New York University Press, 1997, p. 449.

5. Thomas Fleming, *Liberty!*, New York, Viking, 1997, p. 133.

6. See, Barry K. Wilson, *Benedict Arnold: A Traitor in Our Midst*, Quebec City, McGill-Queens University Press, 2001, p. 59. Wilson says that Allen was captured by the British on September 17 and spent the next months in a British jail. He played no further role in the revolution and in fact attempted to become a traitor in 1781 by establishing contact with British General Frederick Haldimand, offering to make Vermont a British jurisdiction in return for keeping it an entity separate from the other colonies.

7. Robert Leckie, *George Washington's War*, New York, HarperPerennial, 1993, p. 199. (Other accounts say Montgomery was forty-one.)

8. Leckie, op. cit., p. 404.

9. Martin, op. cit., p. 385. "Gates chose not to single out for special recognition any division, regiment, or officer . . ." Gates said, "To discriminate in praise of officers would be an injustice," and he took for himself all the credit for Arnold's moves.

10. There are a lot of disagreements in the various accounts as to the horse's color.

11. Leckie, op. cit., p. 546.

12. Ibid, p. 547. Arnold was expected to maintain the expenses of his headquarters out of his own pocket.

13. Johan Huizinga, *Men and Ideas,* Princeton, New Jersey, Princeton University Press, 1984, p. 102.

14. Leckie, op. cit., p. 578. (This would not be discovered until the 1930s.)

15. Harrison Clarke, *All Cloudless Glory,* Washington, D.C., Regnery, 1995, p. 395.

16. Stephen F. Knott, *Secret and Sanctioned,* New York, Oxford University Press, 1996, p. 17.

17. Wilson, op. cit., p. 161.

18. Ibid, p. 225.

19. Ibid, p. 173.

20. George Athan Billias, *George Washington's Generals and Opponents,* New York, De Capo, 1994, p. 188.

Notes on Chapter Sources. For Arnold's background I have relied heavily on James Thomas Flexner, *The Traitor and the Spy,* New York, Syracuse University Press, 1991, Willard Sterne Randall's *Patriot and Traitor,* New York, Quill, 1999, was helpful as was James Kirby Martin. Martin's notes on Arnold as merchant are excellent, and both Leckie and Martin are excellent on questions of grand strategy and Canada.

For the account of the battle of Valcour Island, Martin, Leckie and Flexner, and Fleming were all extremely useful. Balias has good background on Sir Guy Carlyle. David McCullough's *John Adams,* New York, Simon & Shuster, 2001, was helpful in giving a sense of the internal strife and politics of Congress. He also had good information on the Schulyer Gates feud and its background. Bilias was helpful on Gates, as was Leckie. The most in-depth and engrossing account of the battle, which was two battles that took place over seventeen days, is Richard M. Ketchum's *Saratoga,* New York, John McCrea/Owl Books, 1999.

For background on Gates's disloyalty to Washington, Schuyler-Gates feud and other matters related to Arnold, I also relied on A. J. Langguth, *Patriots,* New York, Touchstone, 1989, truly an excellent work.

For Arnold's treachery, I relied on the standard, Carl Van Doren, *The Secret*

History of the American Revolution, Garden City, New York, Garden City Publishers, 1941. Knott provides the matchless portrait of Washington deceiving two spies about to be hanged. Flexner, *Traitor and Spy,* was excellent, although, like Van Doren, a bit dated in places. For providing priceless portraits of Major Andre picking up the John/James Anderson letter, I thank Morton Pennybacker's superb *General Washington's Spies,* Laguna Hills, California, Aegean Park Press, 1930. It's a wonderful work. Only Leckie's work had the amazing confession of Peggy Arnold's ideological seduction of her husband. Also helpful was John Bakeless, *Turncoats, Traitors & Heroes,* New York, De Capo Press, 1998.

For details on Arnold's life in London, high praise must go to Barry Wilson's well researched and plucky book that knocks on the head certain myths that have clung as tenaciously as burs to the Arnold's later history.

I want to also apologize for my truncated treatment of Arnold's military exploits, especially his trek to Quebec and the battle of Valcour and Saratoga, actually two battles that took place in a span of seventeen days. I was compelled to cut the account to the point of mutilation.

THE TRAITOR AS ASSASSIN: JOHN WILKES BOOTH

1. William Tell was the Swiss national hero who refused to bow to the hat of an Austrian Hapsburg monarchy official that had been put upon a pole in the public square of Altdorf. When Tell walked past the hat without bowing, Hermann Gessler, the official was offended in his dignity, and Gessler seized Tell, who was well known as a marksman, and set him a challenge. He ordered him to shoot an apple off his son's head with his crossbow; if Tell was successful, he would be released, but if he failed or refused, both he and his son would die. Tell made the shot, but he had held an arrow back to put through Gessler's heart and when the tyrant asked what the arrow was for, bluntly told him and eventually put it there later, during an ambush. Tell's comrades were supposedly inspired by his act of bravery enough to throw off the yoke of Hapsburg oppression in their homeland.
2. Carl Sandburg, *Abraham Lincoln, The War Years,* New York, Dell Publishing Co., 1959, pp. 857–860.
3. Edward Steers, Jr., *Blood on the Moon,* Lexington, Kentucky, University Press of Kentucky, 2001, p. 45.
4. Bruce Catton, *A Stillness at Appomattox,* New York, Pocket Books, 1958, p. 20.
5. Modern historians believe that Lincoln and Meade had no knowledge of such a plan, but that Kirkpatrick was probably the author of Dahlgren's order. See

James O. Hall, "The Dahlgren Papers: A Yankee Plot to Kill Jefferson Davis, *Civil War Times Illustrated,* November 1983.

6. Eliot Cohen, *Supreme Command,* New York, Free Press, 2002, p. 21.

7. Richard Hofstadter, *The American Political Tradition,* New York, Vintage Books, 1948, p. 116.

8. Steers, op. cit., p. 47.

9. Steers, op. cit., pp. 52–53.

10. William Tidwell, *April '65,* Kent, Ohio, Kent State University Press, 1995, pp. 70–72.

11. Sandburg, op. cit., p. 852.

12. William Tidwell with James O. Hall and David Winfred Gaddy, *Come Retribution,* Mississippi, University of Mississippi Press, 1988, p. 453. Five pictures of good-looking young women were found in the pages of Booth's memorandum book after he was shot, Tidwell says.

13. William Hanchett, *The Lincoln Murder,* Urbana, University of Illinois Press, 1956, p. 12.

14. Barbara Tuchman, *The Proud Tower,* New York, Bantam Books, 1967, p. 124.

15. Tidwell, *Come Retribution,* pp. 5–6.

16. Tidwell, *April '65,* p. 144. The Confederate money handler was a "Mr. Davis."

17. Webb Garrison, *Civil War Schemes and Plots,* New York, Gramercy Books, 2001, p. 173. Confederate agents Jacob Thompson and Clement Clay had a plot to torch the city of New York, according to information developed by the U.S. Judge Advocate General, Joseph Holt. The conflagration was to take place November 8, 1864, election night. A Confederate prisoner, Robert C. Kennedy, confessed in March 1865 that six or seven conspirators were assigned to fire the city. Each man was assigned multiple targets. Kennedy was given Barnum's Museum, Lovejoy's Hotel, the Tammany Hotel, and the New England House. He checked into all three hotels using a different name at each. Another conspirator was assigned to the Saint-Denis Hotel, the Hoffman House and the Fifth Avenue Hotel. For a price a Confederate chemist made 144 four-ounce bottles of Greek Fire, whose active ingredients were phosphorous and hydrogen sulfide. But conspirators, after splashing Greek Fire on the furnishings and lighting it, rushed out and shut the door to the rooms, killing the fires' air supplies. Only one hotel was destroyed. Had it worked, it would have turned crowded hotels and places of public resorts into infernos. Kennedy was found guilty of violating the laws of war and hanged March 25.

18. Steers, op. cit., p. 236. It should also be remembered that Lincoln's war had wiped out Dr. Mudd's wealth in slaves and with the loss of slaves came the lowering of the values of his land. Slaves were needed to perform the task of tobacco farming, and the Emancipation Proclamation put an end to that trade and cost

the members of Charles County millions and millions of dollars. Mudd was full of unexpended, corrosive resentment, see Steers, op. cit., p. 68.

19. Steers, op. cit., p. 79.

20. Steers, op. cit., p. 127.

21. Tidwell, *April '65,* p. 68.

22. Steers, op. cit., p. 86.

23. Tidwell, *Come Retribution,* p. 417. The Azterodt confession was missing for years and discovered only in 1977 by the grandson of Atzerodt's counsel, William E. Doster.

24. Tidwell, *April '65,* p. 146. That Booth's activities were not simply local and his own initiative is made clear when one Henry Finegass testified at the trial of Booth's co-conspirators at St. Lawrence Hall in Montreal, February 15 or 16, 1865, that he had heard a conversation between George Sanders and William Cleary in which Cleary said, "I suppose they are getting ready for the inauguration of Lincoln next month," to which Sanders replied, "Yes, if the boys have any luck, Lincoln won't trouble them much longer." Cleary asked, "Is all well?" and Sanders replied, "Oh, yes! Booth is bossing the job."

25. Tidwell, *April '65,* p. 48.

26. Tidwell, *Come Retribution,* p. 418. New York associates of Booth had come up with a plan to mine the White House and kill Lincoln and others. An entrance had been found on the War Department side where explosives could be planted. But an explosives expert was needed and Booth had no such person. Hence the urgent need for Harney. See also Steers, op. cit., p. 90.

27. Hanchett, op. cit., p. 52.

28. Steers, op. cit., p. 111.

29. William H. Hearndon and Jesse W. Weik, *The Life of Abraham Lincoln,* New York, De Capo Press, 1983, p. 483.

30. Hearndon, op. cit., p. 483.

31. Steers, op. cit., p. 111.

32. Tidwell, ibid, p. 190. Here he notes that on their way to the Garrett farm, Booth and Herold stopped at the home of Richard Henry Stuart, a prominent Confederate citizen of King Georges County. In a later interrogation, Dr. Stuart said that Booth had told him that he wanted to find his way to Mosby. As late as April 24, Booth and Mosby had moved to within twenty-five miles of each other (p. 191). Also, when on April 24 Booth and Herold hired a wagon from a black family to take them to Port Conway on the Rappahannock River, Booth and Herold ran into three Mosby soldiers, including Mortimer Ruggles, son of Confederate general Dan Ruggles and second in command to Thomas Nelson Conrad, the key figure in the earlier plot to kidnap Lincoln.

33. Tidwell, op. cit., p. 190.

34. Tidwell, *April '65,* p. 192.

Notes on Chapter Sources. The key works on Lincoln's assassination are Tidwell's two books and Steers's excellent *Blood on the Moon*. I have drawn from them extensively. As general references I used John Wilkes Booth, www.crimelibrary.com; and Doherty, Edward P., *Pursuit and Death of John Wilkes Booth, Century Magazine XXXIX* (January 1890); Kunhardt, Dorothy, *Twenty Days,* New York, 1965.

William Hanchett's *The Lincoln Murder,* dating from 1986, is a good place for anyone to start because the professor discusses various theories about the Lincoln assassination, inluding the charge that the Confederacy was behind it, and he then shows that each theory is based on speculative and unsupported assertions. Tidwell changed all this. Tidwell was a CIA intelligence professional who had experience in running recruited spies. Having bought a cabin in Virginia that had been involved in Booth's escape, and after studying Booth's escape to Virginia, he quickly concluded that Booth was being "managed" and that "there were players in the drama that did not appear on the stage."

Tidwell unearthed the documentary evidence of Booth's recruitment as a Confederate agent. He also has proved that what previously appeared to be a group of unconnected individuals were in fact associated in various Confederate espionage plots, including Lincoln's kidnapping—a legitimate act of war—but also a plot by the Confederates to blow up the White House. The writings of Steers and Tidwell both rest at key points upon *inference.* In the facts the writers relate there can be seen a certain mutuality of reference and a certain interaction. Inference is merely an attempt to get a hold of the adequate significance of a random collection of existing facts. I think that the way Tidwell and Steers interpreted the facts, although still only a hypothesis, will prove to be definitive after more research is done.

For background on Booth's childhood, I relied on material in Steers's, Tidwell's, and Carl Sandburg's biographies of Lincoln. For material on Mosby, I have relied chiefly on Edmund Wilson's marvelous *Patriotic Gore,* New York, Oxford University Press, 1966. Wilson's section on Lincoln deals wonderfully with Lincoln's dreams and visions. I have read deeply on Lincoln over the years, including several biographies, which I am not listing here simply to avoid appearing more learned than I am.

Some have questioned why I have classed Booth as a traitor because my friends maintain Booth was simply a Confederate sympathizer caught in a civil war. This is not true. Always a Confederate sympathizer, on December 22, 1862, Booth was in St. Louis for a two-week engagement at the Ben Debar's theatre, and there vented anti-Union sentiments including a statement that he wished "the whole damned government to go to hell." That appears mild. But Lieutenant Colonel Henry L. McConnell, provost marshal, Department of Missouri, arrested and fined Booth who then *took the oath of allegiance* to the Union. (Tidwell, *Come Retribution,* p. 258.) This makes him a traitor, period.

THE TRAITOR AS IDEALIST: CHAMBERS AND BENTLEY

1. Barbara Tuchman, *The Proud Tower,* New York, Bantam Books, 1967, p. 112.
2. Whittaker Chambers, *Witness,* Washington, D.C., Regnery Gateway, 2002, p. 180. In a later incident, Whittaker again found his brother unconscious, lying on a couch, his hands cold, and the gas on, in a little workshop behind the main house, and again saved his life before the last, fatal attempt.
3. Bertrand Russell, *Freedom Versus Organization,* New York, Norton, 1962, pp. 71–74.
4. Tuchman, op. cit., p. 73.
5. Isaiah Berlin, *Karl Marx,* London, Oxford University Press, p. 105.
6 Tuchman, op. cit., p. 84.
7. Dimitri Volkogonov's *Lenin,* New York, Free Press, 1999, p. 82. See also same work, p. 237: "Unrestrained, lawless power, based on force in the simplest sense of the word, is precisely what the dictatorship (of the proletariat) is about." Also it should be noted that Lenin's first task as head of Russia was to betray his country. By the end of January 1918, the Germans were advancing on all fronts, encountering little significant opposition. On March 3, Lenin signed the German-dictated treaty of Brest-Litovsk, which ensured Lenin continued German support, for it would take Russia out of the war, a fact of which the Germans were well aware: "The Bolsheviks are the best weapon for keeping Russia in a state of chaos, thus allowing Germany to tear off as many provinces from the former Russian empire as she wishes and to rule the rest through economic controls," said the German Foreign Minister, Admiral Paul von Hintze.
8. William Duff, *A Time for Spies,* New York, Vanderbilt University Press, 1999, p. 57.
9. William Stevenson, *Intrepid's Last Case,* New York, Ballantine Books, 1984, p. 192.
10. Sam Tanenhaus, *Whittaker Chambers,* New York, Modern Library, 1998, p. 110. Chamber bought four rugs for members of his ring and they became "tangible evidence," as he said. Years later, a member of Bentley's ring, which was working with star Treasury official Harry Dexter White, visited White's home and

saw the handsome rug on the floor and said, "Why that looks like one of those Soviets rugs." White became very nervous and when his friend next visited, the rug was gone. (Chambers, op. cit., p. 416.)

11. Tanenhaus, op. cit., p. 384.

12. Charles Bohlen, *Witness to History,* New York, W.W. Norton & Company, 1973, p. 43.

13. Allen Weinstein and Alexander Vassiliev, *The Haunted Wood,* New York, Random House, 1999, p. 13.

14. J. C. Masterman, *The Double-Cross System,* New York, Ballantine Books, 1982, p. 30.

15. Weinstein and Vassiliev, op. cit., p. 47.

16. Manchester, op. cit., pp. 196–97.

17. Chambers, op. cit., p. 460.

18. Herbert Romerstein and Eric Breindel, *The Venona Secrets,* Washington, D.C., Regnery, 2001, p. 124. It was Levine who reported the conversation to Chambers and Roosevelt's "Go Jump in the Lake," was a paraphrase by Chambers of a stronger phrase.

19. Christopher Andrew, *For the President's Eyes Only,* New York, Harper-Perennial, 1996, p. 89.

20. Andrew, op. cit., p. 85.

21. Paul Johnson, *Modern Times,* New York, Harper Colophon Books, 1985, p. 345.

22. Andrew, op. cit., pp. 89–90.

23. According to an interview with a former senior CIA official on April 11, 2003, Eleanor Roosevelt gave the order to dissolve Kelly's department. The author had heard similar allegations from senior U.S. intelligence officials in 1985.

24. G. J. A. O'Toole, *Honorable Treachery,* New York, Atlantic Monthly Press, 1991, p. 327.

25. Lyn Montross, *War Through the Ages,* New York, Harper & Brothers, 1944, p. 828.

26. Montross, op. cit., p. 857.

27. John Keegan, *Six Armies at Normandy,* New York, Viking Press, 1982, p. 25. In fairness, within the next twenty-seven months, the U.S. military had increased its strength eight times, from 190,000 to 1.5 million, says Keegan.

28. John Lewis Gaddis, *The United States and the Origins of the Cold War,* New York, Columbia University Press, 1972, p. 64.

29. Walter LaFeber, *America, Russia, and the Cold War 1945–1975,* New York, John Wiley and Sons, Inc., 1967, p. 14. LaFeber said that until late 1943 Stalin was considering a separate peace with Hitler.

30. John Lewis Gaddis, *Strategies of Containment,* Oxford, UK, Oxford University Press, 1982, p. 20.

31. Gaddis, *Origins*, p. 38.

32. Gaddis, *Origins*, p. 36.

33. Andrew, op. cit., p. 111.

34. Romerstein, op. cit., p. 150.

35. John Earl Haynes and Harvey Klehr, Venona: *Decoding Soviet Espionage in America*, New Haven, Yale University Press, 2000, p. 142. As an example of what a highly placed Soviet spy like Harvey Dexter White could do, the authors relate how White managed to increase the amount of a loan to the Soviet Union for postwar reconstruction. On January 3, 1945, Moscow asked for a loan of $6 billion with generous terms of repayment—over thirty years at an interest rate of 2.25 percent. After White intrigued, the amount of the loan rose to $10 billion repayable over thirty-five years at a rate of 2 percent interest, even though the State Department opposed the loan. Also see Romerstein, pp. 214, 248, on Harry Hopkins, described by Robert Murphy, diplomat and intelligence agent: "Few men in this century have exercised more influence on politics, domestic and foreign, than Hopkins," *Diplomat Among Warriors*, p. 256. Romerstein and Breindel note op. cit., p. 216: "On a number of significant issues relating to the Soviet Union, Hopkins unsurprisingly pressed for pro-Soviet solutions." The authors made the charge that Hopkins was a Soviet agent who had contacts with the Chekist Iskhak Akhmerov, and added he was not only a Soviet agent and was "a very important agent indeed," op. cit., p. 213. But senior former CIA Soviet analyst Fritz Ermarth makes the point that an agent is on the payroll. Ermath doubts if Hopkins was ever an "agent" in the strict sense of the term. Instead he was probably "a trusted person" or KGB intermediary who worked out of conviction, not pay.

36. Weinstein and Vassiliev, op. cit., p. 102.

37. Robert Sherwood, *Roosevelt and Hopkins: An Intimate History*, New York, Harper & Brothers, 1948, p. 363.

38. George Kennan, *Memoirs*, Boston, Atlantic Monthly Press, 1967, pp. 257–69. Kennan said, among many other trenchant things, that "The assertion . . . that we and the Russians were going to cooperate in reorganizing German education on the basis of 'democratic ideas' carried inferences wholly unjustifiable in the light of everything we knew about the mental world of the Soviet leadership," (259), and added of the Soviet occupation of Eastern Europe, "The disaster that befell this area with the entry of Soviet forces has no parallel in modern European experience" (265). See the whole discussion.

39. Rudy Abramson, *Spanning the Century: The Life of Averell Harriman*, New York, William Morrow and Company, 1992, p. 387.

40. LaFeber, op. cit., p. 14.

41. Robert Lamphere and Tom Shachtman, *The FBI-KGB War*, London, A Star Book, 1988, p. 32.

42. Stevenson, op. cit., p. 96.

43. Stevenson, op. cit., p. 107.

44. J. M. Roberts, *Twentieth Century,* New York, Penguin Books, 2000, p. 440.

45. Soviet traitor and British intelligence agent Kim Philby had been quick to alert the Soviets to Bentley's defection.

46. Manchester, op. cit., p. 506.

47. Chambers, op. cit., p. 614.

48. Tanenhaus, op. cit., p. 433.

49. Tanenhaus, op. cit., pp. 433–34.

50. Chambers, op. cit., p. 5.

51. Chambers, op. cit., p. 6.

Notes on Chapter Sources. For general background on America, on the Great Depression, and the country in 1946, I used William Manchester's superb *Glory and the Dream,* New York, Bantam Books, 1975, which gave excellent details on depression and postwar years. His account of the Hiss case is excellent, even if brief.

For family background and Chambers's early life, I relied on Whittaker Chambers, *Witness,* Washington, D.C., Regnery Gateway, 2002. Sam Tanenhaus, *Whittaker Chambers,* New York, Modern Library, 1998.

Details on child labor, Bertrand Russell, *Freedom versus Organization,* New York, W.W. Norton & Company, 1934, and Barbara Tuchman, *The Proud Tower,* New York, Bantam Books, 1967. For material on Marx, I relied on Berlin, on Edmund Wilson's masterpiece, *To The Finland Station,* Garden City, New York, Doubleday & Company, Inc., 1940. Also indispensable: Jacques Barzun's *Darwin, Marx, Wagner,* Chicago, University of Chicago Press, 1941, Paul Johnson's quirky but penetrating *Modern Times,* New York, Harper & Row, 1985, and Robert Heilbroner's masterly exposition in *The Worldly Philosophers,* New York, Touchstone Books, 1972.

For a chilling portrait of Lenin's idolization of force, a work of the first distinction is Dimitri Volkogonov's, *Lenin,* New York, Free Press, 1999. Most of the details of Lenin's fascination with using terror as an instrument of rule come from this book.

For details on Roosevelt and American-Soviet wartime relations, I reread Kennan's *Memoirs,* Boston, Atlantic Monthly Press, 1967; Bohlen's *Witness to History,* New York, W.W. Norton & Company, 1973, and Robert Murphy's *Diplomat Among Warriors,* Garden City, Doubleday, 1964. Murphy, a key U.S. intelligence agent throughout the war, also has a great deal about the American compulsion to please Stalin (pp. 255, 265–83). (It is Murphy's book that the Eisenhower quote, "We must give trust to get trust" applied to the Soviets occurs.) As for Kennan and Bohlen, they were in the U.S. Embassy in Moscow and were firsthand witnesses. Their testimony is invaluable. Also useful was Abramson's *Spanning the Century: The Life of Averell Harriman,* New York, William Morrow and Company, 1992 on Harriman, the U.S. ambassador to Moscow, during the war.

For background on the Spanish Civil War, I relied on Johnson's *Modern Times,* especially George Owell's *Homage to Catalonia,* London, Penguin Books, 1989, and Hugh Thomas's masterpiece *The Spanish Civil War,* London, Penguin Books, 1965. The Cold War histories of Gaddis and LaFeber are incredibly good.

For details of Bentley's life, I primarily relied on her autobiography, *Out of Bondage,* New York, Ballantine Ivy Books, 1988. Bentley's depiction of her ideological seduction by Fuhr is convincing and her picture of her love for Golos is extremely, sincerely moving. This edition also has a long appendix in which a variety of hard-nosed and qualified experts scrutinize, chapter by chapter, the assertions that Bentley made to the FBI. Her allegations, at first greeted with great suspicion because she lacked documents, have invariably proved accurate and have stood examination.

For information about the "Era of Illegals," former FBI agent William Duff's *A Time for Spies,* New York, Vanderbilt University Press, 1999, is compassionate and incredibly knowledgeable—a must-read. Also invaluable was Lamphere's *FBI-KGB War,* especially on the defection of Gouzenko. Stevenson's *Intrepid's Last Case,* New York, Ballantine Books, 1984, provided some key quotes although there were also inaccuracies. For the life of Krivitsky, I used his excellent memoirs, *Stalin's Secret Service,* New York, Enigma Books, 2000, which vividly convey in the man's dauntless strength of life, his tremendous moral courage and outstanding literary style: limpid, direct, full of punch and point.

For details of Hiss's life, Weinstein and Vassiliev as well as Herbert Romerstein were excellent.

For the Chambers and Hiss confrontation, I relied on Chambers's testimony before the HUAC as given in *Witness* (which I edited for sake of space). It occurs in *Witness,* pp. 569–616.

I would also recommend Mark Mazower's *Dark Continent: europe' twentieth century* (sic), New York, Vintage Books, 2000, to discover the degree to which democracy and liberal capitalism or free market economies were under serious scrutiny as failures.

THE TRAITOR AS PETTY THIEF AND NATIONAL CATASTROPHE: JOHN WALKER JR.

1. Ronald Kessler, *Spy Versus Spy,* New York, Charles Scribner's Sons, 1988, p. 20.
2. David Kahn, *The Codebreakers:* The Story of Secret Writing, New York, Signet, 1973, p. 348.

3. Thomas B. Allen & Norman Polmar, *Merchants of Treason,* New York, Delacorte Press, 1988, pp. 8–12.

4. Howe, Russell Warren, *Weapons,* Garden City, New York, Doubleday & Company, 1980, p. 50.

5. Pete Early, *Family of Spies: Inside the John Walker Spy Ring,* New York, Bantam Books, 1999, p. 66. She claimed the relationship lasted ten years. He denied it.

6. Peter Early's marvelous phrase.

7. Early, op. cit., p. 95.

8. John Barron, *Breaking the Ring,* Boston, Houghton Mifflin Company, 1987, p. 23.

9. Allen and Polmar, op. cit., p. 267.

10. Sherry Sontag and Christian Drew, with Annette Lawrence Drew, *Blind Man's Bluff, The Untold Story of America Submarine Espionage,* New York, HarperPaperbacks, 1999, pp. 244–57.

11. Howe, op. cit., p. 54.

12. Sontag, op. cit., p. 295: "U.S. watchers became aware of other new and disquieting changes in Soviet strategy, such as holding strategic missile boats back in the Barents Sea, protected by attack subs and heavily-armed surface ships, so that, if war exploded, the Soviets would be able to salvo missiles by the shortest route—directly across the Arctic Circle—to scream in on targets like Washington, D.C. "or any other location in an arc drawn from about South Carolina through Oklahoma to Oregon."

13. Harold, Nicolson, *Diplomacy,* London, Oxford University Press, 1963, p. 25.

14. Hedrick Smith, *The Power Game,* New York, Ballantine Books, 1989, p. 188.

15. Lehman interview with author at Abington Corp., Washington, D.C., July 1980.

16. Allen and Polmar, op. cit., p. 268.

17. Barron, op. cit., p. 188.

18. John's claim; Laura denied it.

19. Hunter claims that he said the line. Other accounts attribute it to others. I think Hunter should know what he said.

20. A very mild, slightly-built FBI agent said to me in 1985 that nothing would give him more pleasure than to see Whitworth taken into an alley and killed in cold blood. The agent was a real gentleman, of great kindness of heart, and his reaction tells you something about the lethality of Walker's agent. I broke Whitworth's story for McGraw-Hill in 1985.

21. Allen and Polmar, op. cit., p. 250.

22. Sontag, op. cit., p. 343.

23. Former senior U.S. intelligence in several interviews with author in July 2001.

24. Sontag and Drew, op. cit., p. 352.

25. From the former CIA operative who interviewed Solomatin in Paris: "He's dying of a broken heart," the agency man told me. "He really believed in the Soviet system." *Interview,* December 2002.

Notes on Chapter Sources. For constructing an account of Walker's life, between the accounts of Howard Blum, *I Pledge Allegiance . . . ,* New York, Simon & Schuster, 1987, Jack Kneece, *Family Treason,* New York, Stein and Day, 1986, and Pete Early's, *Family of Spies: Inside the John Walker Spy Ring,* New York, Bantam Books, 1999, the last is indisputably a performance of the first order that really grasps its subject. Early, an excellent writer, spent hundreds of hours interviewing Walker and his family and accomplices.

To understand the background of U.S.–Soviet naval competition, the premier book in the field is by Sherry Sontag and Christian Drew, with Annette Lawrence Drew, *Blind Man's Bluff, The Untold Story of American Submarine Espionage,* New York, HarperPaperbacks, 1999. It is excellent in its detail, its grasp of strategy, its ability to tell a story. Also extremely helpful is Thomas B. Allen and Norman Polmar, *Merchants of Treason,* New York, Delacorte Press, 1988 providing excellent information about the world of military communications. Russell Warren Howe's superb *Weapons,* Garden City, New York, Doubleday & Company, 1980, also provided wonderful detail on submarine life and other subjects.

For the hunting of Walker, the investigation and his arrest, I relied on Allen and Polmar, but also the account by the man who caught him, Robert Hunter's *Spy Hunter: Inside the FBI Investigation of the Walker Espionage Case,* Annapolis, Maryland, Naval Institute Press, 1999. Hunter was also kind enough to grant me interviews and supply me with sources. I also found Allen and Polmar helpful again, as well as John Barron's *Breaking the Ring,* Boston, Houghton Mifflin Company, 1987, which concentrates on Whitworth.

For indispensable background about fleet ops and the heightening of Cold War tensions under Reagan, I would recommend Peter Schweizer's *Victory,* New York, Atlantic Monthly Press, 1994, a book about U.S. efforts to undermine the Soviets that is a work of the first distinction. For details about how real the Soviet fear of war was in the early 1980s, definitely consult Christopher Andrew with Vasili Mitrokhin, *The Sword and the Shield: The Mitrokhin Archive,* New York, Basic Books, 1999.

For invaluable detail about how FBI counterintelligence groups are set up I am deeply indebted to Ronald Kessler, *Spy Versus Spy,* New York, Charles Scribner's Sons, 1988.

THE TRAITOR AS PROTEUS AND GOVERNMENT AGENT:
ROBERT HANSSEN

1. David Wise, Spy, *The Inside Story of How the FBI's Robert Hanssen Betrayed America,* New York, Random House, 2002, p. 11.

2. Elaine Shannon and Ann Blackman, *The Spy Next Door, The Extraordinary Secret Life of Robert Philip Hanssen, The Most Damaging FBI Agent in U.S. History,* Boston, Little, Brown and Company, p. 33.

3. When one read of Opus Dei, one recalls Hazlitt's observations about sects: that they "labor diligently, with great success, to exclude all ideas from their minds, which they might have in common with others . . . they retain a virginal purity of understanding . . . and keep up a perpetual quarantine against other people's vices—or virtues." They are not vain, he says, "but conceited: that is, he makes up by his own good opinion for the want of the cordial admiration of others." ("Quakers" from *On the Tendency of Sects,* 1817, quoted in William Hazlitt, *Selected Writings,* London, Penguin Books, 1970, p. 417.)

4. Pete Early, *Confessions of a Spy: The Real Story of Aldrich Ames,* New York, Berkley Books, 1998, p. 263.

5. Early, op. cit., p. 145.

6. Redmond is famous for the bluntness of his speech. A colleague, Jack Platt described it as "Fuck you! Strong note follows."

7. Wise, op. cit., p. 285.

8. Bob Woodward, *Bush at War,* New York, Simon & Schuster, 2002, p. 18.

9. Former CIA official's interview with author, September 14, 2001.

10. Ibid.

11. Wise, op. cit., p. 48.

Notes on Chapter Sources. David Wise is the best writer in America on espionage and his book is a gem. But the books of Vise and Shannon and Blackman were also helpful in providing details although they lacked a sure touch when it came to intelligence matters.

Bibliography

Abramson, Rudy, *Spanning the Century: The Life of Averell Harriman,* New York, William Morrow & Company, 1992.

Allen, Thomas B. and Norman Polmar, *Merchants of Treason,* New York, Delacorte Press, 1988.

Andrew, Christopher, *For the President's Eyes Only,* New York, HarperPerennial, 1996.

———with Mitrokhin, Vasili, *The Sword and Shield: The Mitrokhin Archive,* New York, Basic Books, 1999.

Bakeless, John, *Turncoats, Traitors, & Heroes,* New York, De Capo Press, 1998.

Barron, John, *Breaking the Ring,* Houghton Mifflin Company, 1987.

Barzun, Jacques, *Darwin, Marx, Wagner,* Chicago, University of Chicago Press, 1941.

Bentley, Elizabeth, *Out of Bondage,* New York, Ivy Books, 1988.

Berlin, Isaiah, *Karl Marx,* Oxford University Press, 1939.

———, *The Power of Ideas,* Princeton, NJ, Princeton University Press, 2000.

Billias, George Anthony, *George Washington's Generals and Opponents,* New York, De Capo, 1994.

Blum, Howard, *I Pledge Allegience . . . ,* New York, Simon & Schuster, 1987.

Bohlen, Charles, *Witness to History,* New York, W.W. Norton & Company, 1973.

Catton, Bruce, *A Stillness at Appomattox,* New York, Pocket Books, 1958.

Chambers, Whittaker, *Witness,* Washington, D.C., Regnery Gateway, 2002.

Clancy, Tom, *Submarine*, New York, Berkley Books, 1993.

Clarke, Harrison, *All Cloudless Glory*, Washington, D.C., Regnery, 1995.

Cohen, Eliot, *Supreme Command*, New York, Free Press, 2002.

Duff, William, *A Time for Spies*, New York, Vanderbilt University Press, 1999.

Early, Pete, *Family of Spies: Inside the John Walker Ring*, New York, Bantam Books, 1999.

Fleming, Thomas, *Liberty!*, New York, Viking, 1997.

Flexner, James Thomas, *The Traitor and the Spy*, New York, Quill, 1991.

Gaddis, John Lewis, *The United States and the Origins of the Cold War*, New York, Columbia University Press, 1972.

——, *Strategies of Containment*, Oxford, Oxford University Press, 1982.

Hanchett, William, *The Lincoln Murder*, Urbana, University and Illinois Press, 1956.

Haynes, John Earl and Harvey Klehr, *Venona: Decoding Soviet Espionage in America*, New Haven, Yale University Press, 2000.

Heardon, William and Jessie W. Weik, *The Life of Abraham Lincoln*, New York, De Capo Press, 1983.

Heilbroner, Robert, *The Worldly Philosophers*, New York, Touchstone Books, 1972.

Hofstadter, Richard, *The American Political Tradition*, New York, Vintage Books, 1948.

Howe, Russell Warren, *Weapons*, Garden City, NY, Doubleday & Company, 1980.

Huizinga, *Men and Ideas*, Princeton, NJ, Princeton University Press, 1984.

Hunter, Robert W., *Spy Hunter: Inside the FBI Investigation of the Walker Espionage Case*, Annapolis, MD, Naval Institute Press, 1999.

Johnson, Paul, *Modern Times*, New York, Harper & Row, 1985.

Kahn, David, *The Codebreakers: The Story of Secret Writing*, New York, Signet, 1973.

Keegan, *Six Armies at Normandy*, New York, Viking Press, 1982.

Kennan, George, *Memoirs*, Boston, Atlantic Monthly Press, 1967.

Kessler, *Spy Versus Spy*, New York, Charles Scribner's Sons, 1988.

Ketchum, Richard M., *Saratoga*, New York, John McCrea/Owl Books, 1999.

Kneece, Jack, *Family Treason*, New York, Stein and Day, 1986.

Knott, Stephen F., *Secret and Sanctioned*, New York, Oxford University Press, 1996.

Krivitsky, Walter, *Stalin's Secret Service*, New York, Enigma Books, 2000.

Lamphere, Robert and Tom Shachtman, *The FBI-KGB War*, London, A Star Book, 1988.

Langguth, A. J., *Patriots: The Men Who Started the American Revolution*, New York, Touchstone Books, 1998.

Leckie, Robert, *George Washington's War*, New York, HarperPerennial, 1993.

Manchester, William, *Glory and the Dream,* New York, Bantam Books, 1975.

Martin, James Kirby, *Benedict Arnold: Revolutionary Hero,* New York, New York University Press, 1997.

Montross, Lyn, *War Through the Ages,* New York, Harper & Brothers, 1946.

Murphy, Robert, *Diplomat Among Warriors,* Garden City, Doubleday, 1964.

Nicolson, Harold, *Diplomacy,* London, Oxford Unversity Press, 1963.

Orwell, George, *Homage to Catalonia.*

O'Toole, G. J. A., *Honorable Treachery,* New York, Atlantic Monthly Press, 1991.

Randall, William Sterne, *George Washington,* New York, John McCrae/Owl Books, 1998.

———, *Patriot and Traitor,* New York, Quill, 1999.

Roberts. J. M., *Twentieth Century,* New York, Penguin Books, 2000.

Romerstein and Eric Breindel, *The Venona Secrets,* Washington, D.C., Regncry, 2001.

Shannon, Elaine and Ann Blackman, *The Spy Next Door,* Boston, Little, Brown and Company, 2002.

Sherwood, Robert, *Roosevelt and Hopkins: An Intimate History,* New York, Harper & Brothers, 1948.

Smith, Hedrick, *The Power Game,* New York, Ballantine Books, 1989.

Sontag, Sherry, Christian Drew with Annette Lawrence Drew, *Blind Man's Bluff: The Untold Story of American Submarine Espionage,* New York, HarperPaperbacks, 1999.

Stevenson, William, *Intrepid's Last Case,* New York, Ballantine Books, 1984.

Tanenhaus, Sam, *Whittaker Chambers,* New York, Modern Library, 1998.

Thomas, Hugh, *The Spanish Civil War,* London, Penguin Books, 1965.

Tidwell, William A., with James O. Hall and David Winfred Gaddy, *Come Retribution,* Mississippi, University of Mississippi Press, 1988.

———, *April '65,* Kent, OH, Kent State University Press, 1995.

Tuchman, Barbara, *The Guns of August,* New York, Bantam Books, 1978.

———, *The Proud Tower,* New York, Bantam Books, 1967.

Van Doren, Carl, *The Secret History of the American Revolution,* Garden City, NY, Garden City Publishers, 1941.

Vise, David A., *The Bureau and the Mole,* New York, Atlantic Monthly Press, 2002.

Volkogonov, Dimitri, *Lenin,* New York, Free Press, 1999.

Weinstein, Allen and Alexander Vassiliev, *The Haunted Wood,* New York, Random House, 1999.

Woodward, Bob, *Bush at War,* New York, Simon & Schuster, 2002.

Index